To Paul
Recalling 50+ Years
of Close friendship

Manay
2 Feb 2019

The Dravidian Years

The Dravidian Years

Politics and Welfare
in Tamil Nadu

S. NARAYAN

OXFORD
UNIVERSITY PRESS

Oxford University Press is a department of the University of Oxford.
It furthers the University's objective of excellence in research, scholarship,
and education by publishing worldwide. Oxford is a registered trademark of
Oxford University Press in the UK and in certain other countries.

Published in India by
Oxford University Press
2/11 Ground Floor, Ansari Road, Daryaganj, New Delhi 110 002, India

© Oxford University Press 2018

The moral rights of the author have been asserted.

First Edition published in 2018

ISBN-13 (print edition): 978-0-19-948817-9
ISBN-10 (print edition): 0-19-948817-7

ISBN-13 (eBook): 978-0-19-909359-5
ISBN-10 (eBook): 0-19-909359-8

Typeset in Trump Mediaeval LT Std 9.5/14.5
by Tranistics Data Technologies, Kolkata 700 091
Printed in India by Replika Press Pvt. Ltd.

Contents

PREFACE

I WAS WITNESS TO FUNDAMENTAL CHANGES IN SOCIETAL
structures that occurred in Tamil Nadu after 1967.
As a student, I was witness to the movements against
the forward communities and the revival of Tamil
sentiment and Tamil pride, and later, as a part of the state
administration, working closely with different political
leaders, I saw ideology being translated into policies,
programmes, and their delivery. I do not think such a
change happened elsewhere in India. This is an attempt to
chronicle what happened, and who made it happen, from
the point of view of an insider. The Tamil Nadu archives,
where I spent considerable time, are a treasure house of
documents on the policies and programmes of the time.
These offer insight into the reasons behind several of the
policies, as well as how they were implemented.

The Institute of South Asian Studies, National University of Singapore, where I have been a senior Research Fellow, has supported me enormously in this effort, and I am thankful to Mr Gopinath Pillai, Chairman, the former Director Dr Mitra and all my colleagues there for their encouragement.

I am grateful to Eva Raiber, an intern who worked with me three years ago, for looking up a number of studies on Tamil Nadu by Western scholars. It appeared as though there was a part that was missing—that of politics and administration, and also the expectations of the electorate that changed over the years. This is an attempt to fill that gap, through some examples. Vishali Sairam and Maria Tresa helped me out with several sources. Several of my ex-colleagues in administration were forthcoming with their experiences over this period, and that has enriched this narrative. I am also grateful to the OUP team that worked on the book for their painstaking efforts.

Tamil Nadu is an example of empowering backward classes, and could well set an example for other states.

INTRODUCTION

———

DRAVIDIAN PARTIES HAVE BEEN IN POWER IN THE STATE OF
Tamil Nadu for fifty years, beginning in 1967. In these fifty
years, they have been responsible for changing the social
structure of the state, and for implementing a large number
of welfare programmes for the poor. In terms of economic
performance, social indicators, as well as creating
opportunities for the disadvantaged, Tamil Nadu sets an
example for many other states. Scholars and policymakers
alike have lauded the performance of several programmes,
welfare-oriented as well as those that give opportunities
to the disadvantaged. Academic literature has analysed
the performance of the schemes, and the policies that
drove these schemes. The welfare programmes have
been strongly identified with the ideas and personalities

of the state's charismatic leaders— J. Jayalalithaa, MGR (Marudur Gopalan Ramachandran), and M. Karunanidhi— who have been at the helm of affairs in the state for most of these fifty years. Recent and forthcoming publications on Jayalalithaa, MGR, and Karunanidhi also shed light on the welfare policies of these Dravidian leaders.[1]

The beginnings of Dravidian culture lie in the Social Reform Movement. It eventually morphed into a political movement that gained power and political support. As a person who lived through these changes, and was part of the government machinery at that time, it is interesting to reflect on the transition of the social reform and social justice demands from ideas to a political ideology, and on the administration's role and involvement in enabling this. This book highlights the interaction between politics and the administration. It examines a few programmes to understand political motives, the eventual interpretation of these motives by the administration, and whether the end result served the objectives of the political ideology and the administration. The ideology of the Social Reform Movement, which was adopted in governance by the Dravida Munnetra Kazhagam (DMK) and later by the All India Anna Dravida Munnetra Kazhagam (AIADMK), was to change the balance of social institutions and structures. The attempt was to create a society that was more reflective of the diversity of the Tamil population and to move away from the dominance of the forward communities. This was achieved through the adoption of welfare policies, programmes, and projects. Interestingly, the administration was soon part of this process of change—and in many cases, it even spearheaded these changes. In some cases, political ideology used the administration to achieve its ends, and in others the administration used the ideology to create programmes for the public good. Public pressure for services, which served to enhance the effectiveness of delivery, as well as deliver a political agenda to the people, accentuated this interesting interplay. The interplay between politics, the administration, and the people appears to be unique to Tamil Nadu in the sense that, in other states of India, there is no evidence of a distinct social ideology driving development during this period.

This book draws from archival material as well as personal interactions with several senior colleagues involved in the programmes. The narrative is personal, as several of the actors were close acquaintances. The approach adopted is to examine the political motivation behind every programme, contextualize it within the objectives of the government at that time, look at how the administrative machinery took up and implemented the programme, and finally comment on whether the end result served political ends, public needs, or both. It is seen that in several programmes, even though the origins may be purely political, the way they were implemented resulted in public welfare enhancement that served political ends along with ensuring that sustainable development initiatives were put in place. Such programmes have often survived several changes in governance, primarily because they enhanced public good. The motivations of the politician in charge at that time, those of the key people who implemented them, and the interactions between the two are examined to illustrate the interplay between the administration and politics, and to attempt to explain why these programmes have been successful in Tamil Nadu. Finally, there is clear evidence that public awareness and public pressure have sustained several of these programmes.

I was both witness to and a participant in the changes in the social structure of the state, the enhanced access of the backward classes to higher education and to government jobs, and the evolution of several programmes focused on social welfare delivery. I came to Chennai in 1958, having completed my schooling in Kolkata (then Calcutta). Chennai and Tamil Nadu were not familiar territory for me at that time. Until 1965, all through my BSc and MSc, and two years of teaching Physics afterwards, I lived in a hostel in my college, the Madras Christian College. My hostel, St. Thomas Hall, had over 200 inmates, and all of us had single—albeit small—rooms. Early on, I came in contact with the political sentiment in the state at that time. Some of the students came from English-medium schools from urban spaces within India, there were others from Sri Lanka and Malaysia (Singapore became independent only in 1965), and a majority of students were from Tamil Nadu, of whom several had studied in Tamil-medium schools. Political discourse for this group was centred around E.V. Ramasamy Naicker (popularly known as EVR or Periyar), the Justice Party, and the young DMK. The discourse mainly revolved around opportunities for the backward classes, opposition to Hindi, and pride in the Tamil identity. EVR was more focused on social change in these years, and believed that political change would follow social change. Annadurai[2] differed on this, and broke away to form the DMK in 1949, as he wanted to achieve social change through political power. The DMK considered the Congress to be a representative of the old social order, and was politically in opposition to the Congress.

EVR, however, felt that the Congress under K. Kamraj, the then chief minister, would advance the cause of social justice for the backward classes, and announced his support for the Congress in the 1957 elections. The DMK was a party opposed to the Congress' ideology, and the 1957 elections saw the DMK and Periyar in opposite camps.[3] The Election Commission did not recognize DMK as an official party until 1962, but in 1957, the party won 13 seats through independent candidates. Karunanidhi won from Kulithalai, and when I came to Madras, his speeches in the Legislative Assembly, especially those espousing causes like those of the beedi workers in Nangavaram and of agricultural wage labourers, were part of the hostel discourse in my college. Surprisingly, there was much less empathy for left wing movements like those witnessed in Kerala at that time.[4] Madras was full of Tamil sentiment, and there was opposition to Kula Kalvi Thittam,[5] which was considered to be an attempt to perpetuate the dominance of the upper classes, especially Brahmins. The Social Reform Movement of EVR, and the subsequent discourse leading to the formation of the DMK, had reached the youth in colleges and schools and there was a wave of sentiment wanting change in the existing social order.

DMK oratory, the film dialogues of Annadurai and Karunanidhi, and the movies of MGR were the undercurrent of debates in a college that was still run on staid and conservative Scottish discipline by the Principal, Rev Boyd, and later Rev McPhail.

In the 1962 elections, a number of my college mates and friends actively participated in electioneering for the DMK, and anti-Congress sentiments were already palpable. There was strong objection to Hindi, and my familiarity with that language was looked down upon. In 1963 and 1964, I had been elected Chairman of the College Union, and subsequently Secretary of the University Students' Council and could see that these sentiments were common across all colleges in Madras state,[6] and students were fervently following the speeches and doctrines of the DMK. In my tenure with the University Students Council, I could also see the differences in the attitudes of students from some city colleges, who were more in tune with the earlier colonial and high-caste sentiments, and those of students from Madras Law College and Pachaiyappa's College, representing the new social reality.

Then came the food shortages of 1964 and the anti-Hindi agitations of 1965, in which a large number of my friends and students from the Madras Law College participated, and it was evident from the point of view of the younger generation that the days of the Congress government in Madras were numbered.

I wrote the examinations for the IAS in 1964, as soon as I was eligible in age, and joined the service in 1965. After a year at the National Academy of Administration in Mussoorie under probation, I was posted in 1966 as Assistant Collector (Training) to Salem in Madras. It was in 1967, after the elections that swept the DMK into power, that I was given my first independent posting. Several of my college mates contested on DMK tickets in the elections, and I could see the palpable change in the approach of the administration after 1967.

Over the next two decades, I was intimately involved in the happenings of the state at different levels, as Assistant Collector, Collector, Director of Rural Development, and Secretary In Charge of Rural Development Programmes, which gave me the opportunity to witness policy changes at close quarters. During the DMK regime that lasted from 1967 to 1976, I saw existing institutions being revamped and a new social structure being put in place through reservations for appointments and in higher education for the backward classes. The beginnings of welfare programmes for the poor, including subsidized rice at government outlets, assistance and pensions for the poor and the widowed, and other schemes laid the foundations for welfare programmes in future regimes. I witnessed the social justice agenda being slowly dominated by the upper strata of the backward classes (noted by several academics),[7] and the growth of corruption that eventually led to the dismissal of that government. The subsequent MGR regime that lasted until 1987 carried the social welfare programmes forward, and focused on nutrition and mid-day meals in schools as the instruments to reach the poor and the rural disadvantaged, and there is little doubt that there was a political motive behind these programmes. MGR had risen to power on a populist wave that was enhanced by the fact that he frequently played the role of a saviour of the poor in his films. The big growth in social welfare programmes targeted towards the poor in rural areas arose out of his genuine concern for the poor as well as the image he portrayed on screen.

The Jayalalithaa regime that followed, between 1991 and 1996, focused on the political advantages of the welfare programmes, and was less concerned with the Social Reform Movement ideology. Dilution in policy of the original Dravidian ideology was in evidence in this and subsequent regimes. Subsequent governments, which alternated between the DMK and the AIADMK, carried the concept of social welfare into the realm of granting freebies for election gains.

There is a lot of academic literature on Tamil Nadu for this period. There has been analysis of individual programmes, of their relevance and effectiveness, especially of the nutrition and the noon meal programmes. The midday meals programme was the brainchild of MGR, and involved the supply of hot cooked meals to all children between the ages of 2 and 15 years in the state. Such a massive feeding programme had not been tried earlier, and initial criticisms focused on the waste of resources. However, the discourse gradually changed over the years from the sharply critical to the cautiously laudatory. Other scholars have looked at ethnic mobilization as well as sub-cultures and their changing influence on policy and politics in this period. In later years, the pressures of the Most Backward Classes and the Dalits on governments for greater concessions and opportunities are also well documented. There are a large number of micro studies that look at disadvantaged groups and their struggle for political mobilization as well as asserting their claims to public services. There are comparisons with other states, which invariably highlight how Tamil Nadu has effectively implemented many social welfare programmes, in comparison to several other states.

From the point of view of one involved in administration and implementation, there appears to be one discourse that is missing. Between policy formulation and public claims for services, there is the realm of implementation and the role of institutions and hierarchies that convert ideas into action. The first decade of rule of the Dravidian parties involved significant changes in the social and administrative fabric, and it is relevant to look at how the administration coped with these changes. In the background is the hypothesis (supported by some academic literature) that there was politicization of the bureaucracy, and also that over time, the ideas of social justice of the political class were accepted and adopted by the administrative class, and this constitutes a major reason for the success of the programmes, and also for the administrative changes that followed. Efficiency in administration and programme delivery was always a strength of the Tamil Nadu structure; now that was turned towards achieving goals that were more oriented towards achieving social justice and social welfare.

Fifty years is a long time, and it is a period that has seen a large number of development initiatives, changes in policy and governments. In pursuing this hypothesis, the attempt has been to pick up those initiatives that have had significant impact, that is, the flagship interventions. Further, since the political ideology was based on social justice and social welfare, the choice of cases has been biased towards these, rather than industry, infrastructure, energy, or agriculture. The programmes discussed are those with significant government outlay and expenditure, and a substantial organizational structure. These are programmes that have been commented on by academics, multilateral institutions, and the Government of India and, in several cases, used as models for other states. The study is biased towards specific successful programmes, only because it serves to illustrate the advantages of synergies among politics, administrative capability, and public pressure in achieving welfare goals. There is also an attempt to select programmes from different regimes—Karunanidhi, MGR, and Jayalalithaa, to illustrate the unity as well as diversity in policy and implementation.

The focus of the following chapters is detailed along these lines: at the forefront is the political objective of the programme, which is a reflection of the political ideology, the nature of leadership, as well as the pragmatic politics of that time. The Karunanidhi and the MGR governments were different, and an attempt is made to underscore the differences in approach and the causes thereof. Jayalalithaa set a different trend, which has been followed by successive governments, and the reaction of the bureaucracy to these changes is documented.

There has been an attempt at examination of the extant literature, as well as examination of government documents in the Tamil Nadu archives about the recorded origins of some of the programmes discussed here. There have been several interactions with senior officers in the Indian Administrative Service (IAS) who served in these administrations, as well as other senior people in the know. The files also speak about the way in which the bureaucracy grasped the reins after the formulation of the policy, and the detail and manner in which it ensured execution. The motives for this involvement varied, from the nature of the people involved to a professional drive to perform. Two major programmes, the midday meals programme and the nutrition programme, are examined in detail, as they offer contrasts in ideological origins. One was driven by the chief minister, the other by the World Bank. Yet, at the implementation level, they finally converged on a political objective that was acceptable to politics and participants alike, and therein perhaps lies the uniqueness of Tamil Nadu. Discussions with senior officers involved in implementation have helped piece together a political economy narrative of development. Personal experiences over these years as a witness to such changes, especially from close quarters, on several programmes with anecdotal notes are also documented.

There were also other initiatives, like the public distribution system, separation of public health (with medical education being made a separate organization), and medical education, that were implemented over time and over regimes, and have drawn approbation across the country. The origin and development of these somewhat apolitical programmes is also discussed briefly, to outline the success of the administrative capability of the administrative machinery in Tamil Nadu.

Tamil Nadu was also developing rapidly on all fronts, and the story would not be complete without looking at information on improvements in standards of living, health, education, and infrastructure. Public awareness and participation was an important ingredient in the success as well as sustainability of these programmes, and there is discussion about how this participation gradually developed over the years, synchronizing with rising prosperity, literacy, prosperity, and urbanization.

The current state of politics and administration forms the concluding piece, arguing that the programmes today are but a deteriorated form of the earlier ones, administered by an ever more politicized bureaucracy. The changes in the motives for current policies are also commented on.

While the narrative is intended to inform the general reader, the author has referred to, among other sources, academic work done on these issues, which gives the content its depth. There are chapters where the narrative would be incomplete without reference to academic work done in these areas. There are others, where the narrative flows more from the examination of the decision-making process as found in government files, as well as discussions and interviews with colleagues.

Chapter 1 gives an overview of the Social Reform Movement and how the DMK evolved as a political party. There is reference to several academic studies in this chapter to contextualize the movement and its implications. The references are illustrative, not exhaustive. Chapter 2 is about the years of DMK rule between 1967 and 1977 and is an attempt to narrate how the social reform ideals of the party were converted into policy and implemented, bringing about a fundamental change in social structures of administration, education, and governance. It also explains the origins of the welfare programmes that became significant signposts of the policies of that and succeeding governments. The reference is to government files and decisions. Chapter 3 deals with the MGR years of 1977 to 1987 and the ascendancy of social welfare programmes in the policy agenda as well as the gradual reduction of the Dravidian agenda. During this period, there were two important programmes that were started, the midday meal programme and the Tamil Nadu Integrated Nutrition Programme (TINP). One was the chief minister's initiative, the other, a World Bank initiative. The political agenda, administrative response, and public acceptance for these are discussed in Chapters 4 and 5 respectively. Though distinct in concept, they were merged into the social, administrative, and political agenda, and are presented as two distinct case studies.

Chapter 6 deals with the first five years of the Jayalalithaa administration, from 1991 to 1996, and is a chapter where there is continuity as well as change—from a social welfare objective to a political one. I had left the state in 1992 and returned for a year during 1996–97, and after 1997 was continuously posted to the central government in Delhi. Though my remit in later years did involve periodic interactions with the state government, its bureaucracy, and ministers, I was no longer involved with the state administration. The narratives in Chapters 7 and 8 are based on information from government files and from secondary reports. Chapter 7 deals with the period 1996 to 2006 and Chapter 8 with 2006 to 2016, in an attempt to look at how governance and policies were slowly overwhelmed by the need to have freebies to give to the electorate. The last chapter, Chapter 9, looks at politics in Tamil Nadu in 2017, and the road ahead for politics and governance. All through the narrative is an assessment of how the administration and bureaucracy adapted to the changing political expectations, and the extent to which they were successful in converting these policies into genuine welfare programmes. There is also mention of the aberrations and corruption that occurred during these periods. In the last chapter, there is an attempt to examine the revival of Tamil sentiment and also look at the policies and potential performance of the state in the years ahead. There is a distinct revival of caste sentiments, and of issues of Tamil identity. It is a function of developments in politics as well as economic development in the state. The implications of these developments appear to be significant for politics as well as development in the coming years.

This work is a personal view of the social transformation of the state of Tamil Nadu, from the point of view of one who has lived through it. It is for everyone who has an interest in Tamil Nadu and other states, and in how programmes were implemented there. As it includes public policy and governance case studies, it would be of relevance to academics and policymakers alike. For the general reader, the narrative offers an insight into the people, the times, and the programmes. It is also intended to fill a gap in the academic literature that has so far largely ignored the role of implementation. Youth today, growing up in the post-1967 world, may be interested in how these leaders proceeded to achieve their goals. Most importantly, for the younger generation, this would hold up a mirror to the society they live in, and explain how a transformation happened over the last fifty years.

Notes

1. The books being referred to here are Vasanthi's work on Jayalalitha, *Amma: Journey from Movie Star to Political Queen* (Delhi: Juggernaut Books, 2016) and R. Kannan's *MGR: A Life* (Delhi: Penguin Random House, 2017). In addition, A.S. Paneerselvam is working on a forthcoming biography of Karunanidhi which would also look at seventy-five years of the Dravida Munnetra Kazhagam (DMK) party newspaper *Murasoli*.

2. C.N. Annadurai, a lawyer, writer, orator, and script writer, led the DMK after he broke away from EVR. He was widely popular and respected for his public oratory as well as for the fiery dialogues in films and stage in which he attacked the existing social order in Tamil Nadu.

3. Chapter 1 talks of this divisiveness in detail.

4. E.M.S. Namboodripad had become chief minister in Kerala in 1957, the first state in which the Communist Party had won elections.

5. Kula Kalvi Thittam (Hereditary Education Policy) was an attempt at education reform introduced by the Congress government in Madras. It was intended to enable students to pursue courses in their traditional vocation; for instance, the child of a potter would study pottery under this system. There was opposition to this because it was felt that this was re-emphasizing class and caste distinctions. Rajagopalachari lost his chief ministership in 1954 to K. Kamraj due to public opposition to this policy.

6. The state was named Tamil Nadu in 1969, all earlier references are to Madras and Madras Presidency.

7. See, for example, Narendra Subramanian, *Ethnicity and Social Mobilization* (New Delhi: Oxford: Oxford University Press, 1999).

I

THE SOCIAL REFORM MOVEMENT
Early Years

———

THE DMK CAME TO POWER IN TAMIL NADU IN THE 1967 elections, ending decades of Congress rule. In the fifty years since then, Dravidian parties—either the DMK or the AIADMK—have been in power in the state, and have shaped the political, social, and economic agenda of the state. The changes in the social structure of the state and the development opportunities that have been offered to the backward classes in these two generations have created a social fabric that is quite distinct. It is important to understand the origins and growth of the Dravidian movement in the state, and its metamorphosis from a social justice platform to one focused on economic development and social welfare initiatives.

The origins of the Dravidian movement lay in the Self Respect Movement, which, in many ways, provided the social and political background that led to the growth of the Dravida Kazhagam (DK) and eventually, the DMK. The Dravidian movement had its origins in the struggle between the Brahmins, who were the first to benefit from English education in the southern states of India, especially in the Madras Presidency, and the non-Brahmins, who were later entrants to English education. The movement originated as a protest against the dominance of Brahmins in administration, education, and public services, and sought equal opportunities for all communities. In the British administration, the ruling class belonged mostly to the higher castes that had an interest in protecting their own hegemony. Rich non-Brahmins served as traders and entrepreneurs. They even helped the English-speaking Brahmins get coveted administrative posts so that they could later make use of them for commercial purposes.

English education was more widespread in the south as compared to the presidencies of Bombay and Bengal, possibly due to the services of Christian missionaries. In 1852, Madras had 1,185 mission schools with around 38,000 students, while the Bombay and the Bengal presidencies together had only 472 mission schools, with around 18,000 students. Brahmins formed the majority of students educated in the Madras Presidency, even though they formed less than 3 per cent of the population. The Madras Brahmin was far ahead of his counterpart in the northern states. Between 1892 and 1904, out of 16 Indian Civil Service (ICS)[1] candidates selected, 15 were Brahmins. In the case of engineers, 21 of the 27 selected candidates were Brahmins. It was a similar picture among Deputy Collectors and even the lower rungs of revenue administration in the Madras Presidency. During the years of the freedom movement, the Congress party in the south, in its initial years, was keen on securing senior positions for Indians, which inevitably meant that Brahmins benefitted the most.

There were earlier movements in Tamil Nadu led by the upper castes that led to the abolition of the Devadasi system, suttee, and child marriages. Urban centres also witnessed movements for women's rights. Muthulakshmi Reddy and Annie Besant were at the forefront of several social initiatives.

However, the most significant movement for social reform was a movement for self-respect among non-Brahmin communities, who felt alienated from the processes of administration and governance. It was a movement specifically against the Brahmins, who occupied positions far in excess of the numerical proportion they made up of the population.

Brahmins dominated in all government jobs, the bar, the university, and the Government Secretariat. Their mastery over English was considered a passport to power, influence, and a means to profit. Brahmins domination was felt even in private business companies and mercantile houses. Most of the leading journalists were from the Brahmin community. They virtually controlled the High Court of Madras.[2] Sixty-seven per cent of those receiving baccalaureate degrees from Madras University were Brahmins. Those who occupied the higher rungs of the non-Brahmin castes chafed at this hegemony and wanted the benefits of political and social positions for themselves as well.[3]

The Madras Presidency was not unique in witnessing the growth of social reform movements. The early 1900s witnessed several social reform movements in the Indian subcontinent. The spread of Western education and English in schools carried with it ideas of egalitarianism, rationalism, and a scientific approach. Christian missionary schools questioned the ritualistic behaviour of traditional Indian society. Organizations like the Arya Samaj and Brahmo Samaj strove for a less ritualistic society, one in which the upper castes did not dominate. There was also apprehension that the colonial government in power was advocating social compartmentalization between religions and between classes in an attempt to divide Indian society, so that the freedom movement could be weakened.

The focus in Madras was somewhat different. Rather than reforming social and religious structures, the movement focused on the removal of the dominance of Brahmins in government. In this sense, the movement was very different from the rest of the country, where there was no such move against a single dominant class in a concerted manner.

The non-Brahmin movement advocated the allocation of government jobs according to the numerical strength of the communities, a vision that was immediately attractive to all non-Brahmins. In 1916, the Dravidian association that was formed claimed its purpose to be the establishment of a Dravidian state under the British Raj—a government by and for non-Brahmins. The South Indian Liberal Federation (SILF) became the Justice Party in 1917. In 1920, the first elections under the Montague-Chelmsford reforms saw the Justice Party being elected to power in the Madras Presidency. The Congress party had boycotted the elections in the wake of nationalist sentiment around the inadequacy of the Montague reforms in ushering in self-rule. The Justice Party at this time was supportive of colonial rule, and readily participated in the Madras Presidency elections. The Justice Party, while in power, ushered in a number of reforms that were part of its social reform agenda, including the introduction of a communal rotation roster for government jobs and reforms in temple administration. The party was supportive of British rule, and even its social reform agenda for non-Brahmins was limited to being within the existing structures. The members of the party were largely rich merchants, or from the landed gentry and did not reflect common aspirations. These were the years of the freedom struggle, and the Justice Party soon lost its popularity on account of its implicit support of colonial rule. By 1925, it was looking at opportunities to reinvent itself.

According to N.K. Mangalamurugesan,[4] the genesis of the Self-Respect Movement and the ascendance of EVR in the political landscape of Tamil Nadu could be seen against the background of the increasing trend of Brahmins opposing any change in the caste system and existing customs. Specifically, he talks about the Vaikom Satyagraha (a movement against untouchability) and the Gurukulam controversy (when C. Rajagopalachari, Mahatma Gandhi, and other prominent leaders in the Congress advocated communal restrictions) amongst other movements.

EVR was part of the Congress and had tried, on several occasions, to raise the issue of communal rotation for posts. His final effort was at the Kanchipuram convention of the Congress in 1925. He was outmaneuvered. The Brahmin leaders' unwillingness to agree to communal restrictions, and the lack of consensus among the non-Brahmin leaders eventually led to EVR leaving the Congress.

He then started the Self-Respect Movement (SRM) as a social protest against the Brahmins and it immediately attracted the support of the lower castes and classes, for they considered the Justice Party an elitist organization. For the Justice Party, anti-Brahminism was not anti-religion or anti-Hindu, while EVR's movement was against the entire caste system and Hindu rituals. The leaders of this movement believed that the emergence of the Brahmins as a status group arose from the social, religious, and cultural values that prevailed in society. They felt it was important that these values be proven alien, degrading, and sectarian, and that there was a need to restore the status of the non-Brahmins. They considered the term non-Brahmin a misnomer, and wished to be called Dravidians, as inheritors of a tradition superior to that of Brahminism. Christoph Jaffrelot talks of the concept of ethnicization and Sanskritization in his work on South India.[5] According to him, the non-Brahmin movement was instrumental in engineering forms of caste fusion and it succeeded in endowing lower castes with an ethnic identity. Painting Dravidians as the original inhabitants of India resulted in the following:

- In Tamil country, the multilayered ideology of Dravidianism emerged out of opposition to Brahminism and Brahmin institutions of colonial rule and, in the hands of EVS, became associated with a vision of Dravidian and Shudra primacy against Aryan Brahminism.

- Dravidian politics developed into an inclusive Tamil nationalism, associating the Dravidian community with the non-Sanskritic Tamil language and cultural tradition.

Jaffrelot says that the ethnicization process was fostered by the British policy of compensatory discrimination based on the reservation of seats in the bureaucracy and the assemblies. According to him, the decision to grant statutory representation to different groups contributed to their crystallization into new categories that resented under-representation. He also feels that the British in Madras supported this movement explicitly as a counterbalance to the Brahmin-dominated Congress. The process of state engineering, therefore, went hand in hand with the invention of the Dravidian identity of the lower castes and each reinforced the other. This divide between the forward castes and the other castes remains strong in Tamil Nadu even today, even though all the forward castes together account for only around 5 per cent of the population. The British were also active in stoking the inter-party politics of the Congress, creating schisms among different groups.

Publication of the *Kudi Arasu* magazine started in 1925, and it could be considered to have initiated the spread of SRM ideology. The SRM was more interested in social freedom than in winning political independence, and wanted to achieve some form of social equality before the British left India. EVR believed that social reform should precede political reform. However, EVR did openly lobby for people to vote for the Justice Party. The government order prescribing a community-based rotation for filling vacancies in government posts was issued at this time, and effectively ended the monopoly of any single community on government jobs. Mangalamurugesan also addresses the widely held idea that the SRM evolved out of the Justice Party. In his view, it was only EVR's anger towards the Congress that made him lean towards the Justice Party. Specifically, he talks of how the concept of social freedom can be traced back to the Congress itself. There were always two sections in the Congress—one consisting of higher caste members who emphasized political freedom and the other consisting of members from the lower castes who argued for social freedom. It was the schism between the two groups that culminated in the formation of the Self-Respect Movement. The Justice Party at this time was a party that appealed to the landowning class, the middle and upper middle class merchant communities, and therefore represented the bourgeoisie and lacked popular support. The SRM directed its appeal mainly to the socially and economically weaker non-Brahmin communities.

Some important steps taken by 'Self-Respecters' were to drop caste appellations appended to their names, avoid caste symbols, encourage inter-caste marriages, and other measures that championed social reform. They also argued for the removal of social restrictions that applied to women. Calling for sanctions against Hindu temples, which deprived Brahmins of their income and therefore their power in society was also one of the main focal points of the SRM.

Other significant ideas arose and gained ground around the same time as the inception of the SRM. The Tamil Purist Movement or Thani Tamil Iyakkam began as a movement to avoid loanwords from Sanskrit. The modern revival of the Tamil Purist Movement (also known as the Pure Tamil Movement) is attributed to Maraimalai Adigalar, who publicly pledged to defend pure Tamil in 1916. Kailasapathy talks about how, in many ways, literature was the base for Dravidian ideology. The influences of European writings on the Tamil Purist movement became the basis for the growth of a pure Tamil ideology. Specifically, 'The enthusiasm and thrill with which the European savants presented the salient features of Tamil language, literature, antiquities and religion also instilled in these Tamil scholars a notion of uniqueness about their past glory that set them apart from other races and peoples of India, especially the Brahmin community.'[6]

The launching of the Purist movement coincided with the formation of the SILF (Justice Party). We see broad parallels between both. Both were started by non-Brahmin upper caste personalities drawing support from educated, wealthy, and pro-British personages. Kailasapathy also says that 'they were never really popular movements and hidden within them were several contradictions'.[7] The Justice Party was superseded by the Self-Respect Movement, which in time gave rise to the DK and the DMK. The Tamil Purist Movement on the other hand, was merged with the anti-Hindi protest movement and was later absorbed into DMK ideology.

Academics on the Origins of the Movement

There is a lot of literature on the Self-Respect Movement, its origins, development, as well as its leadership. While an exhaustive analysis may not fit into the current narrative, it is important to examine how the movement has been dealt with in the academic literature.

A.R. Venkatachalapathy's work[8] on the movement attempts to understand the reasons for the success of the SRM within the context of the Saivite movement. The Saivite movement was an anti-Brahmin movement that argued for the superiority of the Vellala caste. S. Vedachalam Pillai, who changed his name to Maraimalai Adigalar, launched the Thani Tamil Iyakkam in 1916. He attempted to divest Tamil of Sanskrit words. He extolled the Vellalla community for introducing settled agriculture in Tamil Nadu, and argued that they were an indigenous Tamil caste superior to the Brahmins. A number of Tamil purist scholars belong to the Saivite movement—including V. Kanakasabhai, Nallusami Pillai, and Sundaram Pillai.

Venkatachalapathy attempts to juxtapose the success of the Dravidian movement with the sectarian interpretation of the 'anti-Brahminism' of the Saivites and the 'anti-patriarchal' content of the Self-Respect agenda. He attempts to differentiate between the Saivite interpretation of history and their anti-Brahmin ideologies, and considers how these differences are interpreted. In the Saivite conception of Tamil society, Saivites replaced the Brahmins, and their scriptures replaced the Vedas. Though caste remained, it was occupation-based with no stigma attached to it. He compares this to the Self-Respect Movement and its conception of an ancient Tamil society that was egalitarian and democratic. Neither religion nor caste existed, and perfect equality prevailed. In both cases, the disintegration of this ideal society was the result of Brahmin invasion into Tamil country. Another important factor that Venkatachalapathy attributes to the success of Dravidian movement is its ability to exclude religious texts, which in the Tamil context consisted mostly of Saivite works.

M.S.S. Pandian[9] discusses the Self-Respect Movement in detail in his work on the history of Dravidian ideology. In specific, he dwells on the reasons why history favoured the Self-Respect Movement over Saivite ideology. He explains that the Saivite movement valorized the Saivite Vellalas and discursively dethroned the Brahmin, replacing him with the Vellala elite. EVR and the SRM criticized Saivism. In EVR's view, Hinduism envisaged multiple levels of power relationships, and the Saivaite movement was inadequate in not recognizing this. During the period 1942–44, EVR's opposition to the Tamil devotional literary works *Kamba Ramayanam* and *Periya Puranam* caused a break with Saivite Tamil scholars, who had joined the anti-Hindi agitations.

For EVR, self respect was something to fight for, and each group should fight for its self respect. He thus expanded the realm of politics to a range of oppressed groups. In his view, the 'telos of history and rationality was interminable, continuously invalidating the past and disclosing newer avenues of freedom all through. Thus, there is no fixed goal—the search for freedom is an ever continuing one.'[10] Also, EVR's conception of disempowerment was qualitatively different and significantly more inclusive that of the earlier Dravidian ideology. Over a period of time, the Tamil Purist Movement waned in the face of the stronger SRM arguments.

In another related work, M.S.S. Pandian[11] critiques the Cambridge school of historiography. Christopher John Baker[12] of the Cambridge school of historiography, who is associated with the Endangered Language and Cultures Group, argues that movements which claimed to protect the minority were a common feature of the new politics of India in this period of councils, ministers, and electorates;

and it was unusual, if not paradoxical, to find a movement
which claimed to defend a majority that included up to
98 per cent of the population and almost all men of wealth
and influence in local society. In this argument, caste
identity becomes inconsequential, which Pandian refutes.
He gives the example of the Dravidian movement as an
example against this theory.

Jacob Pandian's work on Tamil movement revolves
around similar debates. He talks about how specific
ancient symbols acquired meanings of social revolution
and oppression, and how these symbols in turn came to
symbolize Tamil nationalism. He says, 'Tamil re-ethno
genesis and re-invention of tradition of the late 19th and
20th centuries proclaimed the boundary between the
"Dravidian south" and the "Aryan north," and the Tamil
literary tradition, once again, became the vehicle for the
boundary-maintenance, which affirmed the distinctive
linguistic-cultural heritage of the Tamils, providing them
with the Dravidian identity.'[13] For example, he talks about
the story of Kannagi written by Ilango Adigal in the third
century AD. To Ilango Adigal, Kannagi's life and acts
constituted a metaphor for conceptualizing the spirituality
of chaste women, and Tamil values, and of Tamil justice
in particular. An important medium for the transmission
of these symbols was cinema, which we shall discuss later.

In his work on caste and politics in Tamil Nadu,
Hugo Gorringe talks of how the legacies of the
non-Brahmin movement shaped Tamil politics. First
was the institutionalization of communal or caste-based
politics and the belief that social and ritual hierarchies
could be challenged and renegotiated through political
mobilization. The second legacy was the early institution

of affirmative action programmes for backward castes and classes. Gorringe says the communal categories that were established were effective, and new organization forms were directed towards securing economic advancement, jobs, and special concessions.

Kalaiyarasan says that in Tamil Nadu, the village was ideologically seen as the site of oppression while urban space was seen was as liberated. EVR saw Gandhi's ideas on village reconstruction as a political strategy to keep the masses within traditional caste-bound geographical spaces.

Changes in the SRM

According to Mangalamurugesan, a swift turn of events on the international scene had a tremendous impact on the thinking of Self-Respect leaders. In particular, the rise of communism influenced the SRM movement in significant ways. Between December 1931 and November 1932, EVR toured the UK, Europe, and the Soviet Union and was strongly influenced by communist ideals after this visit. The SRM became very active in spreading atheism and communism in the state. The spirit of the Self-Respect and Social Reform movements yielded place to socialism. When EVR returned from his visit to Russia, he chaired the famous general body meeting of the SRM at Erode. He envisaged the formation of two new wings in SRM—the first was the Self-Respect League, which would be a social reform wing, and the second was the Self-Respect Socialist Party which would put up candidates for elections in the provincial councils and local bodies.

An important development during this time was the spread of atheism within the SRM. Regular translations

of works by philosophers like Bertrand Russell, Robert
G. Ingersoll, and atheist propaganda appeared regularly in
Kudi Arasu. In fact, according to Murugesan, the editorials
of *Kudi Arasu* bear testimony to the change of ideals of the
SRM. EVR's disgust with capitalism and his decision to
reconstruct the movement through socialist ideals led to
changes in the SRM.

After his return from a year's sojourn in the Soviet
Union, EVR was full of communist zeal, and in 1934
presented a fourteen-point agenda to both the Congress
and the Justice Party, and said he was willing to join
whichever group accepted the agenda. The Congress was
trying to woo him back into the fold, while the Justice
Party, weakened by then, was looking for a saviour. The
Justice Party was quick to respond, for it had little to lose.
EVR also raised his voice against the introduction of Hindi,
which was being espoused by the Congress.

In the period between 1936 and 1940, the SRM
metamorphosed further. Under EVR's leadership, the
party resolved to make Tamil Nadu a separate state.
The demand for this new Dravidian state became the
fundamental issue of the Justice Party. In this period, the
seed for the future political party, the DMK, was sown by
the entry of C.N. Annadurai. His association with EVR
and the SRM provided, in many ways, the basic political
and social ideals that in turn led to the development of
the DMK. It was also around this time (July 1937), that
Rajaji began to stress the need for a common language
in India and justified Hindi as the appropriate choice. In
keeping with this thought, he made an announcement
for the introduction of Hindi as a compulsory subject in
the school syllabus. The SRM condemned this for two

reasons—one, it would aid the spread of Aryan culture in Tamil Nadu and two, it would benefit only the Brahmins. The anti-Hindi campaign became the foundation for the Dravidian movement's success.

It is also interesting to note that the entire movement until that point was about eliminating the Brahmin hegemony and was against Brahminical rituals and the social order ordained by this class. This was expressed in a demand for greater representation in positions within institutions, whether government, education, or even political parties. It was also a movement against rituals in marriages and religious occasions, which were considered to be Brahminical in origin. According to the 1931 caste census, around 25 per cent of all the Brahmins in Tamil Nadu were living in the Thanjavur district, and it correlates well with the strength and virulence of the anti-Brahmin movement in the Tiruchirappalli–Thanjavur belt.

In spite of EVR's left-leaning views, especially after his visit to the Soviet Union, there is little evidence of the social revolution among the agrarian classes that was being advocated at this time within the SRM. The Justice Party, by its very composition, sought to protect large landholders, and divisions in the party arose over attempts to bring in legislation that would give greater rights to tenants and tillers. The leadership of the Dravidian parties that followed—the DK, DMK, and the AIADMK—did not draw upon the rural agrarian population, a fact that is supported by the policies in regard to the agricultural population that these parties followed while in power. In a sense, the social revolution that ensued in Tamil Nadu after the Dravidian parties came to power is different from a social movement against capital and landowning classes. It had little to do with re-appropriation of capital, and focused on access to public services and positions. Increasing nationalist sentiment and factional infighting caused support for the party to shrink steadily from the early 1930s. Many leaders left to join the Congress. The party was seen as a collaborator, supporting the British government's harsh measures. Its economic policies were also very unpopular. Its refusal to decrease land taxation in non-Zamindari areas by 12.5 per cent provoked peasant protests led by the Congress. Faced with a resurgent Congress, the party was trounced in the 1937 council and assembly elections. After 1937, it ceased to be a political power.

A group of leaders became uncomfortable with EVR's leadership and policies and formed a rebel group that attempted to dethrone him. On 27 August 1944, the Justice Party's sixteenth annual confederation took place in Salem, where the pro-EVR faction won control. The confederation passed resolutions compelling party members to renounce British honours and awards, drop caste suffixes from their names, and to resign from nominated and appointed posts. The party also took the name Dravidar Kazhagam. Annadurai, who had played an important role in passing the resolutions, became the general secretary of the transformed organization. Most members of the Justice Party joined the DK. A few dissidents like P.T. Rajan, Manapparai Thirumalaisami, and M. Balasubramania Mudaliar did not accept the new changes. Led at first by Rajan, they formed a party claiming to be the original Justice Party. This party made overtures to the Indian National Congress and supported the Quit India Movement.

The objective of the DK was proclaimed to be the achievement of a sovereign independent Dravidian republic, which would be federal in nature, with each district having residuary powers and autonomy of internal administration. As in the SRM, one of EVR's basic objectives was to eliminate all 'superstitious belief' based upon religion and tradition. For example, members were urged to boycott Brahmin priests and he campaigned vigorously for widow remarriage and inter-caste marriage. Other ideas that EVR insisted be a part of the DK, like wearing black shirts and boycotting independence days led to the exit of many young leaders from the party including Annadurai, who went on to form the DMK. While the DMK was concentrating on social reform through politics, EVR was cautious in not allowing any of his party members to contest elections. In furthering the cause of social reforms, EVR advocated widow remarriage and a system of 'self-respect marriages' without the intervention of any priests or religious leaders. The DMK also advocated self-respect marriages and these have become a part of the social fabric of Tamil Nadu, replacing traditional Hindu wedding rituals.

Birth of the DMK

According to Robert L. Hardgrave Jr,[14] the Dravidian movement was instrumental in bringing to the people of Tamil Nadu an awareness of themselves as a community. Supporters of the DK engaged in processions featuring the breaking of Hindu idols and the denigration of Hindu rituals and culture. A movement arose within the DK to challenge EVR's leadership. His marriage to Maniammai, who was forty years younger than him, did not go down well with many of his followers. In addition, EVR was clear that he did not want to contest in elections, and that his party would fight for social equality. The dissidents, led by Annadurai, broke away from the DK to form the DMK.

It is worthwhile to look at key aspects of the DMK manifesto and examine how these played an important role in the orientation of the DMK's campaign. The excerpt below from Hardgrave Jr's 1964 work talks of the defining policies outlined in the DMK manifesto. We see how the concept of 'social ownership' and bringing people from the backward castes into the production economy were the most important aspects of the manifesto.

The DMK Election Manifesto, drafted by Annadurai, declared that the party's long-range goal was the creation of a Dravidian Socialist Federation, but that in the meantime it would place before the people an immediate program. In the fifty-page document, the DMK called for the creation of a socialist economy, based on direct taxation and nationalization of banks, big commercial chains, cinema theaters, and transport. If elected, the party would undertake a series of industrial developments, including oil exploration and the construction of an atomic power station. In undertaking all types of industries, the Government would progressively minimize the role of the private sector for the ultimate objective of social ownership of all means of production and distribution. If elected, the DMK would distribute three acres of irrigated and five acres of dry land to each Harijan family without land of its own. It would establish wage boards to fix fair wages for industrial labor and minimum wages for agricultural labor. It would reserve the production of dhotis and saris exclusively for the handloom industries, and it would give 25 percent of membership in all cooperative societies to back- ward communities.

According to Hardgrave, Jr, the fact that the 1965 manifesto received elaborate consideration testifies to a growing concern for a broader social base for the party. The claim for a separate state was shelved in favour of concentrating on the problem of rising prices in Madras, which was of immediate concern to every voter. Through its elaborate structure, conferences and campaigns, and its broad financial support, the DMK sought mass membership as a base for political power. In fact, Hardgrave, Jr notes, the DMK also made concerted attempts to win support from the Brahmins, and party membership was open to Brahmins. However, the thrust of the DMK's expanding social base was directed at areas of central and southern Madras state. Its bastion was the Tiruchirappalli and Thanjavur districts, the fertile plains of the deltaic region, where there was a predominance of Brahmins. It relied on cinema as the most effective instrument of communication and the popularity of film stars was its greatest attraction. Populism was central and sustained in the Dravidian parties, and helped to strengthen party organization. This contrasts with the experience of the Congress, whose turn towards populism in the late 1960s and early 1970s served to weaken party organization. Political activists from modest backgrounds and with views somewhat divergent from those of party leaders had more influence in the DMK than they ever did in the Congress.

Members of this party, including Annadurai, were intimately connected to the film industry. Of course, the film industry's support for the DMK must be the understood in the context of the protection of Tamil as a linguistic medium and as a means of protest against the Congress-supported taxation of the Indian film industry. Both Annadurai and Karunanidhi were eloquent speakers, and wrote passionately about social justice. *Murasoli* magazine was the mouthpiece of the party, and in 2017 celebrated its diamond jubilee—75 years of publication. Karunanidhi had a letter for his party colleagues almost every day, and even during the Emergency years, there were missives conveying allegorically political sentiments. Annadurai and Karunanidhi were both script writers for stage plays and movies. The concept of touring stage players was prevalent in rural Tamil Nadu, where social as well as mythological plays were staged. They formed a very effective platform for the DMK leaders to spread their views.

To put together the timeline so far, 1912 saw the formation of the Dravidian association and 1917 the formation of the Justice Party. EVR launched the SRM in 1922, and the Justice Party and the SRM merged in 1938. In 1944, the name was changed to Dravidar Kazhagam, but EVR withdrew the party from electoral politics and converted it into a social reform organization. He explained, 'If we obtain social self-respect, political self-respect is bound to follow.' 1949 saw the formation of the DMK with Annadurai at its head.

Now that the DMK had become a political party with aspirations to governance and electoral victories, it was important to convey to the electorate what this agenda would mean for them. The election manifesto promised a socialistic pattern of society with nationalized industries and transportation as well as wage guarantees for agricultural and industrial labour. However, this alone might not have been enough to move the voters as this was very similar to what their opposition, the Congress, was offering.

For the youth in Madras and for those that participated in the food[15] and anti-Hindi agitations, and for those who had subscribed to EVR's ideology, bringing the DMK to power offered three distinct advantages. First, there was a promise that the hegemony of the upper classes in society and in positions of power would end and that there would be opportunities for all classes to be appointed to government positions and posts. In a state where traditionally (and even now), government employment is a sign of economic security and social standing, this promise offered an opportunity for moving up the social and economic ladder. This was a powerful expectation. Second, there was an expectation of access to higher education and to professional courses like engineering and medicine that would now perhaps become available to the backward classes, and in rural areas. Again in a state (unlike several states in the Hindi-speaking belt), where professional education was valued, this was a powerful incentive. Finally, there was an expectation that Tamil language and culture would get its due place in society, education, culture, entertainment, and literature. People had not forgotten that in the annual music festival for the saint Thyagaraja in Tiruvaiyaru, on one occasion, the singing of Tamil devotional songs rather than Telugu or Sanskrit had attracted the ire of the upper classes, who insisted on a ritual cleansing of the premises before the event could proceed. There was a strong clamour for the restoration of Tamil pride, and pride in being Dravidian. I could see and experience this almost every day in my college and university days.

In several ways, Tamil Nadu in 1967, was ready for a shift to Dravidian ideology and politics.

Notes

1. The Indian Civil Service—the highest public service position, admission to which required selection through a stiff competitive examination and interview.

2. S. Saraswathy, 'Minorities in Madras State', University of Madras, 1974, quoted in *Socio-Political Situation in Tamil Nadu: A Backdrop*, shodhganga.inflibnet.ac.in/bitstream/10603/20360/6/06_chapter%201.

3. This awareness for the need to achieve social justice was one of the more important factors that led to the rise of the Dravidian movement. Narendra Subramanian's seminal work gives an authoritative view of the development of this movement.

4. N.K. Mangalamurugesan, *Self-Respect Movement in Tami Nadu, 1920–1940* (Madurai: Koodal Publishers, 1979).

5. Christophe Jaffrelot, 'Sanskritization vs. Ethnicization in India: Changing Indentities and Caste Politics before Mandal.' *Asian Survey*, 40(5): 756–66.

6. K. Kailasapathy, 'The Tamil Purist Movement: A Re-evaluation.' *Social Scientist*, 7(10): 23–51.

7. Kailasapathy, 'The Tamil Purist Movement: A Re-evaluation.'

8. A.R. Venkatachalapathy, 'Dravidian Movement and Saivites: 1927–1944', *Economic and Political Weekly*, 30(14): 761–68.

9. M.S.S. Pandian, 'Notes on Transformation of Dravidian Ideology: Tamil Nadu 1990–1940', *Social Scientist*, 22(5/6): 82.

10. M.S.S. Pandian, 'Notes on Transformation of Dravidian Ideology'.

11. M.S.S. Pandian, 'Beyond Colonial Crumbs: Cambridge School, Identity Politics and Dravidian Movement(s)', *Economic and Political Weekly*, 30(7/8): 385–91.

12. Christopher John Baker, *The Politics of South India 1920–1937* (Delhi: Vikas Publishing House, 1976).

13. Jacob Pandian, 'Re-Ethnogenesis: The Quest for a Dravidian Identity among the Tamils of India', *Anthropos*, 93(H. 4./6/): 547.

14. Robert H. Hardgrave, Jr, 'The DMK and Its Politics of Tamil Nationalism', *Pacific Affairs*, 37(4): 396–411.

15. For details refer to Chapter 2.

2

THE DMK AND SOCIAL CHANGE
1967 to 1977

———

THE DMK WAS FORMED IN 1949 AS A POLITICAL PARTY, and initially espoused the cause of an independent Tamil Nadu. The political ideology of the DMK was drawn from the activities of EVR's Self-Respect Movement, and the social agenda of creating opportunities for non-Brahmins and prejudice against Brahminical rituals was also adopted. Pride in the Tamil language and culture and in a Dravidian identity was part of the party's propaganda. The introduction of Hindi as compulsory in schools further strengthened the anti-North and anti-Congress stand of the party. The party believed that their social agenda could be achieved only through political power, and participated in the 1957 and 1962 assembly elections, coming second to the Congress.

The Communist Party of India (CPI) had launched armed peasant revolts in parts of Andhra Pradesh and West Bengal between 1946 and 1953. The government of Madras, under Chief Minister C. Rajagopalachari, came down heavily on the revolts. This repression drove the communists closer to those who were opposed to the Congress, namely the DK and the DMK. The latter provided refuge to communist fugitives throughout this period. The DK campaigned for the communists in the 1952 elections, and this gained the CPI considerable support during the elections, when many communist candidates contested from prison. This was particularly true in the Thanjavur and Tiruchirapalli regions, where both the communists and Dravidian parties enjoyed the greatest support in those days. After the revolts were quelled, the CPI opted for peaceful electoral participation in 1953, but the growth of the DMK weakened the communist movement, with many communists sympathetic to the movement shifting over to the DMK.

Karunanidhi's participation in the Periyar movement, his association with the Dravidian cause, his oratory and literary skills, and his command over Tamil language and literature are all well-known and well documented. Karunanidhi is a great orator. He was always confident that he could reach the poor and the downtrodden directly. He had been subjected to class and caste distinctions as a young boy trying to learn music in the temples.[1] Those feelings of humiliation and being socially ostracized have remained with him. In *Murasoli*, the party daily, he wrote a letter every day to his 'brothers and sisters' in the party, talking about social equality and opportunities for the downtrodden. His reach through the media and films was phenomenal. The movie *Parasakthi* was released on 17 October 1952, on the occasion of Deepavali. The screenplay and dialogues were by Karunanidhi and the film attacked Brahmins and Hindu customs. There is a demand in the film for a separate Dravidian nation, and condemnation of the societal structure of those times. Sivaji Ganesan made his debut as the protagonist in this film, which achieved cult status, resonating with the demands of the Social Reform Movement, anti-Brahmin sentiments, and Tamil pride. There was an attempt to ban this film, which only increased its cult image.

It was in M.G. Ramachandran (henceforth MGR) that the DMK ideology, its message, and connection with the masses found a true vehicle. Karunanidhi had written the story and dialogues for *Marudanattu Ilavarasi* (Princess of Marudu, 1950), with MGR in the lead, a film that enjoyed enormous box office success. The year 1957 saw the release of the MGR-starrer *Pudumai Pithan* (Innovator) with story and dialogues by Karunanidhi. *Mannadi Mannan* (King of Kings, 1960), again starring MGR, had a song specifically for Dravidians. Annadurai scripted the dialogue for *Nallavan Vazhvan* (Good Men Will Prosper, 1961), by which time the Dravidian movement, Tamil identity, and culture were very much part of the public discourse.

The people of Tamil Nadu have always been avid cinema fans. Up to the 1980s, 'touring theatres', basically thatched sheds with a screen, used to be the hallmark of all small towns. The Congress had made use of this opportunity to reach the masses by encouraging the screening of films that had a nationalist sentiment and eulogized the freedom movement. Print media, including dailies like the *Swadesamitran*, carried this forward. The Congress ceased to use films as a medium of propaganda after independence and it was the DMK that transformed this medium into a platform for reaching out to the Tamil people about their Tamil and Dravidian identities. The frequency of people going to the cinema in Tamil Nadu has been very high, and Annadurai and Karunanidhi used films as a major propaganda vehicle for promoting Dravidian ideology. Annadurai's dramas *Nallathambi* (Good Brother, 1948) and *Velaikari* (Servant Maid, 1949) promoted social reform and non-Brahmin self-respect. There were overtones of atheism in these, especially a rejection of idol worship and temple culture. Hardgrave, Jr and Neidhart[2] conclude that the film became a major vehicle for the Dravidian movement in South India, and its effect and penetration may be measured in the spectacular rise of the DMK and in its landslide victory in Tamil Nadu in the 1967 election.

Sara Dickey, in her work on politics of adulation in Tamil Nadu,[3] talks specifically about the effectiveness of films and fan clubs in establishing a party in power. By broadcasting an attractive image, films can overcome a problem faced by many aspiring politicians in developing countries with electoral political systems: garnering widespread voter support where access to voters through mass media is limited. Also, fan clubs have proved to be useful to actors entering politics. They provide a pre-existing network of supporters, often highly organized, that can easily be transformed into a political cadre.

MGR soon became so popular that he could wield substantial control over many aspects of his films, ensuring that they enhanced the party's image in addition to his own. As Forrester (1976) points out, 'always, either explicitly or just below the surface, there was a political message in

his films: the DMK is the party that does in real life what
MGR does in the film, the party that loves and serves the
poor, that does battle with evil, that delivers the oppressed'.

In the mid-1950s, the DMK launched a series of
street agitations, encompassing the major themes of
Dravidianization. There were protests against the name
of a railway station, opposition to the craft education
scheme introduced by the state government in schools
(it was deemed a caste-based programme), and against
Nehru's denigration of Tamil and south Indian culture. Its
periodic agitations in 1959, 1960, and 1963 were against
the commitment of the Indian Constitution to change the
official language of India from English to Hindi.

The Dravidian party was by now strongly on an
anti-Aryan, pro-Tamil platform. By this time, the anti-
Brahminical stand, now metamorphed as an anti-Aryan
and anti-North position, was focused on creating a separate
Tamil identity through political means. The fact that both
Annadurai as well as Karunanidhi were closely associated
with Tamil films, drama, and literature only accentuated
the DMK's Tamil identity. It was no longer about opposition
to Brahminism alone. It encompassed a larger Tamil
identity that included language, culture, and literature
that was considered closely linked to a separate ethnic
identity.[4] It was also a pro-poor, anti-landlord platform.
As a student in Madras those days, I was witness to the
sentiments that these ideas generated among students.
There were Sivaji Ganesan fans and MGR fans, intense
debates about the superiority of one over the other. Sivaji
films were contemporary stories from everyday life, with
a romantic motif and well-crafted narrative. MGR films
centred on social messages, and MGR was careful that even

the lyrics of the songs conveyed a social message about the poor. His films often had scenes with the DMK flag in the background. Among the students, especially those from Tamil-medium schools, the number of MGR fans far exceeded that of Sivaji fans. Debates ranged over film dialogues and over how the DMK in power would deliver all that was promised in the films scripted by Karunanidhi or Annadurai and acted in by MGR.

Hardgrave Jr and Neidhart, in 'Films and Political Consciousness in Tamil Nadu', try to understand the electoral success of the Dravidian parties through the penetration of MGR films. They conducted a survey among 500 urban (Chennai) and 500 rural respondents and concluded that:

- The MGR fan had greater intensity and was a 'repeater' while the Sivaji fan normally went to watch a film only once.
- Also, among those who voted for MGR, a higher percentage expressed an interest in politics.
- Star preference sharply delineated interest in politics. MGR fans were far more interested in politics than Sivaji fans. This was an especially powerful factor, for Sivaji fans had a higher level of education, a variable which itself significantly correlated with political interests.
- The breakdown of the voting figures by star preference was of great significance: Sivaji fans were Congress-inclined; MGR fans, DMK-inclined.

Two important developments between 1963 and 1965 accelerated the DMK's race to electoral success. The first was the announcement by the central government that

Hindi would be the official language and would replace English. The Official Languages Act, 1963 sought to make Hindi the national language, though permitting the continuation of English beyond 1965. The text of the Act did not satisfy the DMK. As the day (26 January 1965) of switching over to Hindi as the sole official language approached, an anti-Hindi movement gained momentum in the state with support from college students. Riots broke out on 25 January in Madurai, sparked by an altercation between students and some Congress party members. The riots spread all over Madras state, continued unabated for the next two months, and were marked by acts of violence, arson, looting, police firing, and baton charges. The Congress government of Madras state called in paramilitary forces to quell the agitation; their involvement resulted in the deaths of about seventy persons (by official estimates) including two policemen. There was firing in Cumbum in Madurai district, with three youngsters killed. To calm the situation, Prime Minister Lal Bahadur Shastri gave assurances that English would continue to be used as the official language for as long as the non-Hindi speaking states wanted. The riots subsided after Shastri's assurance, as did the student agitation, but suspicion towards the intentions of the central government and, by imputation, the Congress, remained.

Another factor exacerbated discontent. At the national level, grain production fell from 89.4 million tonnes in 1964–65 to 72.3 million tonnes[5] in 1965–66, a drop of 19 per cent. Tamil Nadu is a marginal state in food grain self-sufficiency. In some years, the north-east monsoon is good, and it is marginally surplus. In poor monsoon years, it is a deficit state and has to depend on rice from Andhra

Pradesh and other nearby states. With grain being in short supply, the Madras government was forced to purchase rice and wheat in large quantities from Andhra Pradesh and Orissa. It must be recalled that consumption of wheat was not as prevalent in the 1960s as it is today, because it was considered a north Indian food. There was aid from the United States of America, but mostly in the form of flour and wheat. Officers of the food and civil supplies department were deputed to move food grains from the train stations and the port to consuming centres in the districts. In one incident, the Madras collector stopped a consignment of rice belonging to Bhaktavatsalam, the Chief Minister, because the transportation papers were not in order. This made big news and led to the impression that the Congress government was somehow responsible for the food shortage and for hoarding.

On 16 November, the Congress government introduced family cards for rationing provisions in an attempt to tide over the crisis. It was also raining that month. A week later, *The Hindu* reported: 'Despite the rain, men, children and women stick to queues, some without cover, some under umbrellas, or holding a bag over their heads.'

Every adult in every family was entitled to one 'unit' comprising of one litre of wheat and rice, every week. This was an equivalent of just four ounces a day per person. Over 4,40,000 family cards were distributed. The distribution was well managed and a success, but the initiative was too little too late. The spike in the prices of essential commodities, the continued shortage of food, and the feeling of being neglected by the central government alienated voters, causing them to shift support away from the Congress government and towards the DMK.

Among the major electoral promises made by Annadurai before the elections was that he would make available three kilograms[6] of rice for a rupee if the DMK won.

Rajaji had broken away from the Congress and formed the Swatantra party, and grew closer to the DMK as the tempo of anti-Hindi agitations increased and the popularity of the Congress declined. It may be recalled that he had advocated the introduction of Hindi as early as 1954. His education policy of caste-based schooling had cost him the chief ministership, and the Congress opted for a backward class candidate as chief minister in K. Kamraj. Rajaji never forgave the Congress, and the current developments gave him an opportunity to oppose the Congress at the hustings. He noted the emergence of the DMK, and Swatantra and the DMK were electoral allies from 1964 to 1970. Rajaji used his stature as the state's most respected Brahmin politician to help alter the DMK's anti-Brahmin image. He argued that DMK had abandoned secessionism, and had outgrown the casteism that it inherited from the DK. During the 1967 elections, he reminded the public about the DK's implicit alliance with the Congress. The DMK's association with Rajaji contributed significantly to the electoral results of 1967.

Against this backdrop, the Madras assembly elections of 1967 resulted in an overwhelming victory for the DMK, heralding a period of unbroken rule for the Dravidian parties that has lasted fifty years. The DMK won 179 seats and the Congress emerged victorious in 51 seats. This was in stark contrast to the 1962 elections where the seat distribution between Congress and the DMK was 139 and 50 seats respectively. Annadurai was sworn in as the chief minister.

The food shortages and family ration cards, in many distinct ways, were the beginnings of the welfare-oriented policies that are now associated with the state.

One of the first ideas that Annadurai was keen to implement was that of supplying three kilograms of rice for a rupee. The initial interactions at the highest levels in the Secretariat were tentative and inconclusive, with either side not too sure about how to deal with the other. The upper echelons of the Tamil Nadu Civil Service in those years still had several senior officers belonging to the ICS of the British era—the Chief Secretary was an ICS officer. They had grown up in the Congress era. Their work ethic was focused on processes being carried out quickly, ethically, and most importantly, as per rules and procedures. A hierarchical structure clearly defined responsibilities and duties at each level, and an efficient system of monitoring, inspections, review, and correctives made the Madras administrative system one of the best in the country.

There had been innovations after independence. The creation of the community development and the Panchayat and Panchayat Union framework for rural development delivery owed everything to the vision and diligence of R.A. Gopalaswamy, the Chief Secretary in the late 1950s. The structure, programme, and institutions that were set up carried forward the ideas of community development of the visionary central minister S.K. De. In many ways this was a national programme, and community development was the buzzword in all states in the 1950s. As sub-collectors, we had to know the Panchayat and Panchayat Union manuals and had to inspect and monitor the development programmes of these institutions. We had a separate Panchayat Development Wing in our offices. Gram sevaks in each village were village counsellors, development initiators, and helped in agricultural development with assistance from a group of extension officers attached to the nearest Block Development Office. Elected Panchayat presidents, and Panchayat Unions, assisted by Block Development Officers, carried the rural development policies of the government forward, including local irrigation initiatives, rural roads, as well as agricultural extension. Needless to say, the elected representatives were predominantly from the Congress.

R. Venkataraman,[7] the Minister for Industries in Madras in the Congress regime, put in place institutions for small-scale industries, including financing institutions, industrial parks, and other infrastructure. Small-scale industrial estates, the Tamil Nadu Industrial Investment Corporation, encouraging the Government of India to set up large public sector undertakings like Bharat Heavy Electricals and the Neyveli Lignite Corporation were some of his initiatives. The administration absorbed all this, quickly bringing rules and manuals and procedures to integrate new ideas into the existing administrative patterns, creating new review and inspection mechanisms, relying on existing District Collectors to ensure that process-driven development was firmly in place.

Annadurai's suggestion of three kilograms of rice per rupee was none of the above. Earlier administrations were a continuation of colonial policies that were largely top down. Annadurai's was an idea that came from the needs and demand of the people, and hence a bottom-up initiative. Second, it was innovative in the sense that nothing of this kind had been tried before, and it required a rethinking of logistics, financing, and institutions. Third, Madras was used to prudent and conservative financial management that did not like welfare giveaways that would cost the exchequer without any tangible returns. The administration naturally protested and said that this was not possible. They told the chief minister it was unworkable, too costly, and there was not enough rice to sustain all this. Annadurai was a very respected and capable person. He hesitated, but insisted on at least one kilogram of rice per rupee being given through the existing ration card system. This was done, and marked the beginning of direct grant and welfare schemes, which now form a large component of state policy. State finances did not allow the enlargement of this programme beyond Chennai and Coimbatore, and the refusal of the central government to increase allocations from the central pool of food grains made it even more infeasible to do so. Simultaneously, it disturbed the relationship between the higher echelons of the civil service and the political masters. Until now, policies were based on an analysis of needs, balanced with implementation capabilities and invariably implemented through existing structures. The new dispensation had new ideas that would not fit into all this. In the first five years of the new regime, several senior officers retired, some went away to Delhi to take up senior positions, and the new group that came in was more attuned to the aspirations of the new leaders.

Annadurai passed away in 1969, and M. Karunanidhi, the winner of a party election for leadership, became chief minister in 1969. The cabinet consisted of ideologues of the erstwhile anti-Hindi, anti-Delhi movements as well as

young, educated, and articulate persons keen to show that
the government could do as well, if not better, than earlier
governments for development. The policies that followed
between 1969 and 1976 are a mix of these ideas.

There was strategic use of state patronage, and the use
of local party cadres in administration. As a young officer,
I witnessed representations from the public spearheaded
by local party functionaries. This was a change. Earlier,
I used to meet Panchayat Union Chairmen, accompanied by
their officers, on matters pertaining to development. Now,
there were district and local party functionaries, bringing
representations on the availability of irrigation water, food
grains, or the functioning of schools. Suddenly, we had to
deal with representations from the party, rather than from
the hierarchy. Upwardly mobile interest groups emerged,
seeking the support of the party now in power. Initially,
they pointed out public grievances for redressal, short-
circuiting the established channels of administration, and,
over the years, these have grown into assertive demands
from the district administration. Representations from
party cadres in administration are now the norm rather
than an exception. While this serves to articulate public
demands and grievances, it constrains the administration
into looking at things only from a particular point of view.[8]

There was focus on increased representation of other
classes in jobs and in the party cadre as well. Data from the
Tamil Nadu Public Service Commission indicates that,
between 1960 and 1980, the caste composition of those
entering into government service changed considerably,
with substantially a greater proportion coming from the
backward classes. Action for government recruitment
from the backward, most backward, and Dalit castes

ensured that the structure of the bureaucracy underwent a change. Several of the new personnel were from non-urban areas and could understand village-level conditions. The new dispensation was more in tune with the expectations and aspirations of the party in power.

At the cutting edge in administration, at the level of the lower rung of police and revenue authorities, the representation of Dalits and other backward classes it was more marked. The mere introduction of recruitment based on numerical strengths of the communities in society ensured that forward caste representation in new appointments went down drastically, while opportunities for backward castes and for scheduled castes and tribes increased significantly. The proportion of Brahmins recruited into government jobs became smaller in tune with their proportion in the population. As a result, the number of entrants into government jobs became much more representative of the diversity of classes and castes in the population. This was a very significant change. On the one hand, it brought to fruition the proportional representation that EVR had aspired to right from the days of the Kanchipuram Congress in 1925. At the same time, it brought into government people from different backgrounds and aspirations as well as from small towns and rural areas, who were more in tune with the sentiments of the Dravidian parties, as were the students of Madras in my time. This was, and continues to be, a very important step forward in ensuring social balance in state administration and is instrumental in delivering the social welfare and social benefit services in succeeding administrations. The class composition of government service today is totally different from what it was when I joined service in 1965, and is definitely more representative of the diversity of groups in Tamil Nadu.

Given the assumption of the DMK that existing institutions were steeped in Congress ideology and culture, there was some suspicion about existing institutions at the local level. They were considered Congress-oriented institutions, working on an agenda prescribed by the central government. The Rural Development and Panchayat institutions formed one such group. They were subject to central fund grants and review, and could not be dismantled—they were kept at arm's length, and allowed to function. Between 1967 and 1969, I suddenly found focus on the prescribed Rural Development and Panchayat Union and Block level programmes waning, and a greater focus on dealing with public representations.

There was greater reliance on the district administration and on District Collectors. Collectors were the implementing arms of government policies at the district level, and the continuity from colonial days ensured that the administration remained committed to this. As indicated earlier, senior members of the service at the Secretariat level were people who had worked under colonial rule, and the systems and processes that continued were a reflection of those standards. I remember that during my probation at the training academy in Mussoorie, multiple sessions were devoted to the importance of the role of the District Collector in ensuring coherent administration and planned development based on policies laid down hierarchically.

In Tamil Nadu, the situation changed after 1967. The DMK was a party that had emerged from a mass movement. It was important for them to, while in power, listen to and satisfy the expectations of the people. The DMK was also a disciplined organization in which district secretaries had direct access to the top leaders. The district secretaries started interacting with District Collectors directly on matters pertaining to day-to-day administration. The post of District Collector became a powerful and coveted one. There were seasoned collectors like S.P. Ambrose, who had been at the helm of several districts, and was in Coimbatore in 1967. Ambrose initially found the change—of having to deal with the new MLAs—difficult, and mentioned several cases of attempts by newly elected politicians to take the law and administration in their own hands. He said that he had the support of the ministers from the district and the chief minister, who respected the way he functioned.[9]

Gradually, this changed, especially after 1971, when the DMK came back to power with an overwhelming majority, and the party cadres had more influence. The collectors and the party district secretary became the most powerful arms of the state administration in the districts. There was naturally a trend towards state patronage in postings and the politicization of administrative cadres. Senior members of the civil services retired in these years or were deputed to the central government in very senior positions, and the changes in state bureaucracy at the field level were quite palpable. This was true for the subsequent AIADMK regime as well. 'What is significant is that the transformation was enabled seamlessly even as two parties explicitly inimical to each other reigned in Tamil Nadu. The state is often cited as a habitat of politically committed bureaucracy. While this may be true in parts, what is also true is that the system is committed to developing the state.'[10] The politicization of administration as well as the change in the class structure of the administration enabled the DMK to push forward the social justice agenda that had been the basic feature of the Periyar movement.

The industry ministry in the state was under S. Madhavan, a lawyer from Ramanathapuram district who tried to outshine Venkataraman's achievements. The creation of new industrial parks, attracting major industry and industrialists to invest in Tamil Nadu, and fiscal and infrastructure initiatives led to a spurt of industrial development in the state. Corporations for the development and financing of small industries, large industries, and financing and provision of infrastructure were formed and proved very successful.[11] The Tamil Nadu Industrial Development Corporation (TIDCO) invested in several large industries, including the Southern Petrochemical Industries Corporation (SPIC) Limited and South India Shipping. The State Industries Promotion Corporation of Tamilnadu Ltd (SIPCOT) provided land and developed infrastructure as well as project finance. New sugar mills were planned and developed. Between 1973 and 1975, I was part of a team responsible for developing the sugar industry, and six sugar mills in the public and co-operative sector were set up in the state, some of which have a record of quick project execution. There was gradual consciousness that an all-India market for the sale of products as well as raw materials was essential if Tamil Nadu were to progress. The anti-Delhi rhetoric became muted over the years.

In fact, Narendra Subramanian goes on to say that the creation of the DMK aided democracy and tolerance in various ways. The party gave activists and supporters some autonomy in how they responded to leaders' appeals. In the process, they could mobilize widely felt aspirations and reduce caste inequality. The core of Subramanian's argument is that in the politics of Dravidianism, though ethnic appeal has supplied cohesion, the dominant motif and mechanisms have been populist. Therefore, the populist feature of the Dravidian ideology dominates the era.

There was investment in helping the poor. Housing programmes after clearing slums, housing projects for fishermen, police personnel, and for Adi-Dravidars[12] were initiated. New institutions like the Slum Clearance Board and the Harijan Housing Development Corporation were assigned the responsibility to carry out these mandates.

Apart from rice at one rupee a kilogram, there was an effort to extend the public distribution system (PDS). By 1976, the entire state was covered by PDS, which provided rice, sugar, kerosene, and wheat to the card holder, as well as special rations and gifts, including saris and dhotis on Pongal.[13] Other welfare schemes included assistance for marriage in the form of a cash grant for thaalis[14] and also schemes for indigent widows and pensioners. It was not a holistic approach, but rather a grant-based approach towards particular sections of people that the government considered to be disadvantaged or in need of support.

The development indicators for Tamil Nadu increased significantly during this decade. The state domestic product grew by 17 per cent at constant prices between 1970 and 1976, per capita incomes rose by around 30 per cent, literacy rates went up from 39.5 per cent in the 1971 census to 54.4 per cent in the 1981 census. The infant mortality rate dropped from 125 in 1971 to around 103 by 1977. Though significant growth occurred in the years when MGR was in power, the foundations for growth were laid during the initial DMK years. There was also focus on industrialization and infrastructure, as already pointed out, and Tamil Nadu stood next only to Gujarat and Maharashtra in industrial growth during this period.

There were important changes in administration and delivery of services. It has been pointed out that Tamil Nadu was among the top states in process-based administration even prior to independence. The changes brought about in the Karunanidhi era, which included a changeover at the highest levels of administration from the earlier British-era administrators through retirement or deputation, the use of state patronage in the recruitment, identification, and appointment of district-level officers sympathetic to the regime, and the close association of the district-level party leaders with the administrative set up all resulted in a significant change in the implementation of programmes. Coupled with the fact that traditional administrative hierarchies were strong and implementation capabilities time-tested and resilient, this resulted in a slew of development initiatives getting implemented at the ground level. Unlike the past, these initiatives were people- and welfare-oriented, and at every level, had been formulated with the political benefits that might accrue in mind.

Periyar had been attracted to communist ideology and even the DMK election manifesto was a pro-public sector, anti-capitalist statement. However, several actions had already been taken. Land reforms in the form of abolishing the zamindari system and distributing land to the tenants had already been initiated in Tamil Nadu by the late 1950s. The DMK did enact some legislation with regard to minor *inams*,[15] temple lands, and plantations and orchards, but these were more in the nature of completing the reforms picture. Land was very much in the hands of the peasant and the landowner.

The communist movement, especially in Thanjavur district in Tamil Nadu and parts of Andhra Pradesh in the erstwhile Madras Presidency, had been put down by stern police action during the period in which Rajaji was chief minister. In 1967, the organization occupied only pockets in the districts where rights of tenants were affected.

Therefore, policies on agrarian matters, on land reforms, peasant rights and land tenure were somewhat muted. In 1969, after he had just become chief minister, Karunanidhi toured Pudukkottai area, then a part of Tiruchirappalli district. Tiruchirapalli was a traditional stronghold of the DMK, and the Tiruchirapalli as well as the Thanjavur party district secretaries were among the most powerful in the party—even ministers used to defer to them. Pudukkottai at that time was a hotbed of communist activities under Umanath.[16] The peasantry was being organized to fight for their landholding rights against the landlords and *inamdars*—the Minor Inams Abolition Act had just been enacted. I was Sub-Collector in Pudukkottai, and there were law and order problems every day between landlords and tenants. Karunanidhi spent a whole day in that area, and addressed nineteen meetings. His speeches were a treat to listen to, and I listened to all of them that day. He attacked the communists. His argument was that the DMK knew all about agrarian distress, the problems of the poor, and did not need advice on how to deal with agrarian issues. He recalled the agitation that he had led for distressed handloom and beedi workers at Nangavaram in Kulithalai, which was his first constituency. The appalling condition of men, women, and children in this village was the theme of Karunanidhi's maiden speech in the assembly. The speech assailed the class bias of the judiciary and the failure of the state machinery to provide safeguards for the poor and marginalized sections of the society. That day, he asked the communists, 'What do you know about deprivation that I do not know?' All through the DMK regime, there was a duality between association with the left parties for electoral alliances, and a distancing from their land and labour based organizational issues.

The DMK exempted farmers owning five to twelve acres of land from agricultural income taxes. All dry land was exempted from land taxes, benefiting over 4.5 million farmers. In 1971 and 1972, the Tamil Nadu Land Reforms Act was amended, reducing the ceiling of land ownership per individual from thirty standard acres to fifteen. There were other changes which, rather than attempting a wide-ranging policy change in land tenure and concentration of land holding, appeared to be focused on some large landlords in Thanjavur district. Lands belonging to Thiagaraja Mudaliar in Vadapathimangalam near Thanjavur were taken over by the state for sugar cane plantation. The usage of some of the lands belonging to G.K. Moopanar[17] and other large landowning families was restricted to plantations and orchards.

In his seminal thesis, Vivek Srinivasan argues that widespread and decentralized collective action for public services plays a critical role in the delivery and working of public services.[18] At the time, the DMK came to power, and in the years of the Karunanidhi government (1969–76), evidence of collective action determining government policy or even service delivery is not easy to find. It is possible to argue that the Social Reform Movement and Dravidian movement constituted collective action against established class and caste interests, and therefore the party's democratic victory and rule enshrined all public aspirations in the government. It is only later, in the MGR years and subsequently, that we see demand for public services increasing, and collective action becoming noticeable. It was a function as much of the services being provided, such as midday meals and the public distribution system, as of increasing literacy and consciousness among the people.

An important change occurred in village administration. The British system of revenue collection from agriculture was based on the *ryotwari* settlement, with each parcel of land being 'settled' to determine the rent to be paid to the crown. The Madras Hereditary Village Officers Act of 1895 governed posts in the village, and regulated the succession to certain hereditary posts. The management of village accounts was in the hands of the *karnam* (the village accountant) and the collection of revenues the responsibility of the village headman. They were paid a token sum for their services. This team was also responsible for allocating irrigation water from the channels and ponds by a system determined by the district administration. The headman was appointed from the landed class, and it was considered a post of privilege. There were a large number of Brahmins in these posts, especially in the fertile districts of Thanjavur, Tiruchirappalli, and Tirunelveli. Village accountants, though not necessarily landed, were educated people from the other castes. Dalits were employed as village watchmen or water management menials who managed the village irrigation systems.[19] These posts were

considered hereditary posts, and as sub-collectors, one of
our important responsibilities was the appointment of these
personnel to vacant posts. The stratification of eligibility
reflected the caste structures of the village. These were
posts of prestige, sharply competed for by eligible aspirants,
or, appeals against the sub-collector's orders would be to
the Board of Revenue, a hallowed institution of very senior,
experienced civil servants, or, in some cases, to the High
Court. As a sub-collector, one of the great thrills was to
have one's orders of selection of village officers upheld[20] by
the Board of Revenue and the High Court.

It was important for the DMK government to change
this system, bring about social justice in villages, and
end the domination of the higher castes. In 1973, an
Administrative Reforms Commission set up by the state
recommended, among other things, that the existing
part-time village officers be replaced by regular, full-time
transferable public servants who should form part of the
Revenue hierarchy. K. Diraviyam, the Revenue Secretary
at this time, was an outstanding civil servant with a deep-
rooted belief in the need to provide equal opportunities
for all sections of Tamil society. He believed that it was
the role of the government to change existing colonial
structures to provide for such reforms. He was a man of
detail and excellent at implementation, and his role in
the conceptualisation and implementation of the midday
meals programme is discussed in detail in Chapter 4. The
state government accepted this recommendation and
promulgated the Tamil Nadu Village Officers Service
Rules, 1974 on 17 May 1975. This abolished the system
of hereditary village karnam and headman. Village officers
were appointed, recruited eventually through the Tamil

Nadu Public Service Commission. A village office was opened in each village, where the village accounts would be kept and revenue collected. Eventually, in 1981, when MGR was chief minister, this was enshrined in the Tamil Nadu Abolition of Part-time Village Officers Act, 1981. The social hierarchy of villages underwent a significant change as a result of these measures. V.V. Swaminathan was Minister in the MGR cabinet in 1980 and 1984, elected from Bhuvanagiri, and a staunch supporter of the need for changes in the social fabric of the state. The 1981 act was one he strongly supported. Interestingly, the change in the structure of the village officers started during the DMK regime, and was completed during the AIADMK regime, indicating that that there was uniformity of ideology on the need for this reform.

The consequences were threefold.[21] First, villagers, especially tenant farmers, no longer had to depend on the karnam for recording tenancies and collecting revenues from them. To a great extent, the stranglehold of larger farmers over tenants was loosened. Second, the newly appointed village officers came from all classes, and there was an opportunity for even members of the most backward classes to hold these positions of power and prestige in the village. Birth and death certificates, pattas (certificates of land holding), community certificates (for school admissions and concessions), address proof for accessing the PDS, and several other essential certificates were now issued by the village officers, and the change in the system of appointment had a significant impact on the social dynamics of the village and the eligibility of public services to all classes. Third, the newly appointed personnel were more objective and unbiased, thus providing access to services for all communities.[22] In some measure, this led to changes in land holding patterns in villages. Several larger landlords sought to move away from agriculture, as they could no longer command the services of their tenants or agricultural labourers at will. Many Brahmin landlords sold their lands and moved to cities, as their children moved to urban employment.

Villagers were also dependent on an intricate system of co-operative societies for their credit needs as well as for inputs like seeds, fertilizer, and pesticides. These societies also provided the facility of storing harvested grain in village-level warehouses and advancing credit to farmers against produce. The DMK regime changed this system. The co-operatives were systematically dismantled, and the minister for co-operation, Si Pa Adithanar, exercised considerable ingenuity in achieving this. The existing village level co-operative societies were the base for district- and state-level co-operative societies. Access to credit was from the Tamil Nadu Co-operative Central Bank, which was recognized and regulated jointly by the Reserve Bank of India and the Registrar of Co-operative Societies, the latter being an officer of the state government. The pyramidal structure had elected functionaries at every level, and in 1967 was occupied predominantly by Congressmen and, in some instances, those owing allegiance to the Communist Party. Adithanar[23] realized that administrative control was vested with the state. Skilfully, he created a large number of new co-operative societies, called lift irrigation societies, multipurpose societies, and the like, and held elections for these, with DMK candidates emerging victorious. The Tamil Nadu Co-operatives Act was amended in 1970[24] so that these new societies could become members of district and state cooperative federations and banks. Within a couple of years, DMK politicians had secured a majority in all co-operative institutions, agricultural co-operatives, co-operative sugar mills, co-operative spinning mills, and co-operative banks. The administrative structure was overhauled, with new recruits appointed to the posts of clerks, accountants, sub-registrars, and deputy registrars of co-operative societies. There was an emphasis on the recruitment of members of the backward classes in these societies. By 1971, the structure of the co-operatives had changed significantly. As a next step, there was an attempt to avoid fresh elections to the co-operatives. Elected positions, from the smallest member to the highest state-level president, would have meant elections to nearly fifty thousand positions in the state. Later, the Tamil Nadu Co-operatives Act was again amended to provide for the suspension of elected bodies and the appointment of special officers or government functionaries to these positions.

The result of these changes was that the farmer now depended on the new structures, which were administratively managed rather than through local representatives, for all his credit and input needs. Changes in village administration as well as the co-operative structure thus changed the dependence pattern of the villagers from local, village-level functionaries to government-appointed ones.

These changes in recruitment at the village level and state level to government offices, educational institutions, welfare and concession programmes for the underprivileged, and political interventions at the district and village level all resulted in significant changes in the content and delivery of public services in the period 1969 to 1976. At the village level, however, Dalits and members of the most backward classes still had to struggle for basic public services.

The ideology and the thrust for social reform and justice, brought about another major institutional change. Prior to 1967, transport (bus) services in the state were substantially in the hands of private operators. In Madurai, the TVS group ran city and suburban services—a distinguished upper caste family with a hand in different areas of business and manufacturing. In Salem and the surrounding areas, it was in the hands of the traditionally wealthy, and the landlords. Between 1967 and 1971, all bus services in private hands were nationalized, and several regional state-owned transport corporations were set up to run them. There was little compensation to the erstwhile owners, as the operating permits were just allowed to expire and not renewed. Interestingly, the people put in charge of the transition and the running of the new corporations were among the best in the Tamil Nadu Civil Service at that time. Thus, the civil service readily acquiesced and participated in a measure that was essentially taking away assets from one identified class, and nationalizing those assets, again an indication that the administration saw itself in tune with the political ideologies of that time.

The Karunanidhi era was successful in creating a symbiotic relationship between politics, development, and administration, which laid the foundation for many more such programmes in later years. The later MGR movies, *Adimai Penn* (Slave Girl, 1969), *Engal Thangam* (Our Thangam, 1970), *Rickshawkaran (Rickshaw puller,* 1971), and *Mattukara Velan (Cowherd Velan,* 1970)[25] reflected the times. The DMK was already in power, and these films promised that the poor would be taken care of by the state. They presented a leadership that would wipe the tears from the eyes of the poor, grant relief against injustice, ensure employment and livelihoods, and, in short, improve the lot of the people. It is not surprising that MGR, and the DMK which he was a part of at that time, was identified with the ability to craft and deliver social welfare measures aimed at the common man.

It is possible to argue that the policies in the initial years (1967 to 1976) were more in tune with the earlier demands of the Justice Party and the SRM—to provide for greater employment and access opportunities to backward classes and castes in government employment, activities, and development initiatives. There was an effort to change the education curriculum, to emphasize the importance of Tamil, and an attempt to offer grants, doles, and scholarships to open up opportunities for the backward classes.

However, these paternalistic policies were abandoned after 1971.[26] Reduction in rice subsidies and repeal of dry laws (1971) were some measures that were not popular. The identification of the DMK with the emergent backward classes became stronger, further alienating the upper as well as the lower strata. The DMK in power between 1971 and 1976, was a more assured, stronger party. Karunanidhi himself belongs to a backward class, but there were others in the cabinet who were from the landowning, trader, and educated classes. This was true for some of the district secretaries as well. Tiruchirapalli, Thanjavur, and Madurai were headed by such people. During these years, it became evident that the extension of the backward classes' quotas to more affluent castes prevented poorer individuals from accessing these facilities, even though there had been an overall increase in the quota. These translated into village-level jobs as teachers, police personnel, junior assistants in block offices, and the like, which immediately enhanced the prestige of the family and the community in the village, enabling them to organize and access public services.[27] The DMK, in power, consisted of several people belonging to the upper classes among the non-Brahmins. This could possibly be a reason for the feeling that the regime was neglecting the poorer and most backward classes in its policies in later years. As benefits accrued to the higher categories among the backward classes, they exacerbated the difference between the different strata in the villages, leading eventually for the demands, in the MGR era, for greater segmentation in reservation, for the most backward classes (MBCs) and for Dalits. In particular, the Dalits felt that they had not been integrated into the social changes that occurred. The outpouring of Dalit literature in Tamil, especially in the last two decades, is a testimony to the distance yet to be travelled in achieving social balance in the village. This was true of other backward communities as well.

Vivek Srinivasan[28] highlights the role of Vanniyars of South Arcot and Chengalpattu districts for their ability to organise movements for social mobility, by following the practices of higher caste people. The Vanniyars acquired further prominence in the 1980s through the formation of the Pattali Makkal Katchi (PMK). They were able to play a role in state and national politics even though their strength was limited to a few districts. Their influence appears to have waned now. Of late, caste associations including the Kongu Vellalar groups and the Mukkalothar groups have gained prominence, and are more visible in politics and in administration. Caste associations have therefore played an important role in mobilizing communities and representing their causes with the state, a finding that Vivek Srinivasan underlines.

The arguments against caste, gender and social discrimination were taken up by contemporary literary figures as well. The poet Subramania Bharathiar and the saint-poet Ramalinga Adigalar are two examples. Both of them wrote extensively on these issues and on the restrictions faced by sections of the people of this region.

At the same time, village-level studies of Vivek Srinivasan's thesis indicate that there was a dominant landholder in that village, who was a Reddiar, that the villagers had to press their claims for decades before the Dalits got access to roads, education, water, or some semblance of equal treatment. His chronology of action indicates that the development of education and job opportunities had much to do with Dalits successfully accessing public services.

The work of John Harriss, Jean Drèze, and other scholars who have followed the 'Slater' villages[29] seem to indicate that it took until the 1970s and the 1980s before the effects of development opportunities started reaching the Vanniyars and the Dalits in Tamil Nadu. There is even an argument that the Vanniyars' plea for Most Backward Class status was based on their exclusion from opportunities in the government in the late 1960s and 1970s.

The DMK's stance towards the central government, especially towards the Indira Gandhi government, hardened after 1973. There could have been two reasons for this. First, the presence of several erstwhile Tamil Nadu Congress leaders like C. Subramaniam and R. Venkatraman in Delhi in important and powerful positions would have contributed to the DMK's negative image in Delhi political circles. Second, the politics of the state continued to be strongly opposed to the earlier Congress ideology. Congress leaders in the state, like G.K. Moopanar, were still powerful and commanded a following, and were the ears of Indira Gandhi in the state. The legislative assembly also contained a strong Congress opposition, and several stalwarts like P.G. Karuthiruman, S. Bhuvarahan, and K. Ramamamoorthy. At the political level, especially after the massive national mandate for the Indira Gandhi government at the centre, maintaining political space in Tamil Nadu required opposition to Congress ideology and actions. An added issue was that the Indira Gandhi government had incorporated several leftist leaders as advisers, and one of them, Mohan Kumaramangalam from Madras, was to bring in far-reaching changes. This ascendancy of communist ideology did not suit the DMK in Madras. Tamil Nadu was an industrialized state, and it was important for the DMK to find space in the labour union movement in the state that was dominated by the communists and the Congress. It was natural that the DMK found itself at loggerheads with the centre on several occasions.

The problem was that this coincided with a period during which Indira Gandhi was very powerful at the centre, and adopted policies that were leftist in nature. India entered into a bilateral defence protection pact with the Soviet Union. In 1971, India went to war with Pakistan and helped create Bangladesh. Banks were nationalized, as were oil companies belonging to multinationals. Privileges accorded to Indian princes were abolished.

In Tamil Nadu, the DMK had a massive majority in the assembly. The DMK was perceived to be more arrogant and authoritative in governance. There were also murmurs that the benefits of the social justice initiatives were unequal and benefited the upper classes among the backward communities. Others demanded allocation of criteria for the 'most backward' communities. These changes in the DMK's attitude led to a decline in the popularity of the DMK. There were complaints about the growth and increasing openness of corruption and nepotism among party functionaries, ministers, and members of local bodies. Party activists became more demanding at the district and local levels, including demanding the extrication of people accused of crimes from police stations. At the district level, several district secretaries, like the ones in Madurai, were very powerful and could intervene in administrative decisions like contracts and postings. There were larger issues at the state level, including the Veeranam scheme of bringing water to Chennai through pipes using untested technology.[30]

In the political arena, there were changes in Delhi as well, with Indira Gandhi seeking to confirm her hold over the Congress. In the 1971 elections, Indira Gandhi sought Karunanidhi's help which resulted in a massive mandate for the Congress in Parliament and a large majority for the DMK in Tamil Nadu. This had a fallout. Gandhi did not need the DMK any more, while the Karunanidhi regime in 1971–76 became more assertive. Karunanidhi strongly opposed the Emergency of 1975, and paid the price of dismissal of the government in 1976, and the institution of an enquiry commission on corruption in the regime. The Sarkaria Commission did find improprieties in the award of the contract for the Veeranam pipelines, but the issue could not be pursued for want of corroboratory evidence.

After 1972, Karunanidhi was also fighting for political space against the ascendancy of the AIADMK, MGR's newly formed party. The later years of the DMK regime saw gradual defection of women and youth to the AIADMK from the ranks of the DMK.

In conclusion, the period 1967 to 1977 saw the articulation in policy of several of the social justice ideals that the Dravidian movement had aspired to. In integrating these policies with social welfare schemes and with structural changes in administration and governance, the entire government machinery was incorporated into actively participating in delivering this agenda. This identity of interests further developed into a system of effectively managing and delivering other social welfare programmes in the later regimes. In the initial years, this resulted in rapid development of the state, but this identity in later years became a hurdle to growth. This will be dealt with in later chapters.

Notes

1. A.S. Panneerselvan, 'Karunanidhi, Relentless Legislator', *Frontline* (23 June 2017), available at http://www.frontline. in/the-nation/relentless-legislator/article9719331.ece).

2. R. Hardgrave and Anthony C. Neidhart, 'Films and Political Consciousness in Tamil Nadu', *Economic and Political Weekly*, 10(1/2): 27–35.

3. S. Dickey, 'The Politics of Adulation: Cinema and the Production of Politicians in South India', *The Journal of Asian Studies*, 52(2), 340–72.

4. We saw these sentiments resurface in 2017 in the Jallikattu agitations on Marina Beach in Chennai.

5. As a contrast, foodgrain production is a record of over 280 million tonnes in 2017. The population is about 2.7 times what it was in 1965.

6. Actually three 'padi' per rupee—a padi is a local Madras volumetric measure that would hold approximately 1.1 kilograms of rice.

7. He later became Finance Minister in the central government, then Vice President, and then President of India.

8. This is not a feature of Tamil Nadu alone. It exists today in all states, perhaps more aggressively in some Hindi-speaking states.

9. Discussions with S.P. Ambrose, August 2017.

10. http://www.bloombergquint.com/opinion/2016/12/08/lessons-in-progress-from-tamil-nadu-and-dravidian-politics.

11. We are here referring to the Tamil Nadu Small Industries Development Corporation Limited (TANSIDCO), Tamil Nadu Industrial Development Corporation (TIDCO), and the State Industries Promotion Corporation of Tamilnadu Ltd (SIPCOT) respectively.

12. Scheduled Castes were given the nomenclature 'Adi-Dravidars' in Tamil Nadu official parlance to denote that they were the original Dravidians who inhabited Tamil Nadu.

13. Pongal is a harvest festival celebrated around 15 January every year. It is considered a very important festival in Tamil Nadu.

14. A necklace that the bridegroom puts around the bride's neck at the wedding, which she wears all her life, signifying that she is married.

15. Inams were land grants given by erstwhile kings and colonial rulers in recognition of services performed.

16. P. Umanath, communist leader, was the elected Member of Parliament from Pudukkottai in 1962 as well as 1967,

He espoused the cause of agrarian tenants against the landlords, in Pudukkottai area, which was an 'inam' area. This led to violence between the two groups and to law and order problems, the entire time that I was Sub-Collector in Pudukkottai. His wife Papa Umanath was a communist leader in her own right. Umanath was also a trade union leader and Joint Secretary of the CITU.

17. G.K. Moopanar was an important landlord in Thanjavur district and a staunch Congressman. He was the most prominent leader of the Congress from Tamil Nadu, and a confidante of Indira Gandhi.

18. Srinivasan's thesis looks at how Tamil Nadu in Southern India developed a policy priority to deliver basic public services such as schools, child care, midday meals, public distribution, public health, and other services.

19. The administration of villages by a chain of officers one below the other from the headman down to the barber was a feature of Tamil Nadu that had existed for centuries and was known as the *barabuti* system.

20. In almost three years, in two different locations as sub-collector, I had less than 10 per cent of my orders overturned.

21. V.V. Swaminathan, former minister in the AIADMK, calls this one of the most important changes for social empowerment that the DMK brought about (*Nakkeeran*, 30(15): 19).

22. They are also less involved in the village, sometimes not even living in the village, but in the nearest urban centre.

23. S.P. Adithanar, Lawyer, businessman, newspaper publisher, was an important leader of the DMK party. He was an ideologue, and his business acumen helped him find innovative solutions to further party ideology.

24. Act 29 of 1970, 10 November 1970, accessed from Tamil Nadu archives.

25. MGR continued to act in films promoting DMK ideology. *Adimai Penn* is a monumental film in this regard. In this movie, MGR plays both the king (who is killed by the villain) and the prince (who escapes after a long imprisonment). Jayalalithaa also acts in dual roles—as a peasant and as the queen of a neighbouring territory. MGR the Prince and Jayalalithaa the Queen save the kingdom from the clutches of the evil ruler. In *Rickshawkaran*, a movie for which MGR won the National Award for the best actor, he takes on an ineffective justice system and a vast network of criminals specialized in the trafficking of women.

26. Narendra Subramanian, *Ethnicity and Populist Mobilisation* (Delhi: Oxford University Press, 1999), p. 217.

27. Vivek Srinivasan describes this in his thesis. Vivek Srinivasan, 'Understanding Public Services in Tamil Nadu: An Institutional Perspective', *Social Science Dissertations*, 2010, p. 175, https://surface.syr.edu/socsci_etd/175.

28. Vivek Srinivasan, *Delivering Public Services and Beyond Effectively* (Delhi: Oxford University Press, 2014).

29. Gangaikondan, a village outside Tirunelveli in southern Tamil Nadu, was the subject of one of the village surveys conducted by the students of Professor Gilbert Slater from the University of Madras in 1916, and re-studied in the mid-1930s, the 1950s, and 1984, and most recently by the authors in 2008. The paper presents the findings of the most recent study and traces the story of agrarian social change in the village through the 20th century, drawing on the successive surveys. At the beginning of the century Gangaikondan was dominated by Brahmin landlords; by its end the most numerous Dalit/Scheduled Caste community, the Pallars, had more land in aggregate than any other single caste, though most owned only small holdings. They were also pre-eminent in the electoral panchayat institutions of the village. The agricultural economy of the village has

declined fairly steadily, and it might be described as being now 'post-agrarian' in the sense that only a small minority of households depend primarily upon agriculture.

Professor Gilbert Slater was the first Professor of Economics at the new department of Economics at Madras University and chaired the department from 1915 to 1921. During his tenure, he worked on the socioeconomic conditions of several villages in the then Madras state, and these 'Slater' villages have been studied continuously by succeeding economists and development studies scholars. There is rich material of over a hundred years available on these villages as a social and economic narrative, with contributions from several scholars over the decades.

30. This was one of the items investigated by the Sarkaria Commission in 1977, and the contractor was found guilty of corrupt practices.

3

SOCIAL WELFARE AND MGR
1977 to 1987

KARUNANIDHI AND MGR FELL OUT IN 1972, OSTENSIBLY because MGR accused Karunanidhi and the DMK of non-transparency in maintaining party accounts. MGR floated the new AIADMK party in 1972. The MGR films that came later—*Pattikkada Pattinama* (Rural Village/Town, 1973), *Urimai Kural* (Voice of Right, 1974), *Netru Inru Naalai* (Yesterday, Today, Tomorrow, 1975), and *Meenava Nanban* (Fishermen's Friend, 1977)—promoted the AIADMK and MGR's image. It worked because, as Sara Dickey points out, 'MGR did not, however, allow his identity inside or outside the party to become totally merged with that of the DMK. He built up his image as hero by making independent and widely publicized donations to charities, and began to suggest through his films that the ideals he espoused "could be achieved only through a leader like MGR". Eventually, "people began to think that the leader whom they wanted was not somebody like MGR but MGR himself"'.[1]

A.B. Mathur in his work on MGR talks about why the MGR phenomenon worked for both the DMK and the AIADMK. He says,

AIADMK was completely managed and led by MGR and his popularity among the masses being complete and unquestionable; his word was law and his desire a command for his followers. His image as an actor, always a do-gooder, symbolising good against the evil, a friend of the poor and the destitute, projected with finesse and imagination by the party cadres made him a legend in his life-time. Also, he had of course the political sagacity to organise a party which under his charismatic leadership kept a tight control over the masses and the administrative machinery in the state.[2]

Additionally, the AIADMK's attitude generally and MGR's particularly towards the bureaucracy was calculatedly hostile. More often than not, he attributed the party's and government's failures to the callous and unhelpful attitude of the administrative agencies rather than himself. He was always quick to point out infirmities in actions of officers, and to show them in a poor light in front of the public. He had little faith in the processes of the Secretariat, and his notes in files are often complex, and deal with issues beyond the ambit of the matters under consideration. He had little patience with the processes of administration.[3]

M.S.S. Pandian[4] argues that MGR and the ideologies he espoused in his films succeed in the terrain of struggle and produce consent among the subaltern classes. A characteristic MGR role was that of a working man combating everyday oppression. These films are ostensibly about the oppression faced by the poor, with MGR of course being constituted as one among them. By employing a carefully constructed system of visual scenes, these films celebrate his subalternity and create a mood for the audience to identify themselves with him.

The social universe of the MGR films is a universe of asymmetrical power. At one end of the power spectrum are grouped upper caste men/women, landlord/rich industrialists, literate elites, and, of course, the ubiquitous male—all of whom exercise unlimited authority and indulge in oppressive acts of power, and at the other end are the powerless poor.

M.S.S. Pandian notes that in MGR films the closure is such that a neat solution is offered for the injustice within the moral economy of the system itself. In other words, the subaltern protagonist in the film, that is, MGR, establishes what is considered to be just within the system and thus reaffirms the system. In such a construct, there is little room for revolt against the system, as the leader himself identifies with the oppressed and the disadvantaged.

The DMK had, by this time, lost the advantage of representing the backward classes. The earlier Dravidian and SRM ideology was diluted due to the many measures taken during the DMK regime that enabled the backward classes and the rural population to access public services, appointments, education, and other benefits like pensions and subsidies. The DMK appeared to have become distanced from the most backward classes, the very poor, and the scheduled castes.

MGR's approach reached out across caste barriers and focused directly on the poor and women. Women were either mothers or sisters, and the son and brother had an important filial duty to take care of them. This appealed directly to the masses, which were by now having to deal with the DMK party organization headed by the district secretary and the district minister. Here was an opportunity to take their woes directly to the top. In many ways, these changes set the scene for the MGR-led AIADMK regime that followed from 1977 to 1987.

MGR himself was a likable and somewhat complex person. In 1977, when he first became chief minister, he was elected as member of the legislative assembly from Aruppukkotai, a backward rural constituency in the then combined Ramanthapuram district, where I was posted as District Collector. These elections happened in July 1977, and during the period I was in the district, MGR made several visits there, and I had several opportunities to interact with him and his close associates. My impression in the first couple of years was that he was still trying to get out of his earlier movie image of a hero supporting the poor against injustice, and to mature into the role of a head of government. He commanded tremendous adulation among people in the rural areas. Prior to the elections, when he was touring the constituencies canvassing for votes, it was our duty as district administration to provide security and maintain law and order. His programmes always ran over the stipulated time, and it sometimes happened that he would arrive at election rallies several hours behind schedule, in one occasion nearly fourteen hours behind schedule. The crowds in the villages, numbering anywhere from 5,000 to 10,000 would wait patiently for him to arrive. The district administration used to get concerned that crowds would turn restive, until someone thought up the idea of playing his film songs while the crowds were waiting. An open jeep with large plywood standees of his would be sent in advance to the villages, with a music player belting out all his popular songs and dialogues. The crowds loved it and patiently waited for him to arrive.

After MGR became chief minister, during his many visits to the districts, I used to ride with him in his car and found him eager to find out what was happening. He enjoyed programmes where distribution of welfare benefits to the poor was on the agenda. Having experienced poverty himself, he genuinely felt for the poor.[5]

In the initial years, MGR definitely tried to be independent in his personal expenses. I am aware that in the initial visits to the district, he would pay all his bills and that of his large retinue himself. One of his ministers has complained to me about the large personal expenditure that he was incurring after becoming chief minister, while being denied the opportunities of earning as a film star. The dismissal of his government in 1980 came as a shock to him, and in the period after that, we see a different picture. There were whispers, even in 1981, of his closeness to the liquor lobby and liquor barons, and perhaps his reaching out to the poor through the midday meals programme was just a response to this series of events, both political and personal.

In summary, he was MGR, an iconic figure. His party, the AIADMK, was little more than his fan club at that time, and predominantly depended on the support of the poor, women, and the rural disadvantaged. The district functionaries of the party were local leaders only in name, for they knew well that their position in the party hierarchy was only due to their allegiance to MGR. The entire party machinery, until he passed away in 1987, ran by his fiat and his will. It is important to mention this as an explanation of why welfare programmes initiated by him were implemented across all sections of society, even in the remotest villages. MGR had a short temper, and would discard party functionaries whom he considered less than loyal. These functionaries knew that without the shade of his support they would become political non-entities. Political rivals needed only to complain that the existing functionaries were not implementing his programmes well enough for the latter to be shown the door. The party hierarchy was thus feudal, all obeying the wishes of a single undisputed leader. This certainly contributed to the successful implementation of the programmes.

The AIADMK regime between 1977 and 1987 was markedly different from the earlier DMK regime in several respects. At the time of the split from the DMK, the Karunanidhi regime had started becoming unpopular and had gained a reputation of being assertive, militant, and venal. MGR sharply distanced himself from these views. He indicated that he never favoured anti-Brahminism and was also not for strident expressions of state autonomy. He distanced himself on the subject of language for education, saying that the medium of education was for educationists, teachers, and students to determine. His appeal, through his films and speeches, was to the women and to the poor. The DMK appealed through journals and literary pieces to activists habituated to reading, while the AIADMK appealed through films to an audience that was not very politically literate. Against a wide range of journals in the DMK, the AIADMK party organ *Anna* was a poor rival and had a fitful existence. MGR himself did not enjoy the status of Karunanidhi as a public orator, being much more rambling and unfocused in his public speeches. His charisma lay in his ability to talk about, and to the poor, especially through his films.

The party itself was much looser in structure and more unsystematic in its activities than the DMK. Though there were district secretaries, they commanded less influence than the DMK district secretaries. The leader was the source of all authority and all functionaries owed their positions to the leader. Access and closeness to MGR was everything, and ministers as well as members of parliament and some members of legislative assembly who were seen as close to MGR commanded significant political clout. The Chief Minister's office attained enormous significance—a trend that continued into the Jayalalithaa regime.

In this scenario, support for the poor was always much more crucial for MGR than the promotion of the interests of the backward classes. He announced in 1979 that caste would be supplemented by income as a criterion for access to quotas. There was considerable protest against this, with caste associations taking to the streets, and he had to withdraw this announcement. He reintroduced the criteria of caste as the sole basis for backward class preferences in government appointments and admission criteria for tertiary education and, in a sudden turn of policy, also increased the backward classes' quota from 31 per cent to 50 per cent.

This signalled to several interest groups that the regime was willing to accommodate popular demands if it was accompanied by adequate mass mobilization. A new Vanniyar association emerged with demands for a separate quota for Vanniyars. The Vanniyars felt that their gains from the existing backward classes' quotas were not commensurate to their numbers or to their Dravidian subcultures. In the northern districts, this eroded the DMK vote bank more than that of the AIADMK, and the Vanniyars formed the PMK in 1989. In later years, DMK introduced a separate quota for 'most backward classes' and for 'de-notified communities', the latter being castes considered to be criminal in the British colonial era.

Farmers' agitations also grew in the AIADMK rule for increases in rice procurement prices, reduction in power tariffs for agriculture, and protests against measures for recovery of agricultural loans. The AIADMK regime responded by accommodating several of these demands and by also attempting to divide the farmers by granting greater facilities to the smaller farmers, among whom they enjoyed greater support.

This was an expansionist phase for welfare programmes. MGR's mindset grew from his film persona of distributing largesse to the poor, and especially to the women and children.

Major social and citizen welfare programmes were launched during this decade. The most important was the midday meals programme, which is dealt with in a separate chapter. Other welfare programmes included the TINP, an initiative funded by the World Bank; the Integrated Child Development Services (ICDS) programme, a Government of India programme for children; extension of the PDS;

textbooks and notebooks for schools; and several other initiatives. The midday meals were supplemented by other steps to improve rice supply through increase in the number of ration shops and in the amounts of subsidized rice that the poor and lower income groups were eligible for. Unlike what happened during the DMK period, the new ration shops were opened in rural rather than urban areas. A village self-sufficiency scheme, which provided the rural poor with infrastructure and loans, was launched. This decade saw a plethora of programmes, which have continued since then and have been a forerunner of several similar programmes in other states as well as a competition between successive regimes to do one better. All this happened at the cost of industrialization, infrastructure building, and other development expenditure, and saw the beginnings of the development versus welfare debate in the state—one that continues to date. The AIADMK focused on distributing lunches and small loans rather than land or jobs, and could therefore distribute goods more widely than its predecessor.

In the period between 1977 and 1987, there was a change in the pattern of administration at the district level. It has been already pointed out that MGR did not have any great faith in the bureaucracy, nor did he believe in systems and procedures being followed. The administration reacted in a predictable manner. The programmes known to be close to the chief minister's interest were pursued vigorously, and district administrators and departments tried to outdo each other in seeking recognition from the big man. In other areas, such as agriculture, animal husbandry, and even industrial development, activities and actions were sporadic and event driven. Since no one knew exactly what the chief minister was looking for in terms of long-term development policy, administration quickly reverted to process control, efficiency of delivery, and excellence in supervision and monitoring of programmes that had been the hallmark of the administrative system in Tamil Nadu (erstwhile Madras) state. Excellence in programme delivery came back into focus in all review meetings with special emphasis on the few programmes close to MGR's heart. Some of the programmes of this period are discussed in greater detail in the ensuing chapters.

Unlike the Karunanidhi years, we do not see a concerted set of policies that were oriented towards changing social or caste equations in the villages and the towns. To MGR, a poor person was a poor person, and policies were more to help the women and the destitute, than any particular section of backward classes or to redress any particular social grievance.

During this period, we see few initiatives that focus on agriculture or on tenant farmers other than as responses to various agitations that occurred during different parts of the regime. The midday meals programme was the single most important intervention of policy towards the poor that happened in this decade. The causes, institutional responses, and academic and public views are discussed in another chapter. Programmes like the TINP, a World Bank initiative, and the Integrated Child Development programme (ICDP), which was a Government of India initiative, were parallel programmes that happened and served to achieve similar goals. The difference between these externally sponsored programmes and the MGR directed midday meals programme is also of interest and is discussed in detail in a separate chapter.

Apart from the midday meal scheme and other welfare schemes, the most important change that occurred in the MGR era was the privatization of tertiary education. During the period from 1980 to 1985, when the central and state governments were finding it difficult to expand technical education in the country, the governments of Karnataka, Maharashtra, Tamil Nadu, and Andhra Pradesh took the decision to permit private registered societies and trusts to establish and run technical institutions on a self-financing basis. A large number of private financing institutions came up in Tamil Nadu in the early 1980s. This trend only accelerated in subsequent years, with a large number of arts and science colleges, and even medical colleges being set up on a self-financing basis. These private colleges were initially affiliated to a government university, but later allowed to be autonomous in the award of degrees. The requirement of land, capital, and infrastructure could be provided at that time only by a few people who were politicians and who suddenly found themselves, through whatever means, as having access to resources. Today there are over 600 engineering colleges in the state, most of them owned by politicians, current or former. This sudden availability of education opportunities resulted in an alternate career path opening up for even rural youngsters. By 2008–09, Tamil Nadu had the second largest number of engineering colleges among all states. While there were concerns about the quality of education as well as the fee charged, these colleges certainly had the effect of providing tertiary education opportunities even in rural and semi-urban areas. Between 1980–81 and 1990–91, the number of higher educational institutions grew from 382 to 624, and the enrolment increased from 1.9 lakh to about 3.6 lakh.[6]

Along with engineering colleges and higher educational institutions, there was a rapid growth of teacher training schools, private schools, and other vocational training institutions, mostly in the private sector.

This development is significant from two points of view. First, it relieved the state exchequer of investments in higher education and the funds could be used for welfare programmes. The owners of these institutions were usually public figures or politicians, indicating that politics was becoming a route to financial success in Tamil Nadu. Second, it offered enormous opportunities for the rural population to access higher education. Education was the gateway to government jobs, and the reservations system of the government enabled the poor and the backward classes to access opportunities for employment in the government and allied sectors. This raised the status of educated people in the villages, and enabled them to rise above their caste limitations.[7] Vivek Srinivasan and others have recorded the results of these changes in the microcosm of the village studied, and over this decade we see improvement in public services delivery as well as recognition of rights and entitlements in the villages.

There were sharp increases in literacy to 54.4 per cent in the 1981 census and 62.66 per cent in the 1991 census. Life expectancy reached 57.4 per cent for males and 58.4 per cent for females.

In industrial development, MGR was content to allow growth to happen. Institutions that had been set up earlier continued to attract investment in the state because of the advanced infrastructure and good administrative machinery. There was little industrial unrest as MGR did not allow trade unions to challenge his authority.

While he made little personal effort to portray the state as an investment destination, there was indeed one case where he took a lot of personal interest. S. Viswanathan (henceforth referred to as SV) of the Seshasayee Group, a lawyer and a trade unionist, had been an associate of R. Venkataraman for many years. The Seshasayee Group runs a successful paper and board factory near Erode, and has been noted for its ethical business practices as well as technical competence in paper making. SV met MGR in 1977, and over the next few months, MGR came to know about SV's close association with R. Venkatraman, Jayaprakash Narayan, Chandrasekhar, Ramakrishna Hegde, and other leaders and how these leaders held SV in high esteem. MGR developed a close friendship with SV and started taking his advice on many issues. SV was able to persuade MGR that sugarcane waste (bagasse) could be used for making newsprint, though it was a technology quite revolutionary at that time. For some reason, MGR became enamoured with the idea and pushed it through, despite being advised against it by some senior bureaucrats. While some senior bureaucrats advised against it, there were others who championed the idea and carried it forward.

At about the same time, a World Bank consultant was on a scouting mission to identify projects for investment in India. He was impressed with the concept. Seshasayee Paper Boards was appointed consultant to the project, and made a presentation to the head of Industries Division of the World Bank. R. Venkataraman as finance minister had also lent his support to the project. The World Bank funding for state government projects required the support of the central government, as guarantees for repayment had to be given by the central government. The project secured World Bank programme funding, which was quite a feat.[8]

The bureaucracy in Tamil Nadu, especially in the conservative department of finance and expenditure, was convinced that this was a misadventure. It was untried technology, and the size of the plant proposed was quite large. They suggested an alternative which was close to a project that was being implemented by a private entrepreneur based on waste paper. This was the Rs 100 million, thirty tonnes a day mill, promoted by a waste paper dealer. The bureaucrats suggested that the government should implement several such waste paper based projects instead.[9] The opposition parties claimed that this was a ruse for making money for the ruling party.

MGR's motives in pushing through this project might never be known. He undertook a visit to Mexico and Peru accompanied by SV to see for himself bagasse-based newsprint plants in those countries. Perhaps his interest in the project was purely on account of his trust in SV. There were also some in the bureaucracy who were convinced about the project and lent a hand to these efforts. The entire project conceptualization, design, and execution was entrusted to a group of experts from Seshasayee Paper and Boards Limited, who completed the project to the full satisfaction of the project funders. MGR attended the inauguration of the factory as the chief guest, and asked the helicopter pilot to fly over the plant before landing so that he could get a personal view. People present at the event told me that he was moved. The Tamil Nadu News Prints and Papers Limited is today one of the most successful ventures in the paper industry, and has been making profits continuously for two decades. There has been no whiff of scandal associated with this project.

There was another case of Palani Periasamy, who helped MGR when he was in the US for medical treatment. MGR took a liking to him and encouraged him to invest in sugar mills and hotels in Tamil Nadu. Such interest in individual schemes, projects, and policies was sporadic for MGR. The MGR regime saw a definite shift towards large, inclusive, public welfare programmes, which did not necessarily fit into the SRM or Dravidian ideology, but were meant to be focused on the poor. The Karunanidhi regime had laid the foundations of social change, at the village, co-operative, and institutional levels, and the welfare programmes of MGR became the vehicle in which the new structures carried forward the concept of social justice.

The question which arises is why these schemes were started, and what were the institutional structures which implemented the programmes, as well as the demand pressures from below that grounded and perpetuated these programmes. It is possible to argue that the politicization of the bureaucratic institutions in the DMK decade, the changed structure of the implementing institutions, and the social changes that had taken place created an environment where such programmes were accepted and implemented effectively with efficiency and speed by the institutions, perhaps even simply because they would earn the approbation of the chief minister. There was no question, during this period, of earning his disapproval and surviving, whether in bureaucracy or in politics, and the approach was to implement his ideas and earn his approval, or to stay below his radar.

The programmes themselves were quite varied. MGR himself thought of the midday meal scheme. There were other such programmes like the TINP, the ICDS, and the PDS. Even though the origins of the programmes were different—TINP being funded by the World Bank, the ICDS being a Government of India programme, and the PDS historically being a Tamil Nadu programme—as long as they served some welfare and equity goals, the bureaucratic institutions adopted them and implemented them in a manner that became exemplary when compared to several other states.

Tamil Nadu had a number of such welfare programmes. What is interesting to note is that several programmes were not necessarily altruistic in political conceptualization, but proper implementation brought in a transparency in delivery and programme efficiency. This was unique to the state. The golden era of welfare programmes came to an end with the death of MGR in 1987. After 1991, these programmes became mere election winning tools and the social welfare intention took a backseat.[10]

After the death of MGR, there was factionalism in the AIADMK, leading to political uncertainty. After a brief period of President's Rule, the DMK was elected to power. Jayalalithaa had by then emerged as the undisputed leader of the AIADMK, and was able to persuade the Government of India to overturn the elected government in 1991 and she swept into power in the elections that followed.[11]

In 1989, the DMK came back to power. The short period from 1989 to 1991 was an interesting period. Karunanidhi had come back to power after a gap of thirteen years. He was acutely conscious of MGR's charisma and was determined to show that he could deliver better and more efficient administration than the previous decade. Additions were made to the welfare initiatives. Closer monitoring of programmes, reconnecting with the central government (V.P. Singh was Prime Minister), and trying to integrate with the national stream of development were some of the ideas that were followed. Importantly, he tried to reach out to the people through programmes and actions that sought to enhance his image as well as that of the party. I was Secretary of Rural Development at that time, and he used to monitor programmes very closely. We were building a lot of houses in Adi Dravidar colonies, free of charge, for beneficiaries. The programme was quite successful. During the election campaign in 1991, Karunanidhi decided to canvass from a vehicle that was designed to resemble the houses that were being built.[12] This was of little avail, as Jayalalithaa's charisma was very strong at that time, and people still loved MGR.

In conclusion, it could be argued that the period from 1969 to 1976 put in place social changes that enabled access to government employment and public services to those that had been disadvantaged in earlier years, and that the close relationship between politics and administration enabled economic development to be fine-tuned to the essential ideals of the party. In the MGR era, there was a mushrooming of welfare programmes, excellence in whose delivery was made possible both by the social changes in administration that had come before, and also by the traditional nature of the functioning of the Tamil Nadu bureaucracy.

The regimes after the MGR era, that of the DMK and AIADMK from 1991 onwards, have to be dealt with separately, as they represent a paradigm shift from the earlier decades.

Notes

1. Dickey, 'The Politics of Adulation: Cinema and the Production of Politicians in South India'. Even though Sara Dickey wrote this prior to the formation of the AIADMK, the remarks were valid even in later years, for MGR's following was based on an image nurtured assiduously over the the years that he alone could find a solution for the problems of the poor.

2. A.B. Mathur, 'Review: Dravidian Heritage: MGR and Tamil Nadu', review of All India Anna Dravida Munnetra Kazhagam: Political Dynamics in Tamil Nadu by R. Thandavan, *The Indian Journal of Political Science*, 49(1), pp. 121–28.

3. I was witness to one instance. There was a law student in our neighbourhood that had applied for a travel grant to attend an overseas event to which she had been invited as a speaker. The file was rejected, right up to the finance minister. The girl went to MGR, stood in the queue, met him, and pleaded. He told her 'these people are like that' meaning the government bureaucracy, and gave her a bundle of notes for her travel.

4. M.S.S. Pandian, 'Culture and Subaltern Consciousness: An Aspect of MGR Phenomenon', *Economic and Political Weekly*, 24(30).

5. On a visit to Madurai, there was an old acquaintance, an ordinary person whose job was to light up the film sets, who came to see the new chief minister and brought him food. I was witness to his partaking of that meal rather than the lavish spread that had been laid out on the dining table.

6. One lakh is equal to one hundred thousand.

7. The current protests in Tamil Nadu against the NEET examinations for admission to medical colleges stems from this trend of increasing access of rural children to schooling and beyond—a major gain of the post-1967 era, tracing origins of this move to the SRM for equal opportunities.

8. Conversations with Gopal, CEO Seshasayee Papers, and Arun Bijur, Seshasayee Consultants who were involved with this project intimately.

9. This venture was short lived and closed down soon after.

10. This is discussed in detail in later chapters.

11. Governance and programme delivery in the period between 1991 and 1996 and also in the subsequent years require a separate chapter.

12. We custom built this vehicle for him.

4

The Politics of Welfare
A Case Study of the Midday Meal Programme

———

In the budget speech before the Tamil Nadu Assembly on 26 March 1982, the finance minister of Tamil Nadu V.R. Nedunchezhiyan announced that the Government of Tamil Nadu would implement a midday meal programme catering to all children from the age of two upwards. Details of the programme to be implemented were not mentioned in the speech. This scheme was initially named the Chief Minister's Nutritional Meal Programme, since it was the initiative of Chief Minister M.G. Ramachandran. Later, when the DMK came to power, the name was changed to the Tamil Nadu Government's Nutritional Noon Meal Programme. Further, under Chief Minister J. Jayalalithaa it was renamed the Puratchi Thalaivar MGR's Nutritious Noon Meal Programme. The scheme began as the personal initiative of the chief minister, MGR, and the professed objectives were political.

The scheme is an outcome of my experience of extreme starvation at an age when I knew only to cry when I was hungry. But for the munificence of the woman next door who extended a bowl of rice gruel to us and saved us from the cruel hand of death, we would have departed this world long ago. Such merciful womenfolk, who had great faith in me, elected me as chief minister of Tamil Nadu. To wipe the tears of these women I have taken up this project. To picture lakhs and lakhs of poor children who gather to partake of nutritious meals in the thousands of hamlets and villages all over Tamil Nadu, and blessing us in their childish prattle, will be a glorious event.[1]

Early academic comments about the scheme were cautious. While recognizing that this was a massive effort, the efficacy and efficiency continued to be commented on.

This noon meal of 400 odd calories was provided to a large number through 20,747 child welfare centers and 32,470 elementary schools in the State from July 1, 1982. It covered children in the age group from 2 to 10 throughout the year. It is regarded as the most extensive and expensive supplementary feeding program currently undertaken by any developing country using its own internal resources.[2]

It is not inconceivable that there would have been some political agenda behind MGR's statement as well. In 1977, when the AIADMK won the state assembly polls, it had allied with the Communist Party of India and the Forward Bloc. Between 1977 and 1980, when the Congress

was out of power in the centre, the AIADMK government
had extended full support to the Janata government at
the centre, and later, to the Charan Singh government.
Two AIADMK MPs served as ministers in the central
government. In the Lok Sabha elections held in January
1980, the Congress under the leadership of Indira Gandhi
won a large majority of seats. The DMK was their ally in the
state. The Congress-DMK victory in the 1980 parliamentary
election emboldened their alliance and made them think
that people had lost their faith in the MGR government.
The DMK was able to persuade the Indira Gandhi
government to dismiss the AIADMK government in
Tamil Nadu, and to impose President's Rule in the state.
Given the results of the national elections, the DMK felt
that the popularity of AIADMK was over. The AIADMK
ministry and the assembly were dismissed by the central
government and fresh elections conducted in 1980. MGR
had also made what turned out to be a tactical error. When
Mrs Gandhi stood for election in 1978 (after having lost her
parliamentary seat in Allahabad), MGR had promised her
a safe constituency in Thanjavur district of Tamil Nadu.
However, he developed cold feet, and Mrs Gandhi had
to opt for another seat in Chikmagalur in Karnataka.
Mrs Gandhi would not have forgotten the slight, and MGR
found himself on the wrong side of central politics in 1980.
However, in the state, the AIADMK magic was still strong.
The party swept the state polls in May 1980, winning 162
out of 234 seats, while the DMK and the Congress together
could win only 69 seats. DMK MPs in the Lok Sabha
numbered 24, as against none from the AIADMK. MGR
needed to consolidate his political base and needed to do
something for his core constituency, the rural poor.

There was possibly another undercurrent. In 1981, MGR scrapped liquor prohibition in the state, allowing for the manufacture and sale of country and 'foreign' liquor. The DMK under M. Karunanidhi had allowed liquor sales in 1971, but after the split with MGR, the AIADMK had come out strongly against the liquor policy, and the DMK re-introduced prohibition in 1974.

In 1981, soon after coming back to power, MGR reversed this decision, and liquor revenues became a substantial proportion of state revenues. The DMK opposed the introduction of liquor in 1981, alleging that the government was in league with liquor manufacturers. There was also an adverse reaction from the rural women. The AIADMK needed a platform to convey their concern for the welfare of the poor, women, and children. It is possible that the midday meal scheme was an attempt to win back the sympathies of this electorate group. MGR knew that in the films he could do no wrong as long as he portrayed himself as the saviour of the poor and the oppressed. Women were primarily mothers and sisters to be cared for, and family values extended into married life, albeit after some songs and mandatory love scenes in his movies. Therefore this voter group was vital for him—a fact that his successor J. Jayalalithaa recognized right until her last election. The midday meal programme was perhaps one way of winning the sympathies of this voter group.

There were strong evidence-based arguments for the need for such intervention. In the late 1960s, the United States Agency for International Development (USAID) carried out a detailed study on the nutritional status of people in Tamil Nadu. The study appeared to indicate that the levels of calorie supply per capita in Tamil Nadu were lower than those in all other major states in the country. Field investigations in the study identified the greatest deficits in relation to norms among infants below two years of age and adolescents. The study strongly recommended intervention targeted at weanlings, adolescents, and pregnant and lactating women. This major study led, in later years, to the funding of a World Bank-aided project. It also led to a sustained debate on two different strategies, universal feeding and targeted intervention, which will be discussed further in the next chapter.

According to the World Bank evaluation report,[3]

By the second half of the 1970s, India had a variety of public feeding programs. Malnutrition was particularly severe in the state of Tamil Nadu, despite the 25 different nutrition programs operating there which were costing the government about $9 million annually. Evaluation studies showed that these programs were reaching only a small fraction of the most vulnerable groups:

- Because the programs were not targeted on the basis of nutritional criteria, they did not reach their intended beneficiaries. Children most at risk were not identified.
- Feeding on site tended to replace meals that beneficiaries would otherwise have eaten at home.
- Food taken home was shared with other family members, reducing the impact on beneficiaries.
- The food given was too coarse and bulky for very young children to eat.
- Not enough emphasis was given to nutrition education for mothers, nor to the complementary health care interventions needed to improve their nutritional status.

It is unlikely that these arguments came to MGR's notice or that the decision to introduce midday meals had much to do with the analysis offered by the study.

The concept of providing midday meals in schools had its origin in Germany, France, and other European countries, but its rapid development dates back to the 1900s in England. In the US, school lunches were offered from the beginning of the twentieth century as a supplementary feeding programme. In European countries, school meals were offered on the basis of two determining factors, namely, the distance of the home from the school and the financial circumstances of the parents. In India, the midday meals scheme was started for disadvantaged children in the Madras Municipal Corporation. In 1954, UNICEF and the Government of India signed an agreement for the provision of free milk for the needy. This was initially in the Kaira district of Gujarat, but was gradually extended to other cities. Among the reasons for parents not educating their children were abject poverty, and the provision of noon meals served as an effective incentive for school attendance. In 1956, the then chief minister of Tamil Nadu, K. Kamaraj, introduced the mid-day meal for the first time in India. It functioned in 8,000 schools covering 2 lakh children. Initially it was started with purely voluntary contributions from local people, but within a year the government stepped in, contributing a grant of 0.06 rupee per child for schools with the scheme, with contributions from local bodies of 0.02 rupee per child and public contribution of 0.02 rupee. In 1961, Co-operative for Relief Everywhere (CARE), an NGO sponsored by the US government, offered commodity assistance (bulgar wheat), which was accepted and used to expand the implementation of the programme to cover 16 lakh children. The programme, however, wasn't without its share of shortfalls. There was loss of food commodities due to lack of storage facilities; and school teachers and even students were used for cooking of food.[4]

In 1967, CARE provided for the establishment of central kitchens, and the teachers were relieved of cooking. Food was cooked in central kitchens and delivered to schools through vans provided by CARE. Out of 200 prescribed feeding days, 100 days were supposed to be rice days and the balance 100 days for Bulgar wheat. The scheme was popular, though the actual number of feeding days was less than 200 due to shortage of provisions, vehicle breakdowns, and poor roads and logistics problems. The transition from the concern over providing food to one of providing a nutritious meal occurred after the 1982 midday meal programme was launched. However, in providing what was purported to be a 400-calorie meal through the midday meals programme, there is no evidence of any serious nutritional science-based computation of the ingredients of the meal in the original conception. The original order blandly states poverty as the reason for the programme, and far from being targeted nutritional support, it was presented as a universal feeding programme.

The institutional process of converting this announcement into an operational programme started immediately. The chief secretary to the government of Tamil Nadu at that time, K. Diraviyam, took it upon himself to give body and shape to this announcement. The government issued orders on 28 May 1982.[5] In the file, the entire reasoning and justification has been argued in a four page note prepared by the chief secretary. It expands on the brief statement made in the assembly by the finance minister. The note argues that there were approximately 42.14 lakh children in Tamil Nadu in the age group of 2–4 years and another 63.59 lakh children in the age group of 5–9 years—a total of 105.73 lakh children in all. The note then argues that 60 per cent of these are below the poverty line, and approximately 60 lakh children would be covered under the programme. The file does not contain any supporting documents or analysis of how these figures were arrived at. There is also no mention of reduction in poverty targets or reduction in malnutrition objectives.

The note then sets out in detail the implementation of the programme. After the clearance of the finance secretary for the expenditure to be incurred, the chief minister approved the file on 26 May and orders were issued on 28 May. These orders, which should have been issued from the Department of Education, were issued instead from the Office of the Chief Secretary, which was unusual. The finance minister, who had made the announcement in the first place, did not see this file, which is also a departure from established procedure.

Diraviyam reached the highest position in the Tamil Nadu Civil Services, that of Chief Secretary, in 1982. He belonged to the Indian Administrative Service, the premier Indian service, though he had not entered it through the qualifying competitive examinations. A freedom fighter and a Gandhian, he had strong rationalist and atheist views. He was a vehement supporter of the social justice and social reform movements. There was an urge in him to excel, to do better than other administrators. There was also a strong undercurrent in him of resentment of the existing social order at that time, which he considered to be favouring the upper classes. Kamaraj, the then chief minister, had been impressed with his skills and proficiency in Tamil and English,[6] and appointed him part of the Department of

Information and Publicity of the state government. He rose rapidly through successive administrations, and served with distinction in several departments. As Revenue Secretary, he introduced far-reaching changes in village administration, in line with the social reform agenda of the DMK. As Commissioner of Civil Supplies and later as Food Secretary for several years, he ably steered the state through several years of food shortages, and put in place an efficient public distribution system. He understood the problems of logistics and distribution challenges of the new programme. An efficient administrator, he did not suffer incompetence; rather he took on the burden of execution upon himself. The clarity of this thinking is visible in the implementation orders issued for the noon-meal programme.

The structure envisaged the creation of 17,000 centres for the feeding of children between the ages of two and five years. The children would be fed for 300 days a year.[7] The post of a *bal sevika* (child helper) and two *aayah*s (maids) for each centre was approved. The selection of the bal sevika was to be done for each district by a committee headed by the District Collector, the Personal Assistant (Panchayat Development) of the Collector, the District Social Welfare Officer, the District Employment Officer, and relevant Divisional Development Officer. They were to select candidates from a pool of local girls who had passed their school final examinations. Widows or single mothers were to be preferred. The two aayahs were to be appointed from the village where the centres operated, by the Block Development Officer. There were 97 central kitchens in operation at that time in the state, and these were allowed to appoint one cook and two servants each.

Seven hundred bicycles were to be procured to deliver cooked food from the central kitchens to the nearby feeding centres, and a sum of Rs 36 lakh was sanctioned for the purchase of new vehicles.

The meal for pre-school children would comprise 80 grams of rice, 10 grams of dhal (pulses), 7 grams of oil, and vegetables. The total cost was worked out to be 50 paise. Plates and tumblers were approved for purchase at Rs 10 per set, and a sum of Rs 1,500 for cooking vessels per centre. The bal sevika and the school teacher were responsible for acquiring rice, dhal, and oil from the nearest public distribution service centre. The responsibility of the pre-school children-feeding programme was entrusted to the Social Welfare Department of the state, to be implemented through the Block Development Officer.

The programme for children aged between five and nine years was entrusted to the School Education Department, through the local schools. The Extension Officers (Social Welfare), Extension Officer (Education), and the Extension Officer (Co-operation) were all involved with the monitoring and supervision of the programme. Funds for cooking utensils, plates, and tumblers at Rs 2,500 per centre, were sanctioned. Posts for the supervision of the programme at the level of the Directorate of Social Welfare as well as the Directorate of School Education, were sanctioned. The process of withdrawal of funds for the programme was clearly laid out. The District Social Welfare Officer would withdraw funds from the Treasury, and the Collector would allocate the funds to the individual Block Development Officer under his control. All of the above was set out in the first government order, illustrating Diraviyam's attention to details of implementation.

Soon after, the director of school education sent a letter
to the chief secretary that children between the ages of ten
and fourteen were being left out of this programme.
He pointed out that a small sum of 0.1 rupee per child
per day was allocated for this, which was grossly
insufficient. He suggested that children in this age
group should also be covered under the midday meal
programmes at schools, at least for 200 days in a year
(school working days). Diraviyam noted on this that it
was a genuine request, and that coverage should be for
365 days and should cover 1 lakh children, and cost around
Rs 20 million a year. The finance minister and the chief
minister saw the file within two days and issued orders
after the approval of finance secretary for the expenditure.[8]
Interestingly, all the Government Orders (GOs) are slim
files, without any data to support the assumptions, or
even detailed financial calculations. More importantly,
the below-poverty clause that was mentioned in the earlier
GOs is not here in the file notes—a blurring of objectives
that soon led to the midday meals programme abandoning
the fig-leaf of serving those below the poverty line only,
and morphing into a universal feeding programme.

The depth of details of the implementation instructions
is quite astonishing. There were sanctions of staff and
expenditure, of departmental responsibilities, supervision
patterns. In GO 901 dated 4 June 1982,[9] the meal for
the school children was to consist of 100 grams of rice,
15 grams of dhal, and 15 grams of oil per day. (The oil
content was quickly reduced to 8 grams of oil per day per
child by an amending GO, someone must have pointed
out that 15 grams is a lot of oil for a child in each meal.)
The rice, dhal, and oil were to be procured by the Tamil

Nadu Civil Supplies Corporation (TNCSC) for supply to all feeding centres run by the education and social welfare departments. A system of reimbursing the TNCSC for the procurement and transportation expenditure incurred was worked out in the GO in great detail. The names of persons who were authorized to receive the supplies at the centre were to be to be given to the TNCSC who would intimate the timetable for distribution of the commodities.

There was thus great emphasis laid on the performance of the Food Department and the Civil Supplies Corporation. Tamil Nadu has been a marginal state in terms of self-sufficiency in food grains. The public distribution system was managed through local procurement of food grains during harvest. The TNSCS set up a large number of procurement centres in rice cultivating districts (most importantly Thanjavur), which would buy from the farmers at a pre-announced support price. In good rainfall years, there was enough rice for the market as well as the TNCSC. In marginal years, the shortfall had to be made good from allocations of food grains from the central pool. Sometimes, the central pool would allocate wheat instead of rice, which was not much preferred by consumers. The food ministry at the centre had never approved of this approach. The Food Corporation of India (FCI) was designated as the pan-India authority to purchase food grains, both rice and wheat, at support prices announced by the central government. The FCI would set up procurement centres, most notably in Punjab and Haryana for wheat, and procure and store all the food grains. This would then be allocated to the 'central pool' for all the states, depending on needs. Political patronage between the centre and the states was also involved. Tamil Nadu did not join the central pool, primarily because it had a huge internal appetite from its PDS. It did not contribute to the central pool, a point of some disquiet, for a long time for the central food ministry. The midday meals programme suddenly required close to 25,000 tonnes of rice, more than what was being supplied by the PDS. In addition, the TNCSC had to procure dhal and oil, which were not part of its earlier mandate. The food department was quite apprehensive about the responsibilities placed on it by the midday meals scheme. The department approached the central government for allocation of rice from the central pool. They pointed out that it was for the innovative midday meals programme, meant to target poverty reduction and malnutrition. There was no response from the centre.

Mrs Gandhi was the prime minister and Rao Birender Singh was the food minister in Delhi. Mrs Gandhi, as earlier mentioned, was at this time not quite pleased with MGR. Repeated attempts by state government officials to be allocated rice from the central pool were turned down by the food ministry in Delhi. When this was brought to the notice of MGR,[10] he announced in the Legislative Council—which no longer exists—that he would go on a one-day fast on the beach in Chennai, in protest against the centre's refusal to allocate rice for the midday meal programme. The media and public reaction resulted in him being called to Delhi for discussions. When he reached Delhi along with his officials, he found that Bhagwat Jha Azad had taken over as food minister that day. The meeting with him was polite, but negative. The meeting with the prime minister was to be in the afternoon, and considered a courtesy call only. MGR decided to go in alone to have a discussion with Mrs Gandhi. They were together for about twenty minutes, and then MGR came out to announce that all was well. The allocation from the central pool came the next day, and continued thereafter. MGR turned into a strong supporter of the Indira Gandhi government, even to the extent of policies with regard to Sri Lankan Tamils at that time.[11]

Even in the procurement of dhal, the food department faced difficulties. Tamil Nadu is not a significant dhal-producing state, and a small group of traders had oligopolistic control over the market. Dhal was not a commodity that was supplied through the PDS, and the government was purchasing dhal for the first time. When the TNCSC sought to buy dhal for the midday meals scheme, they were confronted with artificially inflated prices. After several attempts, an appeal was made to the traders about the scheme. One of them relented, and the cartel yielded. There was thus early acceptance even from the public about the value of the programme for the poor.

This narrative is an attempt to illustrate that the conceptualization of the programme, the details of the nutritional content, the method of delivery, and the implementation structure did not emerge out of any complex economic analysis or consultant-based approach of needs and intervention methodologies. It was an amalgam of political and welfarist initiatives, which served as a nutritional supplement and for providing employment in the midday meal centres and supporting infrastructure, which was converted into an implementable programme by the bureaucracy. It succeeded in the initial years because of the personal interest of MGR, his unquestioned leadership over his party, and the political support that he enjoyed from the poor and the rural people. It succeeded equally because the entire government machinery realized the importance of the programme, and all departments, all levels of officers committed themselves to its implementation, and were conscious that they were being monitored and judged closely on the basis of the performance of the programme. Finally, it succeeded because of the meticulous planning that went into its implementation, including logistics, staff and supply, and the provisioning of sufficient funds for its implementation. The combination of detailed planning, close implementation, a committed bureaucracy, as well as a watchful and strong political leadership helped institutionalize this programme in the years that MGR was chief minister, and even thereafter. It is possible to argue that in the years after MGR, the programme had become such an expected ingredient of government service delivery in the state, that public expectation about its smooth functioning was a given. Any drop in performance would have resulted in adverse public opinion. A top-down programme, by its very successful implementation, became, over the years, a demand-driven public service.

The funds for the programme came from the internal budget of the government. The original government order assumed that a meal would cost half a rupee per day, and assuming 60 per cent of the children were to be provided for during 300 days in the year, the figure was optimistically put at around a billion rupees a year, which was clearly a back-of-the-envelope estimate. There were no estimates for the costs incurred by the Civil Supplies Corporation in procuring and distributing the food grains, or a true cost of the staff that were employed. In budgetary terms, these expenditures were parked under the individual departments—school education, food and civil supplies, rural development, and panchayati raj and social welfare. Thus fragmented, the total costs appeared quite manageable. As the programmes swelled to include all children of all ages, pensioners, and the menu expanded to include eggs and special rice on occasions, the budgetary commitments rose substantially.

Two features went in favour of the state finances. First, unlike many states, expenditures on infrastructure and irrigation, two main components of the state budget, were quite small in Tamil Nadu. Earlier Congress governments had taken care of rural connectivity, making good use of central grants. Rural electrification was a focus in the Kamraj regime. In irrigation, there were no major projects, and all the smaller projects had been taken up in the 1960s. This relieved the state budget of a major chunk of expenditure commitment.

Second, the removal of prohibition brought in substantial revenues from liquor into the state treasuries, and there have always been caustic comments that the Tamil Nadu welfare schemes are based on revenues from liquor sales.

The management of welfare expenditure has been an important feature of the Tamil Nadu budget for the last thirty years, the narration of which would have to be a separate exercise.

While this initiative had great public support, response from the Government of India and the academic community, both national and international, was not positive.

The origins of these sets of criticisms could also be traced back to two significant policy interventions in nutrition that happened at around the same time. Arising out of a USAID study on nutrition status in Tamil Nadu, the World Bank had put together the TINP, that was launched in 1979, just a couple of years before the midday meals scheme was announced. This focused on children in the age group 0–36 months, provided supplementary feeding of nutritional food supplements, periodic health check-ups at the designated centres, immunization, as well as nutritional education for the mothers. This was a fully funded World Bank programme, with an elaborate institutional staffing and monitoring pattern.

In 1975–76, the Government of India had started Integrated Child Development Services (ICDS) in 33 blocks in the country. This was expanded to 100 blocks by 1981, and by 1985, covered 1,000 blocks. By 1990, 2,452 blocks were running the ICDS programme.[12] The Social Welfare and Women and Child Development departments of the state governments implemented this programme with funds from the central government. In some states, the Rural Development Department was involved as well. Assistance from CARE and the World Food Programme enabled the programme to provide supplementary nutrition to children aged 0–6 months as well as to pregnant and lactating women. A selection of the most needy and malnourished was done at the village level by the programme staff, which would then benefit from the programme.

During this period, there was considerable overlap in Tamil Nadu between the TINP, ICDS, and the mid-day meals programme, as pre-school children appeared to be covered under all of them. The staffing patterns for the schemes were different as also the monitoring and reporting structures. For several years, all the schemes ran in parallel. The second phase of TINP, started after 1980, focused on non-ICDS blocks in Tamil Nadu. Over the years, there has been integration of TINP and ICDS initiatives, though integration with midday meals programme objectives has been more difficult.[13] The TINP is discussed in detail in the next chapter.

Development professionals criticized the midday meals programme as 'not scientifically sound'. It was rejected by the Planning Commission, and had to be implemented entirely out of the state's own resources. In the initial years, there were two major chains of critical comments. The first was about costs. These argued that the expenditure on the programme came at the cost of other development initiatives. It was argued that the expenditure on the programme was higher than sectoral expenditures for agriculture or electricity and that the costs of the scheme each year exceeded total investments in education, urban development, drinking water, and sewage.[14] Universal feeding was considered an inefficient allocation of scarce state resources. The second area of criticism was about the ability of the programme to reach the target population.

.... the design of targeted food interventions has focused almost exclusively on the E-mistake-that of 'wasting' resources by covering some or all of non-target groups. In so doing, it has neglected the F-mistake that of failing to reach the whole target population.

Empirical studies show that in general as E-mistakes are reduced through targeting, F-mistakes are increased. While E mistakes involve additional expenditure, F-mistakes have a different kind of cost which encompasses both the immediate welfare loss and the foregone future income as a result of malnutrition among the 'missed' target group. In line with mainstream theoretical approaches to the evaluation of alternative food interventions, it is proposed that both types of mistakes (i.e. the total mistargeting error) should be considered in designing good schemes.[15]

In fact, even of the TINP, the internal evaluations were critical in the early years. MGR, of course, couldn't care less about the views of the Planning Commission. I was present at the discussions in 1985 in the Planning Commission when MGR came to Manmohan Singh, then Deputy Chairman of the Planning Commission. Five minutes into the discussions, the topic turned to expenditure on welfare. Coffee was being served at that moment. Manmohan Singh asked MGR about the expenditure on universal feeding. MGR pushed away the coffee, got up, and left, with us trotting behind. Manmohan Singh kept asking how he had upset MGR, but to no avail.

The criticisms continued. A mid-term evaluation of this project conducted in 1982 after 21 months of programme operation found no overall improvement in nutritional status of the children. The only improvement noted was with respect to the prevalence of grades III and IV undernutrition in children of the 37–60 months age group. The high 'graduation' rates among children participating in the feeding programme (10 per cent per month and even 20 per cent during certain months) reflected insignificant overall improvement of the nutritional status when all children were considered.[16]

In 1984 and 1985, Berg and Austin of the World Bank wrote a strong criticism of the universal feeding programme, concluding that the opportunity costs of the programme were unacceptably high.[17] They also stated that the nutritional content of the delivery was questionable, and that nutritional benefits of the scheme unquantified. Barbara Harriss in 1984[18] wrote a rejoinder where she argued that there were no magic bullets for tackling the nutrition agenda, and, referring to Schaffer,[19] pointed to several other infirmities in nutrition interventions, including lack of training, ignorance, lack of adequate data, systems, and analysis of food intake habits and policies.

The second chain of criticism was on the effectiveness of the programme. Barbara Harriss' seminal work on the programme through the analysis of two villages in Tamil Nadu showed that not all those eligible accessed the programme. More importantly, the poorer and disadvantaged, especially in the richer village that she studied, did not access the programme. In those villages, not much effect on enrolment was also seen. To quote,

But to say that the noon meals scheme 'reaches children below the poverty line'[20] is less than half the point, when those above it benefit too, and when not all children from poor households with inadequate food supplies are eligible for access. The point is that they do not and cannot benefit from positive discrimination. This intervention cannot be abstracted from the social relations surrounding food.

The 'Long List of Leakages' (Reutlinger and Selovsky, 1976; Knudsen, 1981)—commodities siphoned off for private trade and petty production, salaries for the richer, resources got through corrupt means by the administration, financial and food resources for political patronage, the sharing of food within the household, the interventions reaching those who do not need it as well as many of those who do demonstrate that these food interventions are counter labelled by receivers and participants as resources. The final paradox of targeting is that it is not in practice the poor who are targets. Rather is the intervention best conceptualized as a target, as the object of resourceful attempts to capture by all manner of participants.[21]

There is a volume of critical literature in the period up to 1990 that has focused on these two issues, the effectiveness of reach and access, as well as the cost of the programme and the development opportunities foregone. Broadly, the criticisms argue that supplementary and targeted programmes should be attempted, not universal feeding programmes. When this was brought to his notice, MGR is reported to have commented that supplementary feeding was all very well for those who had food at home, but for most of his programme beneficiaries, especially among girls, this was probably the only meal they got. This was probably not far from the truth. Poverty levels were close to 40 per cent of the population during this period, and per capita incomes, at 1970 prices, less than Rs 2,000 per annum.

By the 1990s, there was greater acceptance of school feeding programmes, and universal school feeding programmes were introduced in several developing countries. By 1995, the concept of noon-meals in schools became an element of the Government of India's policy, though most states baulked at the complexity of logistics and staff costs involved in providing hot cooked meals in schools day after day. In mid-1995, the Government of India launched a new 'centrally-sponsored scheme', the National Programme of Nutritional Support to Primary Education. Under this programme, cooked mid-day meals were to be introduced[22] in all government aided primary schools within two years. It took several years for the

Government of India to enact the Right to Food Act, and it was only in 2001 that the Supreme Court decreed that all school-going children should be given a cooked meal at school. The validation for the iconic midday meals programme had at last arrived, almost a decade and a half after MGR. Even the international agencies are now muted in their criticism of universal feeding programmes. The success of Tamil Nadu in implementing the programme without a break for over 35 years has been commented on favourably in academic journals as well as in policy and administration circles.

Tamil Nadu's noon-cum-nutritious meal scheme is the country's largest in terms of the number of beneficiaries covered. There is little doubt that enrolment and retention of children, including girl children, in schools have shown significant improvement. Besides, drop-out rates have shown a decline. However, as this paper analyses, there is now a need to seriously re-examine the original rationale for the scheme, namely, getting children to school and retaining them. In the two decades of the scheme's existence, the educational profile as well as the nature of problems at the ground level has changed significantly. Much of this is not reflected in the data presented and available with the government. On the other hand, the scheme has not been able to bring all children to school. If the midday meal is to retain its effectiveness and relevance, it may have to be changed in the light of these changes.[23]

Between 2000 and 2006, a number of academic articles started taking notice of this programme. By this time, there was also a policy recognition in the central government that school meals needed to be an important part of the education and nutrition interventions.

The 1999–2000 National Sample Survey data indicates that a large majority of children in India from poorer households did not have access to the meal schemes operational in the country. The only exception to this was Tamil Nadu where the schemes seemed to work the best in rural areas in the age group of seven to nine-year olds, without any discernible gender gap and was well targeted among the needy households. Further, among the poorer children, literacy rate and educational attainment were clearly higher when they had access to school meals perhaps implying that school enrolment and attendance were improving the presence of such schemes. This data however showed rather low coverage of the Integrated Child Development Scheme among pre-school children across all states indicating problems of under-reporting or under-recording.[24]

There is a clear movement of comments from the critical (especially in the early years of the programme) to that of support and appreciation.

A historical review of the noon meal scheme along with the introduction of the CMNNMP in Tamil Nadu has already been discussed elaborately. Among the measures to improve the level of education, the above-mentioned programme has helped. It has increased the enrolment and has brought down the drop-out rate from 40 per cent to 22 per cent. In the organizational set-up, the chief minister has a high level expert committee for regular monitoring and review.[25]

There were also reports of improved enrolment of girl students from disadvantaged families in schools.[26]

An attempt has been made in this paper to gain a better understanding of the quantitative impacts of school nutritional policies on the education of children, patterns of consumption and the overall welfare of a rural community. The data collected from a whole village study conducted in a South Indian village during the first six months of 1984 were used in the analysis.

There is a significant reduction in poverty and inequality among households resulting from the school nutrition programme. It is clear for all types of household that there is a significant increase in the enrolment of children in school and in continuing education beyond the elementary level. However, the results suggest that a stronger incentive is needed to support high-school education as it involves a higher opportunity cost.

School nutrition policies also influence expenditure distribution among food and non-food items. In general, school nutrition helps households to spend less on cereal foods and more on milk, vegetables, and fruit and non-vegetarian food. There is also a substantial increase in expenditure on non-food items in agricultural labour and silk weaver communities.[27]

Much of the success is due to the institutional structure put in place right at the beginning, and the total involvement of all the relevant departments, as well as the district administration, in the implementation.

By 2002–03, the government of Tamil Nadu had internalized the programme into one of nutrition. The main objective of the programme, as stated in 'Policy Note 2002–2003', of the Tamil Nadu government's Department of Social Welfare and Nutritional Meal programme is 'to provide adequate nutrition to economically disadvantaged children to improve the health and nutritional status of children, to develop their mental and physical ability and to increase the enrolment in schools and to reduce the dropouts'.[28] Thus, the main aim was to make available nutritious food to children enrolled in schools as a measure against child mortality, morbidity, and malnutrition. Further, it aimed to enhance the grasping power of children by improving their nutritional levels and also to combat diseases which arises due to malnutrition and deficiencies. Another main achievement of the programme is the reduction in gender disparity in fields of education and nutrition. One among the major, yet overlooked objectives of the programme is the importance given to generating more employment opportunities, especially for women. The programme, hailed as the single largest employment programme for the rural areas in independent India in the last thirty-five years, claims to be the major employment programme and anti-poverty programme for women in rural and urban areas Rajan and Jayakumar, 'Impact of Noon Meal Programme on Primary Education: An Exploratory Study in Tamil Nadu'.[29] An important and interesting feature of the programme is that anyone can access it. While it may appear to have multiple and contradictory objectives, it can be justified on many grounds, say political, nutritional, health, welfare, education, and social.

Children from grades 1 to 10 studying in government schools, local body schools, and government-aided schools, Education Guarantee Scheme and Alternative and Innovative Education Centre and National Child Labour Programme are covered under the programme. The programme was initially launched in rural areas for pre-school children of two to five years and five to nine years in primary school. On 15 September 1982 it was further extended to the urban areas. On 15 September 1984, the programme got extended to benefit the children in the age group of ten to fifteen years. In the year 1989, the programme introduced the provision of one egg to school children once a fortnight. Introduction of pulses—Bengal gram/green gram—and boiled potatoes took place in 2001. Later in 2013, the programme implemented the variety meal scheme along with four kinds of egg masala in one pilot block of each district. In 2014, the Variety Meal Programme along with four kinds of boiled egg masala was extended to all blocks in the state.[30]

During 1983, pensioners came under the purview of the programme. Later in 1984, the programme was again expanded to cover older urban school children up to fifteen years of age. In the mid-1990s, the government felt that the programme should stay and also felt the need of bringing pregnant women under the programme. As a result, from December 1995, women were also provided noon meals for a period of four months of their pregnancy. Therefore, we can say that the programme is a combination of a hunger–health–nutrition effort with social security for the old, destitute, and widows. School children have their noon meal at school, while the other categories, that is, pre-schoolers, pensioners, and pregnant and lactating women eat at the pre-school centres.

For primary school children, 100 grams of rice per child per school day is provided. At the same time, for the upper primary section, 150 grams of rice per child per school day is provided. Along with the meal, all children enrolled are given an egg with minimum weight of 46 grams (which provides 6.12 grams of protein and 80 kcal of energy) on all school working days. This cost is fully met by the state government. Banana weighing 100 grams (which provides 1.2 grams of protein and 116 kcal of energy) is provided as an alternate to children who are not accustomed to eating egg. During the first and third weeks of a month, on Tuesdays, 20 grams of black Bengal gram is provided to each child in the form of pulao, which is expected to provide 72 kcal of energy and 3.42 grams of protein. During the second and fourth week of a month on Thursdays, 20 grams of green gram is provided to each child in the form of sundal,[31] which is expected to provide 67 kcal of energy and 4.8 gm of protein. It was from November 2001 onwards, the late Chief Minister Jayalalithaa introduced the new scheme of 20 grams of potato, green gram, and black Bengal gram per beneficiary in a week instead of egg. As per this new scheme, it was estimated that the children are now getting 158.2 calories of energy and 8.54 grams of protein instead of the earlier 79.6 calories of energy and 6.5 gram of protein.[32]

Supply of double fortified (iron and iodine enriched) salt is one of the innovations of the midday meal scheme. Considering that iron deficiency/anaemia is one of the common disorders prevalent among students from two to fifteen years of age, iodized salt is used in the preparation of the meals. Another support is the provision of uniforms to midday meal scheme beneficiaries. Four sets of uniforms are delivered free of cost to the children registered under the mid-day meal programme. Moreover, the programme is also involved in the organization of the School Health Programme. Health check-up camps are conducted in schools regularly and micro-nutrients and deworming medicines are provided to the children. In addition, eye camps are conducted and free spectacles are given to those students with defective vision.

As we see, with the reformulation of the noon meal programme in 1982, there has been frequent introduction of nutrition elements in the meal, which clearly explains the fact that the scheme has turned into a nutritious meal programme rather than just a midday meal programme.

Another key aspect is the modernization of the kitchen and work areas. The state government provides Rs 22,000 for civil works, stoves, and liquefied petroleum gas (LPG) connection to each centre. This is done in a phased manner. A sum of Rs 83 crores was allotted from the state budget for modernizing the kitchen with LPG connections. Every year Rs 5 lakhs is allotted for the procurement of plates and tumblers to the midday meal beneficiaries per district in a phased manner.

In each noon meal centre (NMC), an organizer, a cook, and a cook assistant is employed for the better implementation of the scheme. The employees are provided salary in the Special Time Scale of Pay. All retired noon meal employees are provided with Rs 1,500 as monthly pension. Upon retirement, the organizer is given Rs 60,000, and the cook and the assistant cook are given Rs 25,000 as lump sum payment. In addition to this, a special amount of Rs 15,000 is provided as Special Provident Fund. All categories of NMC staff are enrolled under the GPF (General Provident Fund) Scheme. All noon meal employees are covered under the health insurance scheme in which Rs 150 is recovered as monthly subscription. The TNCSC supplies rice, dhal, oil, and salt at the door step of each NMC in order to ensure quality and quantity.

There was an elaborate organizational structure with responsibilities, duties, and reporting structures that was created even in the initial years. The academic arguments about nutrition and educational attainments, as also access to programmes and the costs, were certainly in the minds of the programme implementers, but did not determine the scope or extent of programme content or commitment to programme delivery. This approach of the administration and political hierarchy led to incremental additions to the programme like the adding of eggs, health check-ups, and so on, more or less in ad-hoc manner, with little analysis or enumeration. The administration willingly took up these additional tasks.

Diraviyam passed on in 1983 and subsequent Chief Secretaries did not involve themselves as actively in the programme, leaving the management to a specially created noon meal department under their wing. By 1984, MGR had become unwell, and the state administration between 1984 and 1987 more or less ran on auto-pilot. In later years, it no longer remained a political statement, but a carefully implemented, well thought out logistical exercise, where several government departments had their performance being monitored right up to the highest level. Within a short period, due to the political commitment as well as the official machinery in place, programme delivery became an expected norm in the villages and rural areas, and thereafter, in the urban areas. After a while, the expectation of the programme delivery from the public served to ensure accountability of the ground level officers to performance, and the public pressure kept the programme functioning smoothly. This peculiar case of the programme, maintaining a 'sandwich' structure, with a unique combination of pressure from above through the political will and from below through public expectations is a unique aspect of Tamil Nadu. Political pressure from above, public expectation, the importance given to the programme regardless of the party in power, successful implementation through administrative competence are special features that have contributed to the success of the programme.

It is important to look at the structures to recognize the extent to which large parts of the government machinery got involved in the implementation of the programme. The organization structure for the implementation is given below:

The District Collector has a nodal role in the implementation of the programme, and is assisted by a senior officer called Personal Assistant (noon-meals). The Chief Education Officer is responsible for all the schools in the district and Rural Development department for delivery to pre-school centres. Apart from the Rural Development, the Director of the Social Welfare department coordinates with the Ministry as well as with the Department of Social Welfare in supervising and monitoring the scheme through monthly review meetings for various aspects of the district performance. The Department of Municipal Administration and the Department of Rural Development run the urban and rural NMCs respectively. The total expenditure for the implementation of the programme is allocated in the budgets of the departments of school education, rural development, municipal administration, and civil supplies. Since 1995, the central government has been providing free rice for ten months a year at the rate of 100 grams per day for every student in the classes I to V under the scheme National Programme of Nutritional Support to Primary Education (NPNSPE). Under this scheme the state government places request through the civil supplies department for free supply of rice to the Food Corporation of India. For this, the state government has

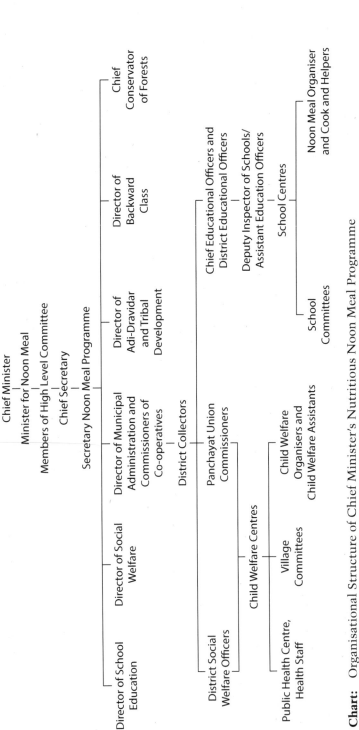

Chart: Organisational Structure of Chief Minister's Nutritious Noon Meal Programme

Source: R. P. Devadas, 1987, *An Appraisal of Chief Minister's Nutritious Noon Meal Programme,* Government Press, Madras.

to provide the central government details relating to total enrolment in the primary schools which are under the purview of the programme. Since the central government provides assistance in kind and also because of the budget of the state government is exclusive of the cost of this supply, naturally, the actual cost of providing noon meals to the school children should include the imputed cost of the central government's supply of free rice for the programme. Along with this the Department of Social Welfare, Department of Elementary Education, Department of Finance, and also the Department of Health have a role in the implementation process. The state government, time to time develops the scheme activities. For example, the Karunanidhi government passed an order under NPNSPE action plan for the release of central assistance towards the Management, Monitoring, and Evaluation (MME) component of the mid-day meals programme. Further an Action Plan was released for the first instalment of central assistance towards MME for the year 2007–08. For this purpose, Rs 79.56 lakh was sanctioned. The government of Tamil Nadu in the same year renamed the NPNSPE as NPMDMS (National Programme for Mid Day Meals Schemec) and extended the scheme to the upper primary classes (from class VI to VIII) in forty-four educationally backward blocks (EBBs).

The state government has also set up coordination committees at various levels. There is a State Monitoring Committee, which is chaired by the chief minister, in order to review the programme annually. In order to review the programme periodically, there is an Intersectional Coordination and Monitoring Committee for the State, chaired by the chief secretary.

The personal assistant to the collector for the Noon Meal Programme is responsible for the implementation of the programme at the district level. He coordinates with the District Collector and the District Rural Development Agency (DRDA) and reviews the performance and implementation of the programme at this level and provides instructions to improve the programme. At the district level, the Department of the Noon Meal Programme is responsible for the implementation of the programme. District Level Coordination and Monitoring Committee headed by the District Collector look after the various issues associated with the midday meal programme. The committee also includes the district level officials of Social Welfare, Health, Rural Development, Agriculture, Food and Civil Supplies, Industry, Municipal Administration and Water Supply, School Education, Adi Dravida, and Tribal Development. The committee also includes the elected leaders of Panchayat and Municipalities and local non-governmental organizations (NGOs) selected by the District Collector.

The responsibility to look into the implementation of the programme at the block level is given to the Block Development Officer and the Extension Officers of the Noon Meal Programme. These officers work under the supervision of the District Collector and hold the responsibility to inform the district authority periodically about the food procurement and the distribution aspects and issues. They make a compulsory monthly review and verify the stock of the food and other necessary inventories. They maintain an attendance record, grant finances for the transportation charges, and also provide financial support for the infrastructural development of

Table 4.1   MDMS: Physical and Financial Achievements

Year	Physical Achievement		Financial (₹ in crore)	
	No. of Noon Meal Centres	No. of Beneficiaries	Target	Achievement
2012–13	43,787	50,14,245	1,520.89	1,229.55
2013–14	42,490	53,52,111	1,588.65	1,473.54
2014–15	42,619	54,62,978	1,622.48	1,522.34
2015–16	42,970	55,15,613	1,470.53	1,428.34
2016–17	43,047	55,05,847	1,644.52	

the schools. They are also involved in making payments to the cook and other staff in the meal centres. Their major task is to monitor the quality and quantity of the food as per norms.

At this level, the school principal is given the overall responsibility of the implementation of the programme. The members of the parent teachers association, the head master, and one of the teachers of the school supervise the functioning of the programme in the school. The organizer is responsible for the procurement of food supplies required from the officials and distributes the daily required food grains to the cooks.

To take an example, in 2016–17, the Programme Approval Board of the Mid-Day Meal Scheme (PAB-MDM) approved an outlay of Rs 43,226.60 lakh (central share) for the year 2016–17.

The total expenditure for the provision of noon meals to school children was in two parts:

- Capital expenditure for the buildings of the NMCs, vessels, and other fixed asset requirements.

Table 4.2   Releases and Expenditure under MDMS to
Tamil Nadu (Rs in Lakhs)

Year	Funds Allocated	Release	% Release
2007–08	18031.19	17170.39	95.23
2008–09	29467.64	26448.85	89.76
2009–10	45757.19	30575.44	66.82
2010–11	44250.57	42231.04	95.44
2011–12	40333.68	40879.27	101.35
2012–13	70054.38	45269.07	64.62
2013–14	49354.83	48470.17	98.21
2014–15	63059.56	63991.10	101.48
2015–16	46356.00	46266.04	99.80
2016–17	43226.60	23400.91	54.13

Source: Social Welfare and Nutritional Meal Programme Department—
Performance Budget, 2016–17.

- Current expenditure on food grains, vegetables, salaries for the staff:
  - Expenditure for payments towards salaries, wages, honorarium, dearness allowances, loans to employees, and repayment of these are grouped under the head 'salary and other allowance'.
  - Office expenses include expenditure related to maintenance of office such as stationery, travel expenses, petroleum, and other such items.
  - The total money spent on purchase of rice (excluding the free supply of rice by the union government), oil, pulses, condiments, vegetables, salt, and fuel are grouped under 'feeding and dietary charge'.
  - Other miscellaneous expenditure is grouped under 'other expenses'.[33]

A study conducted by Swaminathan, et al. has found that one of the main recurring expenses, namely salary, has been increasing though the number of children being fed has increased either very marginally and/or is stagnant.

Data from the Department of Social Welfare indicates that in 1984–5, there were 63,582 centres operating, including all pre-school centres. The total number of beneficiaries was 83.09 lakhs. In 1995–6, the total number of centres had gone up to 68,544, but the number of beneficiaries had dropped to 73.27 lakhs. The drop in the age group two to five is noticeable. The costs of the programme to state had, however, gone up threefold during this period, as already pointed out.

The Social Welfare Department, in its submission to the legislature in 2016, has pointed out some challenges faced by the programme:

- *Inflated number of beneficiaries*: The enrolment figures, especially for the lower classes, exceed the number of children in that particular age group. This inflated number directly results into larger quantities of ration than what is actually required. Estimates regarding the actual number of beneficiaries in an NMC have to be verified by the panchayat union officers by conducting surprise checks in these centres. The problem here is that the officers who can conduct the visits are actually very few and these available officers are often burdened with other work and they also lack transport facilities.

- *Supply of less than stipulated ration*: The civil supplies corporation is entrusted with the supply of dry rations to the NMCs according to the requirement. The delivery challan mentions the quantity of each item that has to be delivered at each NMC. However, the actual quantity delivered of each item is less than the quantity mentioned in the challan. The result is lesser ration to cook the meal and the organizer is forced to reduce the ration from the stipulated 100 grams per child.

- *Leakage of rations at the local level*: Often the organizers and the cooks reduce the per capita allocation per child. As a result, children started bringing side dishes from their respective homes.

- *Poor quality of ration*: It is often argued that the dry ration supplied to the NMCs by the TNCSC is extremely poor in quality and as a result children find it hard to eat and there is more wastage. Inferior quality of pulses takes longer hours to cook. Field visits and surveys conducted by researchers have proved that whatever little pulses are used in the *sambar* (vegetable stew) are usually half cooked.

- *Condition of kitchen and vessels*: NMCs were built under different schemes years back and there were no provisions for the maintenance of these buildings. Many of the vessels got replaced over the years, but still some NMCs are using old aluminium vessels. The state had ordered the supply of stainless steel, mainly for health considerations, that is, cooking in a stainless steel vessel is less hazardous than in the aluminium vessels.

- *Non-payment of fuelwood costs*: It is often complained that, though there is provision of firewood, cooks were not paid money for the same, and they were asked to collect the required firewood during their spare time.

- *Inadequate washing facilities*: The problem of drinking water has been solved to a large extent in rural schools. Tanks have been constructed in schools for the provision of drinking water. However, with regard to the availability of water in the NMCs and kitchens for the purpose of cleaning and washing, fewer initiatives were taken. Many taps in the kitchen were found leaking during the field surveys conducted by the researchers.

It is a reflection of the quality of attention being paid to the implementation of this programme by the administration that it was able to identify all these infirmities and bring it to the attention of the legislature.

Recent studies have proved that only 33 per cent of schools are using LPG in their mid-day meal centres and 39 per cent of the kitchen-cum stores have not yet started functioning. There is also the issue of less coverage of primary school children in four districts (Madurai, Tuticorin, Ramnathapuram, and Tiruchirappalli) and upper primary school children in Madurai, Tuticorin, Tirunelveli, and Chennai, against the state level coverage of 85 per cent.

Another important problem faced by the programme is with regard to the employment status of the personnel employed for the midday meal programme. They are not treated on par with other government employees in the sense that they are not eligible for the monetary and miscellaneous benefits to which the government employees are eligible. The eligibility norms based on which noon-meal functionaries are appointed are not made apparent, thereby making it difficult to decipher the basis on which appointments and remunerations are arrived at.

Several of these problems are endemic to most government schemes. Ability to enforce quality, timeliness, and control over expenditure are important in all government programmes. As far as the midday meals scheme was concerned, during the MGR years, the close attention paid by the chief minister ensured that any slippages would not be tolerated. The DMK years of 1989 to 1991 were those in which the political administration did not want to disturb a popular programme. It was only in the later years of Jayalalithaa's first tenure of 1991 to 1996, that complaints of corruption and neglect appeared to be significant. The local body elections of 1996 ensured that the locally elected representatives were answerable to the people in the village, which improved programme delivery. Finally, by this time, the levels of education and awareness in the rural areas had increased considerably, and people would protest strongly if there were complaints.

The institutional structures were put in place in the initial years of the programme. Departmental structures, with clear responsibility and reporting mechanisms, ensured that the programme ran successfully. By the mid-1980s, the entire administrative structure was well geared to implement the programme on an uninterrupted basis.

MGR passed away in 1987, and there was political uncertainty until 1989. In 1989, the DMK came back to power, but their tenure was short. The government was dissolved in 1991, and Jayalalithaa led the AIADMK to victory in 1991. Between 1989 and 1991, the DMK did not disturb the functioning of the midday meals scheme. They owned and embellished it when finally in power, with foods (adding a fortnightly egg) which made no sense at all in terms of nutritional cost-effectiveness. In the 1990s, when the AIADMK swung back to rule, soya and corn flour were added for meals during school holidays along with sweet *pongal* (a sweet porridge or rice and lentils) to celebrate the birthdays of AIADMK party luminaries.[34]

The Jayalalithaa regime of 1991 to 1996 was characterized by a number of allegations of corruption. The criminal case in which Jayalalithaa and her companion Sasikala were arraigned arose out of misdeeds during this period. The case against Jayalalithaa abated after her death, but the final conviction of Sasikala and others lends credence to the allegations of this period.

The midday meals programme did not escape this unscathed. There were allegations about the purchase of eggs for the scheme and also lack of transparency in appointments. Theft of around 6 per cent of the grain and bribes of up to Rs 7,000 for employment have been reported.[35] Post 1996, while some investigations were started, they did not turn up any significant points for action. However, these aberrations had an effect on the total programme expenditure. By 1996, nearly 1,00,000 people were employed in the scheme in various departments, and the total cost to the state had gone up from around Rs 120 crores in 1982 to over Rs 388 crores in 1996.[36] Within it, delivery charges rose to 29 per cent. The total outlay on nutrition alone would be greater than that of all the states put together, at the end of the millennium.

However, the programme had developed a momentum of its own. There was the large institutional infrastructure that had been created, consisting of personnel, facilities, and commodities. There was also the continued expectation that the programme would go on uninterrupted.

The 1999–2000 National Sample Survey data indicates that a large majority of children in India from poorer households did

not have access to the meal schemes operational in the country.
The only exception to this was Tamil Nadu where the schemes
seemed to work the best in rural areas in the age group of seven to
nine-year olds, without any discernible gender gap and was well
targeted among the needy households. Further, among the poorer
children, literacy rate and educational attainment were clearly
higher when they had access to school meals perhaps implying
that school enrolment and attendance improved in the presence
of such schemes. This data however showed rather low coverage
of Integrated Child Development Scheme among pre-school
children across all states indicating problems of under-reporting
or under-recording.[37]

Vivek Srinivasan's thesis brings this out very clearly.

Compared to most other states in India, Tamil Nadu is noted for
widespread provision of education, primary health care, nutrition
support, rural roads, electricity, water and other public services.
These services are typically well planned and tend to work well.
I examine what determines Tamil Nadu's performance. I argue
that widespread and decentralized collective action for public
services plays a critical role in it but such collective action is
a new phenomenon, dating back to the seventies. I also argue
that normative challenges by major social movements, changing
influences of various social groups and raising individual
capabilities among common people played an instrumental role
in enabling such collective action that ultimately had an impact
on public services.[38]

Srinivasan argues that common people command a
considerable amount of influence in Tamil Nadu, and
this ensured that norms that were adverse to their
interests could not be enforced easily. In looking at the
National Rural Employment Guarantee Act (NREGA)

programme, he concludes that individual resistance and collective action played the critical role of ensuring that the aspirations of common people are taken into account by the institutional structure. He identifies collective action for public services as 'new phenomena'. According to him, the disadvantaged classes have a greater ability to influence the system than before.

Srinivasan's thesis is from 2010, and it is not certain that the social empowerment that he perceives now existed in Tamil Nadu in 1982 when the noon meal programme was started. The empowerment as well as national policy may be relevant for the continuation and ongoing success of the programme, but the initial years owed substantially to the commitment of the administration and institutional structure put in place. By 1995, the government of India had announced the nutrition for school children programme, and by 2001 the Supreme Court had made it mandatory to supply a hot cooked meal, something that Tamil Nadu had been doing since 1982. The noon meal programme is here to stay, along with the large number of paid staff in the Rural Development, Social Welfare, School Education, Civil Supplies, and Noon Meal Programme departments. The costs of the programme will continue to rise. It is, however, interesting to note that the persons accessing midday meals has not changed very much in a decade. It is around 50 lakh children for the school programme, somewhat lower than numbers that the programme started with in 1982. There could be several reasons for this. On the one hand, it could be due to improving incomes and living standards in Tamil Nadu, making available better nutritious food to children in their own homes. It could also be due to greater urbanization, for school meal centres in urban areas have always had lower attendance than rural centres. It could also be due to alternate educational opportunities available in private schools, and the preference, with improved incomes, for parents to send their children to private schools.

At the same time, public pressure, the large staff component liability, and the sheer overhang of the MGR aura will make it extremely difficult for any elected government in Tamil Nadu to do away with the programme or to replace it with other, alternative models. After the Government of India introduced the centrally assisted school meal programme in 1995, they have been providing financial support for it. They have also been monitoring and supervising implementation. Monitoring is through Joint Review Missions sent out by the Ministry of Human Resource Development (HRD) at Delhi, and these review missions have generally appreciated several best practices in Tamil Nadu.[39]

- Nutritious meal is being served to 88 per cent of the enrolled children on an average.
- The government of Tamil Nadu is providing four sets of school uniforms, school bags, *chappals* (slippers), and geometry box to each student.
- Eggs are being served to all students on all school days by the state government from its own resources. The eggs are marked in different colours on each day so that stale eggs are not served to children on the next day.
- The state government has introduced a variety meal in one block of all districts on pilot basis. This variety meal is very popular amongst the children.

- The state government is making e-transfer of funds at all levels.
- The state government has set up an administrative structure and posted regular staff for effective implementation and monitoring of the scheme at state, district, block, and school levels.
- Noon meal functionaries consisting of noon meal organizers, cooks, and assistant cooks are available in all the visited schools. The state government has appointed them as regular employees and they get their salaries regularly as per their pay scales. The state government is also paying pension, lump sum payment at the time of their retirement, Special Provident Fund besides giving them promotional opportunities to become office assistants and teachers in schools.
- All cooks have been trained by the state government.
- TNCSC procures pulses, oil, and salt in bulk quantity through a centralized tender process and delivers them to the NMCs. Buffer stock of food grain, pulses, oil, and salt for more than one month was available at all NMCs.
- The state government has made route charts for supplying pulses, oil, salt to all NMCs between the 15 and 25 of every month to service the following month's needs. Foodgrains lifted from FCI is also delivered with the above ingredients.
- Kitchen devices are made available in government and local body NMCs.
- All the NMCs are to keep food samples in air tight containers for testing.

- The state government is also serving midday meals to school children studying in grades 9 and 10 from its own resources.

The state can always argue that it has been the first to start the midday meals programmes for children and, because of political will and administrative capability, it has done a good job.

Appendix

Puratchi Thalaivar M.G.R. Nutritious Meal Programme

1. Date of commencement

01 July 1982: The scheme was launched in rural areas for pre-school children of two to five years and five to nine years age in primary schools.

15 September 1982: Further extended to urban areas.
15 September 1984: Extended to benefit children in the age group of ten to fifteen years.

03 June 1989: Introduction of one egg once a fortnight.
12 September 2001: Introduction of pulses such as bengal gram/green gram, and boiled potatoes.
20 March 2013: Implementation of variety meal scheme along with four kinds of egg masala, in one pilot block of each district.

15 August 2014: Variety meal programme along with four kinds of egg masala was extended to all blocks throughout the state.

2. Objective

    i. To maximize enrolment and reduce school dropout rates with a view to universalize elementary education.

    ii. To provide nutrition to the underfed and undernourished children in rural areas.

    iii. To empower women by offering employment opportunities.

3. Nature of Assistance

    i. Primary school children in the age group of five to nine years and upper primary school children in the age group of ten to fifteen years are provided with hot cooked nutritious variety meals inside the school campus itself, for five days a week for a total of 220 days in a year.

    ii. The children enrolled under the National Child Labour Project Special Schools in sixteen districts namely, Kancheepuram, Vellore, Tiruvannamalai, Namakkal, Dharmapuri, Krishnagiri, Salem, Coimbatore, Erode, Tiruppur, Tiruchirappalli, Dindigul, Virudhunagar, Tirunelveli, Thoothukudi, and Chennai are also provided with hot cooked nutritious variety meals for 312 days in a year.

    iii. Food grains (rice) at 100 gram per child per school day for primary children (standard one to five) and 150 gram for upper primary (standard six to ten) is provided.

iv. Along with hot cooked nutritious variety meals, all enrolled children are provided with an egg with minimum weight of 46 gram on all school working days. An egg weighing 46 gram provides 6.12 gram of protein and 80 kcal of energy. The cost of these eggs is fully met by the state government.

v. A banana weighing 100 gram is provided as an alternate to children who are not accustomed to eating eggs, which provides 1.2 gram of protein and 116 kcal of energy.

vi. During the first and third weeks of a month, on tuesdays, 20 gram of black Bengal gram is provided to each child in the form of 'pulav' which provides 72 kcal of energy and 3.42 gram of protein.

vii. During the second and fourth week of a month on thursdays, 20 gram of green gram is provided to each child in the form of sundal, which provides 67 kcal of energy and 4.8 gram of protein.

viii. On all fridays, to increase the carbohydrate content, children are provided with 20 gram of chilly fried potato, which has 19.04 kcal of energy and 0.32 gram of protein. The amount for the procurement of 20 gram of potato has been enhanced from 16 paise to 40 paise.

ix. In order to address iodine and iron deficiency among children and as a part of health intervention programme, double fortified salt is used for cooking which prevents iodine deficiency in children, thereby preventing goitre.

x. During important occasions, sweet pongal is served to children by using jaggery and ghee.

Table 4.3 Nutritious Meal Programme in Anganwadis

1.	Date of commencement	In rural areas 01 August 1982
		In urbanareas 15 September 1982
2.	Objective of Scheme	To improve the nutrition status
		of children and also to the
		children in the 54439 AWCs
		In the age group of 2+ to 5+

Year	Physical Target	Achievement (Nutritious Meal)	Financial (in lakh)	
	Unit	Strength	Target	Achievement
2012–13	54,439AWC	11,56,017	8,014.20	7,986.50
2013–14	54,439AWC	11,04,148	8,196.15	6,210.23
2014–15	54,439AWC	11,04,148	8,061.13	6,690.74
2015–16	54,439AWC	11,07,738	8,999.12	8,311.04
2016–17	54,439AWC	13,97,465	8,999.12	–

Source: TN Government Social Welfare Department Performance Budget, 2016–17.

Notes

1. Quoted in Barbara Harriss, *Child Nutrition and Poverty in South India—Noon Meals in Tamil Nadu* (Concept Publishing House, 1991), p. 19. Also quoted by several writers who have written about this programme.

2. S. Jayakumar and A. Irudaya Rajan, 'Impact of Noon Meal Programme on Primary Education', *Economic and Political Weekly*, 27(43–44).

3. World Bank Impact Evaluation Report, Tamil Nadu Integrated Nutrition Programme 1994, available at http://documents. worldbank.org/curated/en/851821468771671074/pdf/ multi0page.pdf.

4. Anuradha K. Rajivan, 'History of Nutrition Schemes in Tamil Nadu', mimeo.

5. GO Ms 857 and 858, Public Department, Government of Tamil Nadu, accessed at Tamil Nadu archives, 28 May 1982.

6. He used to say that his proficiency in English was honed by Srinivasa Sastry ('silver tongue Sastry') who was his teacher. Mrs Indira Gandhi always asked him to translate her speeches from English to Tamil whenever she spoke in Tamil Nadu.

7. This was subsequently changed to 365 days—all days in the year, though there are no files with economic arguments for this.

8. GO Ms 1000, Public Department, accessed at Tamil Nadu government archives, 24 June 1982.

9. GO Ms 901, Public Department, accessed at Tamil Nadu government archives, 4 June 1982.

10. As told by N. Krishnamurthy, food secretary at that time.

11. To recall, this was a time when Delhi was backing Prabhakaran of LTTE, and MGR was also in the know.

12. Michael Lokshin, Monica Das Gupta, Michele Gragnolati, and Oleksiy Ivaschenko, 'Improving Child Nutrition-The Integrated Child' Development and Change, 36(4): 613–40.

13. An interesting by product was that senior officers of the Tamil Nadu government, who were in charge of the TINP and ICDS programmes, became personal champions of their individual programmes, and critical of the others. Several of these were picked up by multinational agencies like the World Bank and the UNDP due to their commitment, and had successful international careers. There was little international support for the mid-day meals programme.

14. Harriss (1986) in Public Administration and Development.

15. Two errors of targeting by Giovanni Andrea Cornia* and Frances Stewart**;* International Child Development Centre UNICEF, Florence.

   ** Queen Elizabeth House, University of Oxford

16. Revised Report on Evaluation of TINP (Nutrition Component) in the Pilot Block; Phase I), Evaluation and Applied Research Department, Government of Tamil Nadu, 1983.

17. Alan Berg and James Austin, 'Nutrition Policies and Programmes: A Decade of Redirection', *Food Policy*, 9(4): 304–11 and Berg, et al., 'Guidelines for Work in Nutrition', Technical Note 86–12, World Bank, Population, Health, and Nutrition Department, Washington, DC, 1986.

18. Harriss, 'Magic Bullets and the Nutrition Agenda', *Food Policy*, 9(4): 313–16.

19. B.B. Schaffer, 'To Recapture Policy for Politics', Institute of Development Studies, Sussex, 1981.

20. *Financial Express*, 14 September 1984. quoted in Harriss, 'Meals and Noon Meals in South India: Paradoxes of Targeting', *Public Administration & Development*, 6(4): 401–10.

21. Harriss, 'Meals and Noon Meals in South India: Paradoxes of Targeting', p. 401.

22. Jean Drèze and Aparajita Goyal, 'Future of Mid-Day Meals', *Economic and Political Weekly*, 38(44): 4673.

23. Padmini Swaminathan, J. Jeyaranjan, R. Sreenivasan, and K. Jayashree, 'Tamil Nadu's Midday Meal Scheme: Where Assumed Benefits Score over Hard Data', *Economic and Political Weekly*, 39(44): 4811–21.

24. Brinda Viswanathan, 'Access to Nutritious Meal Programmes: Evidence from 1999–2000 NSS Data', *Economic and Political Weekly*, 41(6): 497+499–506.

25. S. Irudaya Rajan and A. Jayakumar Source, 'Impact of Noon Meal Programme on Primary Education: An Exploratory Study in Tamil Nadu', *Economic and Political Weekly*, 27(43/44): 2372–80.

26. Reetika Khera, 'Mid-Day Meals in Primary Schools: Achievements and Challenges', *Economic and Political Weekly*, 41(46): 4742–50.

27. Suresh Chandra Babu and J. Arne Hallam, 'Socioeconomic Impacts of School Feeding Programmes: Empirical Evidence from a South Indian Village', Iowa State University, USA.

28. Padmini Swaminathan, J. Jeyaranjan, K. Jayashree, and R. Sreenivasan, 2004, 'Tamil Nadu's Midday Meal Scheme Where Assumed Benefits Score over Hard Data', *Economic and Political Weekly*, 39(44): 4811–21.

29. Rajan and Jayakumar, 'Impact of Noon Meal Programme on Primary Education: An Exploratory Study in Tamil Nadu'.

30. The stages of the programme are in the appendix to this chapter.

31. Sundal is made from different types of gram, which is soaked for a few hours and then lightly fried with oil, salt and mild spices. It could be made of red or white beans, dhal, or chana. It is high in protein content.

32. Swaminathan, et al., 'Tamil Nadu's Midday Meal Scheme Where Assumed Benefits Score over Hard Data'.

33. Swaminathan, et al., 'Impact of Noon Meal Programme on Primary Education: An Exploratory Study in Tamil Nadu Impact of Noon Meal Programme on Primary Education an Exploratory Study in Tamil Nadu'.

34. Harriss, 'Nutrition and Politics in Tamil Nadu', p. 53.

35. Harriss, 'Nutrition and Politics in Tamil Nadu'.

36. Harriss, 'Nutrition and Politics in Tamil Nadu', p. 54.

37. Viswanathan, 'Access to Noon Meal Programmes Evidence from 1999–2000 NSS Data', *Economic and Political Weekly*, 41(6): 497–506.

38. Vivek Srinivasan, PhD thesis Syracuse University, 2010.

39. JRM Mission Report 2013, Ministry of HRD.

5

THE TAMIL NADU INTEGRATED NUTRITION PROGRAMME

A Case Study

AN EXTERNALLY FUNDED PROGRAMME, THE TINP INITIATIVE arose out of the report of a USAID study in the late 1960s on the nutritional status of people in Tamil Nadu, which suggested the need for intervention as the incidence of nutrition deficiency was very high in the state. This analysis, termed the Tamil Nadu Nutrition Study was conducted in 1970 and mainly focused on the consumption aspect of nutrition, food production and processing, and the relationship between income and employment growth and nutrition in the state. The project was picked up by the World Bank, which agreed to fund an intervention programme in Tamil Nadu to improve the nutritional status of children. The project was called the Tamil Nadu Integrated Nutrition Project (TINP 1). The scope of the project was reduced based on considerations of management and cost-effectiveness. It was assumed that large numbers would be difficult to manage and an attempt to do so would lead to inefficiencies. Two important conclusions made by the study attracted the curiosity of development scientists studying nutrition: first, there was a strong two-way relationship between high levels of child mortality and high levels of child malnutrition and second, child malnutrition was high in parts of the state even where income levels were relatively high.

The first of these conclusions explained the emphasis on health investment in the TINP. The second one suggested that the most important constraint to improving nutrition in Tamil Nadu was in the areas of behaviour at the household level, therefore the need of priority interventions in the form of information, education, and communication (IEC) arose.

The programme, as recommended by the study, focused on weanlings, adolescents, and pregnant and lactating mothers. The first phase of the project ran from 1980 to 1989. The study focused on the mismatch between those who were benefiting and those who were in need. It was found that malnutrition was concentrated among pregnant and the lactating mothers and pre-school children. The programme initially targeted only six to thirty-six month old children, but this changed during the implementation to zero to six months as awareness grew about the importance of nutrition, particularly breast feeding, during the first six months of a child's life.

During TINP I, only children who were severely malnourished or those whose growth failed to increase adequately over three consecutive monthly weighings were eligible for the supplementary feeding programme. This was called the growth factoring criterion for supplementation. Children entering the feeding programme were supplemented for ninety days and then exited from the programme, provided they were once again growing properly. Within two years of the programme beginning in any Community Nutrition Center (CNC) area, the number of severely malnourished children fell by half, with the result that at any one time no more than about 25 per cent of the zero to three age group (including both severely malnourished and growth falterers) were in supplementation. In addition, 30–60 per cent of pregnant and lactating women, who met certain technical entry criteria, were supplemented. Limiting supplementation to a minority of beneficiaries helped reduce dependency on the programme, as well as making managerial, nutritional, and financial sense.

In 1982, the state had announced the midday meals programme, which was a universal feeding programme. In 1980, the Government of India expanded the ICDS into Tamil Nadu as well, and soon there were three overlapping programmes in the state targeting women, nutrition, and children. Barbara Harriss notes that between 1981–82 and 1994–95, the state's current outlays for nutrition increased 'by a factor of 100 to stand at Rs 388 crores'.[1] By the turn of the millennium, its outlay on nutrition alone was greater than that of all the other states put together.

Harriss' argument is that there were three distinct forces of change working at different levels and emanating from different sources of politics and policymaking activity. First, the international aid agencies, second, state-level political party competition, and the third, the reaction to the opposition demands about food security concerns. She says that 'the first linked World Bank's nutrition policy advisers with village level nutrition policy workers that they have identified. The second combines party patronage with a parallel nutrition bureaucracy that reaches into the villages'. There was also the benefit to public sector workers, the transporters, and the civil supplies corporation, as well as to a mass of voters below the poverty line.

It is important to look at the implementation of the three programmes from the point of view of the bureaucracy and the implementing agencies. It was clear that the structures for implementation of the three programmes often competed with each other due to the individual nature of the institutional support put in place for their implementation. There was competition and rivalry between the advocates of the programme. In the initial years, as already pointed out in Chapter 4, development professionals viewed the noon meal programme as not scientific and it was rejected by the Planning Commission, which meant it needed to rely on the state's own budgetary funding. There was considerable debate decrying the principles of universal feeding against targeted nutritional assistance.

In MGR's government, the chief minister was not necessarily engaged with the differing objectives of the three programmes. As long as the programme closest to him, the midday meals programme, was being implemented, he was tolerant about other initiatives. In any case, he had no intention of facing up to either the international agencies or the central government. Therefore, enormous budgetary resources went into all the programmes put together. The net benefits for nutritional attainment in Tamil Nadu will be discussed separately, but it is possible to argue that a multiplicity of programmes for nutrition would have diverted state resources away from other pressing development expenditure like infrastructure and industry.

From the point of view of the institutions and the bureaucracy, all the programmes were implemented vigorously and efficiently. The state government provided adequate staff and resources for the implementation, and the supervision and monitoring mechanisms, which the Tamil Nadu administration is famous for, ensured that programme delivery was quite up to the expectations of the donor agencies. Separate staffing patterns, training content, as well as infrastructure creation enabled the establishment of a large hierarchy of personnel and services in each of the programmes, which became, over time, a compelling argument for the continuation of these programmes and for the continuation of the personnel involved. The TINP, ICDS, and the midday meal programme together accounted for over 200,000 personnel employed at various levels, and by the end of MGR era, constituted a pressure group that was politically impossible to overlook. It is a comment on Tamil Nadu bureaucracy that these somewhat overlapping programmes continued without any serious analysis of whether efficiencies putting all of them together could be achieved. Since the TINP and the ICDS differed very much in concept and delivery from the midday meals programme, it is interesting to look at the programmes from the point of view of content, delivery, and benefits in order to analyse how three programmes so different in policy origins, could all be carried out simultaneously and efficiently.

Tamil Nadu's community nutrition programme has progressed through three distinct phases, parallel to the three consecutive World Bank assisted projects which have financed it. The first project, TINP I, ran from 1980 to 1989, and the second, TINP II, from 1990 to the end of 1997. At this point, a decision was taken to convert TINP into the ICDS programme, which was already operating in several districts of the state. The third phase of Bank assistance came from the Woman and Child Development Project (WCDP), a project financing ICDS, which began in 1999 and is on-going.

TINP I

The core of TINP I was a growth monitoring, nutrition education, and food supplementation programme which were implemented by CNCs at the village level, and targeted at pregnant and lactating women and at children under three and their mothers. Under the project, about 9,000 CNCs were opened, each serving about 1,500 people, and in total covering less than half the rural area of the state. The programme had three components—nutrition, health, and communications. Along with the cost of establishing the CNCs, the other expenses incurred by the state were:

- Salary costs for one Community Nutrition Worker (CNW) per CNC, together with a helper who assisted with supplementary feeding, and a network of supervisors and trainers at different levels.

- Food, vitamins, iron supplements, and deworming drugs.
- A training programme and an interpersonal and mass media IEC programme.
- Project Coordination Office (PCO) in the Department of Social Welfare at the state level.
- Monitoring and evaluation system.

TINP is frequently thought of only as a nutrition intervention. But, no less than 43 per cent of TINP I's USD 66 million cost was allocated to investments in the health sector, the most important of which were constructing, staffing, equipping, and running 1,600 Health Sub-Centres, building and running ten centres for training multipurpose health workers, and establishing field training wings at 39 Primary Health Centres, which are the first line referral facilities for Health Sub-Centres. The project was also responsible for providing drugs, vaccines, supplies, vans, jeeps, motorcycles, and bicycles for field health staff and their supervisors.

This part of the project was managed on a day-to-day basis by the state's Department of Public Health (DPH). The project helped to train one Multi-Purpose Health Worker (MPHW) in a health centre for a population of 5,000. The MPHW was expected to deliver her package of maternity and child health services through the CNC, with the help of contacts and records of the CNW. They would make joint visits for the purpose of nutrition and health education.

The TINP focused on the human resource development of the nutrition staff. The key players were the CNW and the Community Nutrition Instructress (CNI), both categories recruited exclusively for the project. For the

CNW, great emphasis was placed on her residence in the village and age and educational qualifications were often overlooked at the time of recruitment in order to meet this criterion. As a local woman and mother of a healthy child, the CNW enjoyed considerable credibility in the community and her own motivation to serve was high. Her presence in the village made it possible to establish contact with mothers outside normal working hours when most of them were unavailable or preoccupied with other duties.

The Communications Component was evaluated to have been fairly effective. Significant improvements in knowledge, attitudes, and practices (KAP) of diarrhoea management and immunization were recorded. A wide range of skilfully packaged, appropriately targeted, and appealingly presented communication materials was developed. Instructional materials for project functionaries and their training in communication skills have been particularly good. The component also played a significant role to bring about inter-agency coordination at various levels in the organization. It was felt that consistent monitoring and the development of a coherent communication strategy with frequent feedback of results could improve the effectiveness of the component.

Targeting improved the nutrition education component of the programme. Growth monitoring and promotion was implemented since feeding hinged on the results of weighing and mothers had to be educated as to why some children were selected for feeding and not others. It led to cost effectiveness since the percentage of children being fed was only one-third of all children. There was an active effort to recruit those at risk through house visits rather than operating the centre on a drop-in basis. Targeting also helped maintain the CNW's workload at a manageable level, enhancing the quality of her output. Selection was important in terms of preventing social and psychological dependency on the supplement and caused the project to focus on information and education as a means of sustaining community interest.

The design of TINP necessitated the full cooperation and acceptance of the community for project implementation. Basic to project design were at least three activities that flouted convention and were highly unacceptable to the community. The first was weighing, that was thought to attract the evil eye; the second, selection for supplementation, which was contrary to all other feeding programmes then implemented; and the third was nutrition education by the relatively young CNW in the face of conventional wisdom and traditional practices recommended by village elders. The success of TINP can be judged by the extent to which these three activities have become fully institutionalized. It is indeed remarkable that the project staff was able to persist with an unpopular design and subsequently win full acceptance and participation in the project.

The project employed a series of mechanisms to be able to win community support. First, the CNW was a local mother who had a healthy child of her own and enjoyed high credibility in the community to begin with. Her ability to communicate effectively was a criterion for her selection and these skills were further enhanced by constant training and a wide range of communication materials to assist her in her role as educator. She received back-up support and reinforcement from the MPHW, the

Community Nutrition Supervisor (CNS), the CNI, and the block-level trainer, in her recruitment and education activities.

A second mechanism to win community support was the Women's Working Group (WWG). A group of fifteen to twenty women, identified by the CNW as progressive, capable of working together, and interested in the activities of the CNC, was formed to promote project activities. The group was initially given health and nutrition training and some members are now quite proficient in using flipcharts and flannel graphs. The group meets once a month at a cooking demonstration where nutritious and easy-to-make weaning food recipes are demonstrated by the CNW. To sustain the interest of the WWG members over the years, the project recently experimented with community self-survey and 'adoption' of families by the WWG members.

One of the most significant experiments in the project was the use of the WWG for local food production. The preparation of the weaning food for supply to local centres by WWG members under the guidance and supervision of the Taluk Project Nutrition Officer brought the community much closer to actual project implementation. It also had the side benefit of providing some economic incentive to women who had been actively promoting the project activities on a voluntary basis. The educational impact in terms of the preparation of appropriate weaning foods must also have been considerable. Local food production met about one-third of the project's need for the supplement. Standardization and quality control were problems with this type of production and it is now proposed that local production would be transferred to better equipped and better monitored women's cooperative societies in each block.

In TINP, a wide variety of communication materials was produced and used effectively as a back-up support to the interpersonal contact established by the front line project functionaries. The use of mass media such as films, filmstrips, slides, posters, and a wide range of printed matter (including flipcharts, flashcards, pamphlets, and so on) was effective. Traditional folk media was used not only by enabling project messages to be incorporated in scripts used by professional troupes but also by organizing competitions, skits, and performances in the villages.

As a government-sponsored project, TINP enjoyed the full support of authorities at all levels. Two existing government departments—the Directorates of Social Welfare and of Public Health and Preventive Medicine—were responsible for implementing the nutrition and health components respectively. The Project Coordination office, which was set up exclusively for the project, was responsible for coordination and communication and monitoring activities. On the nutrition side, project activities did not overlap with any other programmes in the Directorate, most of which were small, scattered, and directed at older children. Some of these programmes were discontinued when the project began. An excellent hierarchy was also newly established and project implementation proceeded apace. Mid-way through the project, nutrition services were further strengthened by the appointment of the Project Coordinator as Additional Director of Social Welfare.

TINP II

At the end of TINP I, the state government took over the costs of all the above activities, thus ensuring their sustainability, and TINP II financed only new activities over and above those of TINP I. Some of the changes made in TINP II are as follows:

- For the physical investments financed under TINP II, only about 10 per cent of the project's USD 139 million cost was allocated to health, especially in hardware and software.
- With regard to the physical investment on the nutrition side, TINP II had two main thrust areas, the first being to expand the CNC network (which went up from 9,000 to around 18,500, covering about 80 per cent of rural Tamil Nadu). The second one was to amalgamate the TINP programme with the state's NMP, which was also managed by the Department of Social Welfare. The amalgamation was intended at avoiding duplication of nutrition centres in the villages and also involved:
  - Combining the TINP and NMP centres in over 6,000 villages where both programmes operated.
  - Adding a CNW to provide TINP services to children under the age of 3 in about 10,000 NMP centres in parts of the state not covered by TINP I.
  - Developing about 2,000 new combined centres in parts of the state which had not previously been served by either TINP or ICDS.

The joint CNCs under TINP II were operated by a CNW providing TINP services to children up to three year old and their mothers, and a Community Welfare Organizer, the NMP programme worker, providing a noon meal to four to six year olds (when the two programmes were united, the target group of the NMP was changed from 3–6 year olds to 4–6 year olds, to avoid replicating services to the 0–3 years age group). The combined programmes came to be known as the 'two worker model'. TINP I and II were managed from a PCO, located in the state government's Social Welfare Department, which was divided into four units, responsible singly for Nutrition, Communications, Training, and Operations Research and Monitoring. The PCO increased gradually in size as TINP expanded, and by the end of TINP II, it had about eighty professional and support staff. The programme was physically expanding over time, but the quality of the project management varied considerably. According to World Bank's view, project management was more effective and efficient during TINP I and also during the first year or two of TINP II. But from about 1993 to 1995, 'there was a significant fall-off in commitment, integrity and supervision, which percolated down to all levels, adversely affecting morale and motivation'.[2]

Integrated Child Development Services

Tamil Nadu launched the ICDS programme in 1976 on a small scale (only in three blocks) covering 0–6 years age group for the first time and combining supplementary nutrition with other child development services. Shortly after ICDS began, in 1980, the TINP was introduced on a pilot basis in another block. With funding and support from the World Bank,[3] TINP focused on an even younger age group 0–3 years old children. According to Rajivan,

these early years are the hardest to reach—being very young, children under six do not assemble every day at a place like a school and need an adult to bring them to a facility. Yet from a nutrition perspective, this is efficient as interventions reach the most important age group. The pre-school age, especially below 36 months, is a nutritionally most vulnerable period when rapid growth takes place. Deprivations in this age group can create irreversible damage which later feeding cannot fully compensate.

This is the only national programme which takes into consideration the nutrition requirements of children under the age of six years. The main broad objectives of the programme are to improve the health, nutrition, and development of children. It provides health, nutrition, and hygiene education to mothers, non-formal pre-school education to children aged 3–6 years, supplementary feeding for all children and pregnant and nursing mothers, growth monitoring and promotion services, and links to primary healthcare services.

The objective of ICDS was to enhance the nutrition status, health, and overall quality of life for adolescent girls, pregnant women and lactating mothers, and children below six years by providing them with the required supply of nutritious food, hot cooked meals, training for adolescent girls, and pre-school non formal education to children below six years and providing noon meals to old age pensioners. Another important objective was the proper implementation of centrally sponsored schemes like the Kishori Sakti Yojana and SABLA, the self-employment programme for the adolescent girls.

Moreover, the programme is also aimed at creating awareness of various policies and programmes of the government through events such as drama performances, exhibitions, and dissemination meets. The broad objectives of the programme are: 'Coverage in terms of both children and adults have expanded over the years. Pregnant and nursing women are eligible under the ICDS. Old age pensioners, the disabled, widows and destitute also avail of the daily lunch as the marginal cost of adding them to the already large list of eligible persons was found to be relatively small'.[4]

The main services delivered under ICDS are:

- Early childhood care, antenatal care, and postnatal care;
- Growth monitoring;
- Supplementary nutrition;
- Health services by health personnel (village health nurse and medical offices);
- Referral services;
- Non-formal pre-school education imparting pre-school education to bring about holistic development of the child through play-way method;
- Nutrition and health education;
- Nutrition and life skill education for the adolescent girls;
- Provision of nutritious hot cooked meal for children in the age group of two to six years and old age pensioners for 365 days;
- Under Rajiv Gandhi Scheme for Empowerment of Adolescent Girls (SABLA), Supplementary Nutrition in the form of Weaning Food (THR), life skill training

and vocational training are given to Adolescent Girls
in 139 Blocks in nine districts;

• Creating awareness mainly through the IEC
activities.

Most centres operate in Panchayat Union buildings
or other public buildings, specially constructed feeding
centres, or rent-free private buildings. School centres run
in school buildings. Centres are equipped with cooking
utensils, plates and tumblers, play equipment, weighing
scales, and mats for children to sleep on. For pre-school
education centres, charts, toys, and other educational
material are provided. Local communities also provide
items required by these centres such as cooking gas to
replace the firewood, additional toys and kitchen gardens,
and so on. Also, former NMCs have become ICDS and vice
versa enabling integration. Each centre has its own staff
for cooking, cleaning, and also for training the children.
In the case of ICDS, the staff is all women and for the noon
meal scheme, staff is drawn from both genders. When
sponsored aid from the World Bank stopped at the end of
TINP II, Tamil Nadu was faced with taking on the costs
of the 11,000 TINP II CNWs in addition to the 9,000
TINP I workers already on its payroll. As a result, Tamil
Nadu chose to move from the TINP to the ICDS pattern.
With respect to staffing, this meant a move from the two
worker model back to a one worker model, since ICDS has
only one worker (again assisted by a helper) to give both
nutrition and pre-school education services to the entire
0–6 years age group (one reason why ICDS has been much
less successful than TINP in reaching the under threes,
the age group at highest nutritional risk). It was later

agreed that attrition, rather than the firing of more than 20,000 village level workers would achieve this result.[5] The majority of village nutrition centres in Tamil Nadu, therefore, continue, for the time being, to follow the two worker model, with one worker financed by the state and the other by the central government. As workers retire, the ICDS model will be adopted, the central government will continue to finance one worker per centre, and the state government's salary costs will gradually be eliminated. Political considerations were evident in this decision, which was not the optimum one from the point of view of resource allocation. However, it would have caused considerable loss of political goodwill to reduce staff, especially women, at the village level, and neither party was willing to bite this bullet.

During the designing stage of the TINP I, ICDS was in its stage of infancy. But during TINP I, ICDS was adopted by the central government as India's national nutrition programme, and by the end of TINP II it had expanded to cover about three quarters of the country. These programmes have different scopes, different organizational structures, and most importantly different strategies for nutrition improvement. In addition, differences with regard to programme financing were also at place. ICDS is conjointly financed by the central government and the states, with the centre picking up the salary costs of the programme, and the states the food supplementation costs. TINP I and II, on the other hand, were state projects not following what became the national nutrition programme model. As a result, Tamil Nadu became the only state in the country not benefitting from central financing for its village nutrition workers.

The three programmes differed in objectives. This has to be borne in mind while evaluating these programmes. In the Tamil Nadu Chief Minister's programme which is a massive operation covering children above two years of age and costing over Rs 2 billion annually, no deliberate selection of beneficiaries is involved, except that children below two years (the crucial age group) are not included. A midday meal is offered each day of the year to all children above two years who care to come to the several thousands of centres in the state. Any 'selection' that takes place is not what is imposed by the sponsors but by the socio-economic imperatives operating at the community revel. Children belonging to the more affluent sections and 'higher castes' often do not turn up, with the result that the overwhelming majority of beneficiaries are the 'poorest' sections of the population for whom one good meal for the children is indeed a great boon. This programme must be treated as a 'special case' and was sustained almost wholly by the deep personal commitment of the Chief Minister of Tamil Nadu to address poverty in a manner that he felt was most effective.

The TINP adopted an elaborate and somewhat complicated approach to nutrition intervention, for infants up to 36 months of age. The rationale was that an infant up to 11 months of age gains weight at 500 grams per month, between 12 and 14 months of age at 200 grams per month, and between 15 and 35 months of age at over 150–175 grams per month. The programme lays down that a weight gain of just 300 grams per month during the 6–12 month age period, and 100 grams per month after this period, may be considered quite adequate, because according to the sponsors of the programme, a child that is malnourished (first to third degree malnutrition) and gaining weight at these lower levels 'will still maintain his or her nutritional status quo'.[6] Thus, the objective is just to ensure that children in moderate grades of undernutrition, with body weight deficits up to 40 per cent of the normal expected standard weight maintain their 'status quo' and do not sink further down into the more severe grade III.

In reality, this could lead to the exclusion of many needy children. It is well known that monthly attendance in weight sessions, especially of the sick and malnourished children is irregular. Because of this, many malnourished children may not be picked up at all till they reach the qualifying grade III and may be missed out as an integrated package of health services and the selection of beneficiaries for the feeding operation is based on their current weight-for-age status. Children visiting the *anganwadis* (welfare centres) are weighed, their ages ascertained, and the weights are plotted on a growth chart, which uses reference lines demarcating 'normal', I, II, III, and IV grades. According to this classification, based on the recommendation of the Indian Academy of Paediatrics, children with weights for age up to '80% of the standard (50th per-centile of the Harvard scale) are considered "normal", those between 80 and 70 per cent as grade I, those between 70 and 60 per cent as grade II, those below 60 per cent as grade III, and those below 50 per cent as grade IV'. A notable and gratifying feature is that all nursing mothers with infants less than six months of age also qualify for supplements.

The probability tables provided by the sponsors themselves admit that nearly 20–25 per cent of undernourished children 'eligible for feeding' even on the basis of the rigid criteria laid down in the project could be excluded. A lower order than this 'acceptable' level must persist for two to three consecutive months, before the child qualifies for attention. Thus, for example, if a child in the 12–35 months age group has gained less than 100 grams per month in the previous three months he is considered 'at risk', but he is not selected until the next month's evaluation.

It was determined that there had been a reduction in the infant mortality rate and a clear decline in the incidence and hospital treatment of diarrhoea. Diphtheria, pertussis, and tetanus (DPT) immunization was found satisfactory. With respect to other services, however, the coverage was determined to have been quite low and the nature of services provided quite weak. The input special to the project on the health side (that is, the referral of children to the Primary Health Care system on failure to respond to supplementation) was also poorly implemented. Health service delivery was hampered by a number of structural problems within the health department, including multiple directorates, duality of control over key functionaries, a large number of vacancies, frequent transfers, and lack of adequate training. The government of Tamil Nadu has independently appointed an expert committee to go into the structural deficiencies of the health system. It is likely that significant changes in the existing structure will be recommended.

There was considerable overlap with existing MCH services and the project was mainly seen as providing additional infrastructure and drugs. Although the MPHW (female) was originally hired under the project, she was soon entrusted with a gamut of public health responsibilities, including those of the male workers, many of whom were not in place. Further, she was also made responsible for achieving family planning targets set by the Directorate of Family Welfare.[7]

A mid-term evaluation of this project conducted in 1982 after 21 months of programme operation found no overall improvement in the nutritional status of the children.[8] The only improvement noted was with respect to the prevalence of grades III and IV undernutrition in children of the 37–60 month age group. The high 'graduation' rates among children participating in the feeding programme (10 per cent per month and even 20 per cent during certain months) was not reflected in the significant overall improvement of the nutritional status when all children were considered. In fact, a study carried out by Nirmala Murthy (Suggestions for simplifying monitoring system, 1982) showed that nearly as many as 25 per cent of these 'graduates' had reverted to their erstwhile 'undergraduate status' within a few months; considering that entitlement to even the undergraduate process involved a test procedure of up to three months, it is likely that several malnourished children may be left out of the process. The evaluation confirmed that monthly attendance in weight sessions, especially of the sick and malnourished children is irregular. Because of this, many malnourished children may not be picked up at all till they reach the qualifying grade III stage of severe malnutrition. The probability tables provided by the sponsors themselves admit that nearly 20–25 per cent of undernourished children 'eligible for feeding' even on the basis of the rigid criteria laid down in the project could be excluded. Apart from the fact that the 'acceptable' levels of weight gain adopted in this project, are of a much lower order than weight gains of normal children, the project envisages exit of the children who have met the weight gain criteria three months in a row.

Another article[9] questioned the principles of determining malnutrition. It argued that there is a mismatch between how malnutrition is defined, measured, and evaluated by the World Bank, and how it is lived and experienced in the affected communities. This article has argued that insufficient attention has been paid to structures constraining individual agency, both in impoverished communities and within the World Bank. More attention should be paid to the circumstances within which house-holds and individuals make choices.

There were other criticisms as well. There were criticisms that the statistical data on the success of TINP was not robust, and many of the improvements in nutritional achievements were anecdotal rather than real. Past documentation on the claimed impact of the TINP is unconvincing, as it is based on rather simple statistical comparisons.

The TINP evaluation reports profess that in the pilot block, third and fourth degree malnutrition decreased from 20.4 per cent at baseline to 15.7 per cent in 1984 and in the control block it increased from 15.1 per cent at baseline to 17.8 per cent in 1984. This indicates a 23 per cent decline in the pilot block compared with a 17 per cent increase in the control block. This result has been interpreted to indicate a 40 per cent net decline in third and fourth degree malnutrition due to the project.[10] The terminal evaluation report further claims that within the category of 6–36 month age group, a higher rate of reduction of severe malnourishment has been recorded in the subgroup of 13–24 month age group. Another section claims that the impact is greatest in the 37–60 month age group. These and other inconsistencies detract from the validity of these conclusions.

Many TINP beneficiaries overlapped with the Noon Meal Programme after two years of age. Thus, the NMP inputs offer a competing explanation for nutritional improvements in children older than two years. In children younger than two, programme impact (after accounting for secular trends) could theoretically be attributed to TINP. But TINP reports show a greater impact in the 13–36 month and 37–60 month age groups and less so in the 7–12 month age group. Corrections also need to be made for secular trends before observed improvements in nutritional status can be attributed to programme impact.[11]

Other comments were that claims of successful growth monitoring have not separated benefits of growth in the programme from other interventions that have been implemented with growth monitoring. Claims of successful growth monitoring, as in TINP have been based on anecdotal or impressionistic evidence. Gopalan's article[12] questions the effectiveness of growth monitoring as a measure of determining malnutrition status. In comparison, the evaluation reports of the World Bank consider it a success.

According to the World Bank,[13] the success of the programme in abating severe malnutrition in the project areas was unambiguous. Survey and project growth monitoring statistics for TINP I indicated that during the programme, severe malnutrition reduced between a third and a half among those in the 6–24 month age group, and by about half among those in the 6–60 month age group. During TINP II, the growth monitoring statistics showed a higher reduction in severe malnutrition than what was found under the independent survey data which shows that severe malnutrition declined by about 44 per cent over the five-year period of TINP II.

Reduction in moderate malnutrition was much smaller and significantly below the targets. By the end of TINP I, moderate malnutrition declined by only 14 per cent in the first project areas to be developed, and had increased in the areas coming on stream in the second and third phases of the project. In the areas of TINP II (which were not covered by TINP I), a 23 per cent reduction in the moderate malnutrition was achieved. Also TINP II did not achieve its overall objective of raising the number of children with either normal nutrition or mild malnutrition by 50 per cent in new project areas and by 35 per cent in existing (that is, TINP I) project areas. Based on this, the World Bank concluded that it was the targets themselves rather than the level of achievement which were the problem. As there is a fall in the severe malnutrition, there will also be a corresponding increase in the moderate malnutrition in the short run. When severe malnutrition is high as it was in Tamil Nadu at that time, moderate malnutrition cannot be expected to decline by as much as severe malnutrition over a five or six year project life. This logic was not considered while setting the targets to be achieved. Looking into the reductions of severe and moderate malnutrition independently of the targets, the Bank estimated that there was significant reduction in both severe and moderate malnutrition compared to other nutrition programmes. This was the conclusion reached by the Bank's Operations Evaluation Department during their evaluation of TINP I. The evaluation was principally based on a sample of TINP data from 1,100 randomly designated CNCs, provided by an independent researcher, Meera Shekar,[14] at Cornell University. These were stratified into three groups, representing project areas which had been in operation for five, seven, and eight years respectively, and the data was examined in terms of the internationally accepted NCHS (Nattional Centre for Health Statistics) standards (or Z-scores). The evaluation concluded that, in the three areas, malnutrition (defined as weight for age of more than two standard deviations from the NCHS reference standard) had gone down by 1.5 and 2.4 percentage points per year, a decline 'unprecedented in other parts of India and elsewhere in the world where large scale nutrition interventions have been implemented'.

As per the evaluation of the World Bank, the issue is not whether the level of malnutrition has declined significantly, but how much of that decline can be attributed to TINP as opposed to the involvement of other nutrition programmes in the state. The observed improvements in the rates of nutrition can be attributed to TINP only if the effects of other factors can be separated out. This was done in two stages: in the first stage, the changes or improvements in the TINP districts were compared with those in the non-TINP districts; in the second stage, the differential impact of other programmes (noon meal programme) with that of TINP was considered. It concluded that the TINP model works to achieve considerable reductions in malnutrition.

The data collected by the National Nutrition Monitoring Bureau (NNMB) found that the improvements occurred in the TINP areas (Madurai 1.96 per cent, Ramanathapuram

1.07 per cent, Tirunelveli 1.75, Chengalpettu 1.61, and N. Arcot 0.83) were much greater than what occurred in the non-TINP areas (Thanjavur 0.26, Nilgiris 0.79, and Kanyakumari 1.12).

An interim survey conducted by NNMB in 1984 also found that much of the decline in the underweight prevalence in Tamil Nadu occurred after 1983 with practically no change between 1977 and 1982. This was the time when TINP I was actively prevalent in many of the districts in Tamil Nadu.

Another factor which has contributed to reduction in malnutrition is the improvement in the per capita income of the population. In Tamil Nadu, between 1982 and 1990, per capita GNP at constant prices increased by about 22 per cent.

It is important to step back and look at the three programmes being run concurrently in the field of nutrition in the state. The nature of governance was benevolent, welfare oriented, and generally unfocused, except with respect to schemes that the Chief Minister was personally interested in. The nutrition programmes served an important political purpose, that the government was seen to be active and concerned about the poor in the villages. Rajivan[15] attributes the successes to political will, public policy attention, and public participation which ensured accountability, quality, and continued budgetary support. Padmanaban, Raman, and Mavalankar[16] echo this view and comment that political commitment and proactive administration have resulted in the improvement in indicators of maternal health over the years.

Most importantly, the programmes provided employment opportunities for women in villages and also encouraged community participation.

During TINP I, the selection criteria for the staff included a requirement of residence in the village, preferably eight years of schooling and communication skills. In addition, whenever and wherever possible, women who were both poor and who had healthy and well-nourished children were chosen to showcase as examples. During the TINP II, the local residence criterion was not strictly followed and by its mid-term a quarter of the CNMs were non-residents and their proportions were higher in some districts. These had major drawbacks, the most important of all being that the non-residents were hardly known and trusted by the clients. Also, since they had to travel to work, they had less time to provide services. There were also allegations that many CNWs who were hired, had made substantial payments for their jobs. If these allegations were true, then it had serious impact on the programme implementation—the amount paid to the CNWs was so less that they could only have recovered the cost of the bribes by making money off the programme, perhaps by selling some of the food supplements. During TINP I, CNWs received a monthly honorarium of Rs 90. Although this rate appeared very low and many of them felt that they are underpaid, it should be noted that TINP I was paying more than the agricultural wage rate availed by women in Tamil Nadu during that period. The arguments put forward by the TINP programme managers and the officials at the World Bank in favour of paying a small honorarium were that this increased the accountability of the CNWs to the community and to the programme for delivering results. Further, it was argued that since workers were paid, the programme did not suffer from high drop-out rates. During TINP II, the Chief Minister of Tamil Nadu decided to make the CNWs permanent employees of the state civil service, a policy decision which was strongly opposed by the World Bank, not just because they feared that it would lead to inflation of the wage bill, but also because the bank feared that it would distance CNWs from their communities, who might come to see them as representatives of the government, rather than as their own community workers.

It is clear that at the community level, local political level, as well as the state level, creation of opportunities of large-scale employment in the state government was an enormous benefit. It raised the stature of the local politicians, gave them benefits of patronage, and created a willing and committed voter bank.

The policy of recruiting a large number of village-level functionaries has been a feature of the DMK regime as well. Between 1971 and 1972, the DMK created a 'Prosperity Brigade' of village level and urban volunteers, paid a small honorarium, ostensibly to assist in the creation of rural infrastructure and social development projects. They were largely DMK cadre who paid a dole from the state exchequer. The MGR regime, in agreeing to an army of village-level staff, largely women, created a huge cadre of formally employed rural personnel, who could be, if needed, used for political ends. Between 1989 and 1991, the DMK, then back in power, created village-level welfare workers pool 'makkal nala paniyalarkal' (meaning, public welfare workers), selection to which was purely on the basis of recommendations from the local political functionaries. The continuance of these staff members in the succeeding AIADMK administration faced challenges, and they were again reinstated when the DMK returned. Primarily, they were political appointees, without any specific task or programme to be allocated to, and hence did not fit into the institutional structures of governance. On the contrary, the TINP and the ICDS workers as well as the midday meal workers were well integrated with government activity at the village level and could pressurize the government in power for their continuance and their livelihoods. The approach of the MGR regime, in allocating these workers to genuine nutrition and meals programme can be argued to be more sophisticated and more in tune with the development and welfare needs of the state.

More than in the midday meals scheme, the TINP and the ICDS projects enabled the workers to interact with the communities they were working in; for example, the duties of the CNWs included:

- Registering all pregnant and lactating mothers, and weighing children under three on a monthly schedule and children from four to six years on a quarterly schedule;
- Providing nutrition counselling;
- Providing supplementary feeding based on the entry and the exit criteria;
- Providing basic advice on feeding sick children;
- Quarterly deworming of children under the age of six;
- Keep records of birth, death, and illness of children under the age of six.

The very activities of the programme enabled closer engagement with the villagers in a manner that the DMK's Prosperity Brigade and the Makkal Nala Paniyalarkal could never do. Programme activities also legitimized the concern and the involvement of the government with the rural people.

There were other features in the TINP as well that accentuated community involvement, which included:

- Formation of women's groups prior to introduction of services;
- Involving these women's groups in actively explaining the service package to the clients;
- Involving the mothers in keeping a growth chart of their children, and making them understand when growth supplement was needed;
- Visits by community workers to the home of the defaulters.

An innovation in the project was the methodology of training for CNWs. Instead of the usual residential programme in a training institution, CNWs were trained at the block headquarters (population 0.1 million). This arrangement enabled the CNW to commute daily and obviated the necessity of requiring village mothers to stay away from their families for any length of time. Secondly, the syllabus and training plan were designed by the CNIs who were both instructresses and second level supervisors. This had a double advantage: one, the training programme exhibited great familiarity with field situations and second, it enabled the instructress to continue to monitor the trainees and provide support in the field after the formal training was over. Great emphasis was placed in developing the communication skills of CNWs during training. Role play, group discussions, and training in the use of communication materials were all carried out.

The last ten days of the CNWs training was done jointly with the MPHW and the workers were taught to develop project objectives in the context of their own villages. The training culminated in a meeting of the CNW with the village leaders to explain the programme and win endorsement for the project. A comprehensive manual for the field workers was developed by the communication wing.

As mentioned earlier, the CNI made continuous in-service training of the CNW possible throughout the life of the project. Bi-monthly review sessions were used to sharpen skills in taking weights, plotting charts, and keeping records. Special attention was paid to workers whose performance was identified as weak. As the basic skills and knowledge of the CNWs improved, in-service training was formalized by devising modules for training in specific skills and using district training teams of nutrition, health, and communication staff in each block.

The training and supervision programmes administered to the CNWs, gave them status, prestige, and confidence. There was one supervisor for every twelve to fifteen CNW. All training (both pre-service and in service) was carried out in the block level.

It has been necessary to discuss the nutrition programmes in Tamil Nadu to understand the political developments and the changes in the social structure that were brought about due to these programmes, which were the largest interventions that happened in the period 1967 to 1989, and more so in the latter half, the MGR era.

These programmes attracted considerable academic scrutiny. It is interesting that over the years the government of India came around to view the food for all programme as the most direct intervention for child malnutrition. The Supreme Court judgement mandated that a hot cooked midday meal be served to every child attending school. MGR obviously was vindicated, and the criticisms of the initial years gave way to cautious praise, and eventually to wholesale adoption.

From the political point of view, all the programmes were enormously successful. As pointed out, they served as a source of patronage for employment; enabled the Government to be seen as pro-poor and active in villages; gave status and prestige to those employed; and, by making them government employees, secured a long-term livelihood for over two hundred thousand persons.

The higher bureaucracy, those at policy and programme management levels, quite happily fell into the intellectual satisfaction of a good programme being implemented efficiently and winning laurels. A series of mechanisms to bring about coordination between health and nutrition personnel at various levels were planned. The MPHW was intended to supervise and visit the CNW frequently. At the Primary Health Centre, monthly meetings were to be convened by the Medical Officer with the health and nutrition supervisors. The Taluk Project Nutrition Officer, the Medical Officer, and the District Health Officer were also expected to meet once a month. Similarly, monthly meetings were planned at the state level and meetings of Secretaries to Government through an empowered committee chaired by the Chief Secretary were part of the project review. There was wholehearted involvement among the higher levels of administration in the implementation of all these programmes.

For the staff, there was an opportunity to become a cohesive pressure group for state benefits in pay, privileges, and positions for advancement. Given the sources of recruitment, which were from the village, often composed of people with educational attainments of class ten and lower, there were opportunities to rise in the supervisory scale, access to government and politicians, and most important, ability to create pressure groups of employees that the state could not ignore.

It is not clear whether MGR saw all these benefits as accruing, but certainly the AIADMK, and his personal political strength, benefitted substantially from these programmes. It is also not clear why Tamil Nadu invested so heavily in nutrition. There was lack of attention to other programmes, most importantly infrastructure including roads, irrigation, and power generation, while attention to industrialization was sporadic.

Yet the parameters of Tamil Nadu's growth were quite excellent during this period. Gross State Domestic Product (GSDP) growth was steady between 5 and 6 per cent, resulting in a steady growth in per capita incomes of around 7–8 per cent every year.[17] The opening up of a large number of private schools enabled access to children in the most rural areas to education. We see the benefits of this in the next decade, with a large number of students accessing tertiary education, most importantly, engineering.

Perhaps there was a unique combination that made Tamil Nadu successful in programme implementation. The combination consisted of a well-planned programme, involvement of the village-level workers in implementation and giving them a livelihood stake in the programme, and the infusion of political patronage in recruitment, management, and supervision of the programmes, that actually gave some material to everyone involved. This is a unique Tamil Nadu combination that has perhaps no parallels in any other state, for it requires strong leadership, good programme concepts, and, more mundanely, a delivery of some tangible benefits for everyone connected, whether it be employees, politicians, transporters, or suppliers.

It was only a natural leap of policy to conclude that this would be the certain approach to winning elections, and we shall see in the subsequent chapters, how all aspects of the formula—a willing bureaucracy, enlightened public consciousness of political realities, as well as rent seeking politicians—were the architects as well as the beneficiaries of a an ever increasing crescendo of welfare and giveaway programmes that followed.[18]

Notes

1. Barbara Harriss, 'White: Nutrition and its Politics in Tamil Nadu', *South Asia Research*, 24(1): 51–71.
2. World Bank, 1998, 'India - Second Tamil Nadu Integrated Nutrition Project', World Bank Group, Washington, DC, http://documents.worldbank.org/curated/en/844271475083700450/India-Second-Tamil-Nadu-Integrated-Nutrition-Project. Probably due to the fact that in the Jayalalithaaa regime, the department was managed by a minister who was later arraigned for several misdemeanours. This affected the performance of the programme.
3. Anuradha Rajivan, 'ICDS with a Difference', *Economic and Political Weekly*, 41(34): 3864–88.
4. Rajivan, 'ICDS with a Difference'.
5. The existing workers had become a pressure group and the government found it infeasible to disband them.

6. TINP Plan of Operations, Annex. 6, p. 1.

7. TINP Mrs J. Balachander.

8. Government of Tamil Nadu, 'Revised Report on Evaluation of TINP (Nutrition Component) in the Pilot Block (Phase I)', Madras: Evaluation and Applied Research Department, 1983.

9. Devi Sridhar, 'Hungry for Change: the World Bank in India', *South Asia Research*, 28(2): 147–68.

10. Government of Tamil Nadu, 'Revised Report on Evaluation of TINP (Nutrition Component) in the Pilot Block (Phase I)'.

11. Sabu George, Michael Latham, R. Abel, N. Ethirajan, E.A. Fragillo Jr, 'Evaluation of Effectiveness of Good Health Monitoring in South Indian Villages', *The Lancet*, 342(8867): 348.

12. C. Gopalan, 'Choosing Beneficiaries for Feeding Programmes', NFI Bulletin, www.nutritionfoundationofindia.res.in/pdfs/.../Pages%20from%20nfi_10_84.2.pdf.

13. http://documents.worldbank.org/curated/en/844271475083700450/India-Second-Tamil-Nadu-Integrated-Nutrition-Project.

14. Meera Shekhar, 'TINP: A Review of the Project with Special Emphasis on the Monitoring and Evaluation System', Working Paper, CFNNP Publication Department, Washington, DC, 1991. Also see, M. Shekar and M.C. Latham, 'Growth Monitoring Can and Does Work! An Example from the Tamil Nadu Integrated Nutrition Project in Rural South India', *The Indian Journal of Pediatrics*, 59(1): 5–15.

15. Rajivan, 'ICDS with a Difference'.

16. D.V. Padmanaban, P. Raman, P.S. Mavalankar, 'Innovations and Challenges in Reducing Maternal Mortality in Tamil Nadu, India', *Journal of Health, Population, and Nutrition*, 27(2): 202–19.

17. Department of Statistics, Government of Tamil Nadu.

18. In web 90.worldbank.org/oed/oeddoclib.nsf.

6

THE AIADMK AFTER MGR
Jayalalithaa and Welfare

———

THE ARGUMENTS SO FAR HAVE BEEN THAT THE SRM IDEOLOGY became the plank on which the DMK as a political party came to power. They took advantage of the food shortages prevailing at that time to announce subsidized rice from public distribution outlets in Chennai and Coimbatore and also to expand the PDS system throughout the state. The PDS was the largest of the welfare programmes in the post 1967 administration, though there were several others. Most importantly, governance and policy was focused on implementing social changes that were the inherent arguments for the SRM. By 1977, several structural changes in the institutions at the village and institutional levels had been made. Focused recruitment of backward classes and the limited opportunities available to forward classes changed the class structure of the administration and created a governance structure more in tune with the social aspirations of the party in power and also sympathetic to the efforts being made to provide greater opportunities to the backward classes. It has also been argued that towards the latter part of the DMK regime, the paternalistic policies that were earlier adopted were abandoned. The identification of the DMK with the emergent backward classes alienated both the upper and the lower strata, as they felt that the extension of backward class quotas to more affluent castes prevented poor individuals from accessing these quotas.

Into this breach, so to speak, stepped the AIADMK of MGR. Coming from a personality-based party, MGR moved away from identification with individual castes, and focused on his core clientele, the women and the young. He was genuinely pro-poor. He increased quotas for the backward classes to 50 per cent, and embarked on a massive scheme of welfare programmes that would reach governance down to the village level. His motives in launching the noon meal scheme may be somewhat ambivalent, but he was quick to see the political benefits of implementing large programmes at the village and rural level, which involved providing employment to local people, especially poor women, and also extended the patronage of his party functionaries at the village level. Added to these were the two schemes, the TINP and the ICDS, which were similar and therefore served the same political purpose. It is difficult to find why nutrition was chosen as the lever for achieving these ends, but it is true that in the 1980s, Tamil Nadu was allocating a significant proportion of its budget to nutrition. The detailed narration of the midday meals scheme, TINP and ICDS, was intended to illustrate the relationship that developed between the administrative hierarchies, which had already become politically in tune with the government in power. They were able to seek out and enthusiastically implement these programmes, to the approbation of the funding agencies. Tamil Nadu had created a name for itself for running welfare schemes well. The large number of staff at the village and district level who were employed in these programmes, were incorporated as government functionaries, thus providing these numbers with livelihoods as well as creating a strong pressure group at every local level, which succeeding parties in government would find it difficult to ignore. The symbiotic relationship between the staff at the local level, the local politicians, as well as the concerns of the programme administrators created a sustainable ecosystem where the programmes were in everyone's interest to continue and to succeed.

When MGR fell ill in 1984, and three years thereafter, governance was on auto pilot. It is a tribute to the Tamil Nadu administrative machinery that it withstood the challenges of lack of strategy and direction. Normal activities touching the citizen's life, including registration of documents, births and death certificates, community certificates for admission to educational institutions, and all other matters pertaining to the schemes in place, PDS, pensions, grants, and the like happened in a routine manner. The administrative departments conducted reviews and implementation monitoring on a regular basis. The cabinet consisted of several senior ministers with considerable experience in running their departments. MGR was still in control, though the extent of his engagement with government matters was known only to a few officers of the chief minister's office. He would attend meetings, and his faculties were quite intact, but he tired easily. In politics, he was well aware of what was going on, and still kept a watch on his colleagues.

The big change that occurred was in levels of corruption and rent seeking. The sudden spurt of privately financed educational institutions, which included engineering colleges, polytechnics, and teacher training and nurses training institutions indicated that private funds were increasingly becoming available. The ownership of these institutions was, in a majority of cases, in the hands of politicians, and the size and investment in the institutions could perhaps be a measure of their political clout in administrative matters. It is important to mention that this development set the stage for the Jayalalithaa government that followed, and for several actions of that government.

During the period 1988 to 1989, Tamil Nadu was under Governor's rule. P.C. Alexander, the Governor, was an eminent administrator, and was ably aided by two advisers. They sought to focus on development and delivery, and all the administrative departments were energized into completing tasks that devolved on their development responsibilities. As usual, the bureaucracy responded, and significant progress was made in scheme implementation, especially those programmes that were centrally sponsored and funded.

When the DMK came back to power for a short period between 1989 and 1991, they aligned themselves with the V.P. Singh government. In administration they decided to continue with existing programmes, as well as the schemes in operation during the period of Governor's rule. S. Guhan was the adviser to the chief minister, and focused on state central relations and fiscal autonomy issues. DMK in power after thirteen years was feeling its way in, but the V.P. Singh government as well as the succeeding Chandrasekhar government were short lived, and they were politically anxious that their mandate could be overturned by the AIADMK. This happened, and Jayalalithaa was able to persuade the central government through the Congress to get the DMK dismissed and fresh elections mandated.

Jayalalithaa's AIADMK along with its ally the Congress won 225 seats in the 1991 elections, trouncing the DMK and its allies, which won only seven seats. Out of these, the Congress won 60 seats. The AIADMK vote share at 59.09 per cent was the highest ever. DMK by itself won only two seats; in the 1989 elections they had won 150 seats. The message was clear. The people of Tamil Nadu recognized Jayalalithaa as the inheritor of the MGR mandate and resoundingly announced their empathy with MGR.

Jayalalithaa had joined the AIADMK in 1982, at the behest of MGR, who anointed her as the propaganda secretary of the party. She had not expressed her interest in politics earlier, but she had withdrawn from films by the early 1970s. By then, she had starred in many films opposite MGR, and the two names were closely associated in the film industry. However, by 1973, she had parted with MGR. The period 1973 to 1982 was a quiet period for Jayalalithaa, for having moved away from films, and distancing herself from MGR, she was lost to the public eye.

The rapprochement with MGR came after a decade. Vaasanthi says that when MGR was on an official visit to the US, Jayalalithaa who was also there for medical treatment, met him through the good offices of a common friend.[1]

The timing was fortuitous. MGR needed someone to carry the party forward, and he felt that none of the second rung leaders could do so. The party had grown and consolidated its position on the basis of public adulation, a hype that all policies were directed towards the poor, and that women and children and the poor always came first. This idea had to be nurtured for the future. For MGR, the party was in need of a crowd puller. As the chief minister, he was less visible at public meetings, and Karunanidhi had gone on a spree of vitriolic attacks on him at public meetings. MGR decided to make use of her for public meetings. Jayalalithaa instantly scored and the DMK were startled by the crowds that came to her meetings. Being intellectually accomplished, she was able to counter the DMK barbs effectively. R.M. Veerappan, close adviser and associate of MGR, and a few others started actively working against her, as he feared that as a member of the party, she could not be taken lightly, and would have serious ambitions. R.M. Veerappan was the production manager for a number of MGR films and handled his finances as well. He was a patron of the MGR Manrams association, and it was initially felt that all the MLAs would back Veerappan in a leadership struggle.

However, her speeches made her an instant crowd-puller, and the AIADMK secretaries in the different districts immediately recognized her value as a political asset for the

party. They recognized her leadership qualities and were
clear that after MGR, it would be her. MGR, of course,
did not want her growth to be totally unconstrained, and
in 1984, he made her an MP in Rajya Sabha. Her maiden
speech in the Rajya Sabha was on 23 April 1984. I was a
Joint Secretary in the Ministry of Energy at that time, with
P. Shiv Shankar as the powerful minister for petroleum,
coal, power, and renewables, posts which are held today by
four different cabinet ministers. He was informed that her
speech would be on energy-related issues, and called me
to find out what she would say. I had not been following
events too closely and had no idea. I quickly put together
some facts and a brief for him and accompanied him to
the Parliament. He was seated directly in front of her
in the treasury benches as he spoke, and was very self-
conscious. It was a surprise that Mrs Gandhi, then Prime
Minister, came to the House to listen to the speech. It was
a very well crafted, excellently delivered speech, and she
received accolades. It must be recalled that Jayalalithaa
was among the more distinguished of the public and film
personalities in the Parliament at that time, and because
of her intelligence coupled with beauty, she was instantly
popular with MPs and media alike. She made several
interventions during her tenure in the Rajya Sabha, and
without exception, all her speeches were well thought out
and excellently delivered. She made a significant impact
as an MP. It was during this tenure that she became close
friends with Rajiv Gandhi, and was able to persuade him
to overturn the DMK Government in Tamil Nadu in 1991.

MGR was also conscious at this time of the weakening
pulse of the Dravidian movement. He had distanced
himself from opposition parties that demanded more power

for the states and did not take part in the walkout at the meeting of the National Development Council that year. He also did not criticize the dismissal of the N.T. Rama Rao government in Andhra Pradesh. It was natural for Mrs Gandhi to consider him an ally, even though for MGR and Tamil Nadu, this came at the expense of Dravidian and SRM credentials. Jayalalithaa, his propaganda secretary, was a Brahmin. The AIADMK could be divided between those who went back to the Dravidian movement roots and those who were less steeped in the ethos of Dravidian politics. It was at this stage that emphasis on social justice, Tamil identity, and separatism started taking a back seat in academic and political discourse.[2]

MGR's health was none too good at this time, and he used to neglect it a bit. He was fond of sweets even though he was highly diabetic, and at all the official meetings as well as at cabinet meetings, there would be his favourite sweet *basandi*, an excessively sugared milk sweet, for everyone. This neglect led to further deterioration, and MGR fell ill in October 1984, with what was diagnosed as renal failure and other complications, and there were days when doctors had to struggle to keep him breathing. Mrs Gandhi flew down to see him at the Apollo Hospital, and ordered an aircraft to be stationed at Chennai to fly him to the US for treatment. When she was assassinated on 31 October, MGR was already in the US.

The prospect of a politically incapacitated chief minister threw the party into disarray, and immediately led to factional tussles within the AIADMK. One of the first political casualties was Jayalalithaa. For nearly two years, MGR had antagonized almost every senior leader in the party by pushing Jayalalithaa to the forefront. Orders were issued that cabinet ministers should stand up when she arrived to address a public function—which had the immediate result of ministers being reluctant to share a platform with her.

With MGR ill and incapacitated, the party bosses lost no time in getting their own back. When Jayalalithaa visited the hospital to call on MGR, she was denied access. She was given no say in any of the consultations in his treatment. In a desperate attempt to stay in the limelight, she issued a statement saying that the doctors had called in Japanese specialists to take a look at the chief minister, but the party general secretary P.U. Shanmugam denied that the statement had been issued by the party office.[3] The MGR fan clubs did not come out in support of her, and with virtually every politician of note in the state writing off her political future, her isolation seemed complete.

MGR recovered, and in the elections in 1984, the party won a resounding victory.

But after MGR returned, and during the period 1985 to 1987, she was at his side, and we in the bureaucracy believed that several decisions at that time were influenced by her. At his death, there were efforts to prevent her from accompanying the cortege to Marina Beach for burial, and it was clear that the senior leaders did not wish for a future for her in the AIADMK. They propped up MGR's wife Janaki as the leader. In the assembly session that followed, there was pandemonium. The government was dismissed, and a short period of Governor's rule followed. Jayalalithaa had to wait until the 1991 elections to don the mantle of MGR in the party. Rajiv Gandhi, who had helped in the dismissal of the DMK, had been assassinated, and it was an uncertain political landscape that she faced. At the Centre, P.V, Narasimha Rao had become prime minister. The Indian economy was in crisis, and in Tamil Nadu the implications of the fight between the Sri Lankan government and the Tamil Tigers had its repercussions in law and order and political issues.

Jayalalithaa had faced innumerable obstacles to reach this position. In her younger life, as well as in film world and in politics, the going had never been smooth for her. It is a tribute to her mettle and strength of character and will that she fought all odds to achieve to the highest position in the state. At the same time, it is important to recognize that she had little knowledge about the economic or social conditions in the state. Her world was a world of entertainment and cinema, and of political sycophancy, which waxed and waned along with the fortunes and health of MGR. All of us believed that she saw government papers in the interregnum when MGR had returned to power and was not fully active, that is, between 1985 and 1987, but this is just internal gossip from the CM office, not verifiable. Certainly she had been witness to the venality and corruption that was becoming rampant in Tamil Nadu politics, and perhaps her later actions were conditioned by it.

Jayalalitha had not been an active member of Dravidian politics, and far from being an atheist, she was an extremely religious person, with belief in rituals, and committed to the upkeep and improvements of temples in Tamil Nadu. Reservations and caste equations during this and the succeeding periods were calculations at vote gathering and election winning strategies rather than any core belief in social justice, reform, and empowerment. The first five years of Jayalalithaa's chief ministership from 1991 to 1996 was evidence to this.

In retrospect, it must be recognized that it was for actions during this period that a criminal case of accumulation of assets was launched against her, which lapsed only on her death in December 2016, while several of her accomplices including her close friend and companion Sasikala had to face prison sentences. The Karunanidhi regime that came after, in 1996, also filed a number of criminal cases against her, which included ministers and officials, but most of them did not end up in conviction, either through lack of evidence, political will, or through neglect.

Working in the bureaucracy in this scenario was quite a challenge. There were clearly two streams visible. There were ministers like G. Viswanathan in the Food Ministry and Muthusamy in the Health Ministry who saw their role as an opportunity to improve governance and to contribute to development. In most cases, these ministers were ably supported by their secretaries as well as the departmental staff. Considerable progress and improvements were made in PDS and in public health, which are described below.

There were ministers and officers who were differently inclined and several departments, including the noon meal department and the rural development department, witnessed actions that were questioned after 1996 and several criminal cases were filed against decisions taken there. Some of the officials had to undergo trial and also punishment.

It was interesting that in both streams, the bureaucracy was in tune with the political hierarchy. It was also interesting that at the highest level, from the point of view of the chief minister, both streams were allowed to operate.

This was also the period when the welfare programmes increasingly became giveaway programmes that focused entirely on distributing goods and goodies with sole objective of winning votes in the next elections. These included a wide range of goods. Rice in the PDS was subsidized further. Girl students were given bicycles to go to school.

The Health Department illustrates what could be achieved even during these turbulent times. On 22 February 1993, Health Minister S. Muthusamy sent a four page note down to his secretary in the Secretariat.[4] Jayalalithaa had been Chief Minister since 1991, and had already set the tone for an autocratic administration. There were a few officers, including the chief secretary, and a few police officials who had access to her, apart from the Chief Minister's Office. Tamil Nadu administration functioned as before, politically sensitive, yet efficient in performance.

Muthusamy had been a close favourite of MGR and had served in the MGR government as transport minister. He had accompanied MGR on his overseas trips. He told me that on a visit to Japan, MGR, who was very fond of watches and electronics, asked Muthusamy to find him a wrist watch which could also be a television. MGR had heard that such a product had just become available in Japan. Muthusamy said that he missed some official meetings while scouring Tokyo for such a watch, and finally found it and gave it to MGR. He told me MGR was thrilled with it and wore it on several occasions. Muthusamy was one of the earliest to announce support for Jayalalithaa after MGR's death, and the initial years after 1991, was one of the strongmen of the party, trusted by Jayalalithaa very much. The political proximity did not last as he fell out with other power centres in the chief minister's proximity, but it is important to understand that as a senior minister from MGR's time, his approach to administration and governance still reflected an earlier era.

Even then, sending a note down on policy and programme matters was unusual for a minister. The note, in Tamil, pointed out that there were difficulties in the procurement of medicines by the government hospital, and he had noticed difficulties in procurement and purchase and in the local procurement processes. There was no clarity in dealing with excess stocks, or in ensuring that unnecessary medicines were not purchased. The note pointed out shortcomings in quality, delays in purchases of medical equipment, as well as delays in installing them and putting them to use. There were places which were neglected, and others which had a lot of equipment. There was no clarity in the operation and maintenance procedures, and even for furniture maintenance.

The note then proposed the establishment of a separate government company with headquarters in Chennai for this purpose. The note suggested that this corporation should have two wings, one for medicines and the other for medical equipment. The corporation would set up warehouses across the state where the medicines would be stored and distributed to the hospitals and dispensaries according to need. The budget for all medicine and equipment purchases would be centralized, and all procurement and purchases done by the corporation.

The hospitals and dispensaries could indent from the corporation requirements, according to budgetary limits fixed for them, and payments to the suppliers would be the responsibility of the corporation.

This was quite a novel suggestion. Until this time, each primary health centre and hospital had a separate medicine and medical equipment budget, and the processes for purchase were quite cumbersome. It took a long time for procurement, with suppliers often complaining of delays in payment. This also led to lack of availability of essential medicines at the primary health centres.

It is not very clear what led to the new policy initiative. There had certainly been complaints about the availability of medicines in government hospitals and dispensaries. The complaints had escalated to a level where there were raids in the offices and home of the then health secretary by the tax authorities. That person was shifted, but there rumours of kickbacks in medicine purchases reaching the highest levels, and incorporating all persons in between.[5] It is certainly true that the raids shook up the establishment and the government. Those in the know argue that the entire initiative did not have any transparency or altruistic motives, but were actually centralizing processes for corruption. Instead of purchases from several locations, now they would all be centralized. The secretary who succeeded took the process forward, and approval for the Corporation was obtained from the chief minister and orders issued.[6] The process of preparing the articles and memorandum of association in consultation with the law department and the bureau of public enterprises took a while. In March 1994, Niranjan Mardi[7] was appointed as the Managing Director of the Corporation. In May 1994,

the government sanctioned[8] Rs 4 lakhs for the initial
expenses of the corporation, and it was in business.

By then the health secretary had changed and
R. Poornalingam had taken charge. A technocrat, with
clear ideas on management and implementation, he set
about laying the foundations of the new Tamil Nadu
Medical Services Corporation. In discussions, he said[9] that
he was only sure that the processes should be clear and
transparent, and that opportunities for wrong practices
should be reduced as much as possible. He assembled a
group of experts from medicine, drug manufacturing,
and technology and logistics services and asked them to
come up with solutions. They opted for technology based
solutions. The standard list of drugs would be the World
Health Organisation approved list of common drugs and
the quantities would be arrived at putting together the
requirements of all the using centres. An initial list of
225 drugs was prepared for dispensaries and hospitals.
Purchases would be done by the corporation on the basis
of open electronic (computer based e-tenders) mode, and
confirmation orders were to be issued electronically. The
opportunities for interfering with purchases was reduced
significantly.

Two other significant steps followed, and the files on
these make interesting reading. Having centrally procured
the drugs and medicines, it was necessary to distribute them
across the state. The minister's note had conceptualized
warehouses in each district. There was the Danish-aided
programme (Danida that was functioning in the state in
some districts, and the funds could be utilized for the
construction of a few warehouses). There is an interesting
exchange in one of the files where the Health Secretary

asked the Finance Secretary for funds for construction of warehouses in other districts—a sum of Rs 3 crores, which finance refused, on expenditure concerns. And then the file records a plea from the Health Secretary for a personal discussion—'why won't you give me a cup of coffee' after which, a sum of Rs 1 crore for the corporation is agreed to, in addition to the corporation borrowing an additional amount of Rs 1 crore from banks for this purpose.[10]

The context of these deliberations and orders is important. By 1995, the perception of the administration and the regime had changed significantly. The ostentatious wedding in 1995 of Sudhakaran, the foster son of Jayalalithaa, was in the news as an exhibition of pomp and excess. It was clear that several of the ministers as well as some of the top bureaucracy were in league for personal benefits. Every department that had lucrative contracts, including rural development, midday meals programme, and nutrition had their tales of misdemeanour. There were complaints in the midday meals programme of overpayment for provisions, especially eggs. There were complaints about the orders for textbooks for schools as well as the notebooks and uniforms intended for school children. The Rural Development Department saw several orders where funds from Government of India were misused. Yet amongst all this, there was this island of propriety in medical services.

I asked Poornalingam how this happened. He said[11] he is not sure why he was allowed to function with independence. He attributes in part to the administrative and political culture of the state, and that there was always a strong opposition party ready to criticize and ready to take over the reins. Politicians, in his view, allow work to be done, as they are interested in a good name. He continued to take further steps. He also feels that Tamil Nadu governance, though corrupt, is performance oriented. He said that there was a discipline and a culture of compliance with orders.

Poornalingam continued his efforts. The drug manufacturers were told that all supplies to the Tamil Nadu Medical Services Corporation had to be marked 'tn' in English or Tamil. Each capsule had to bear the mark, as well as the foil sheet and even the bottles, syringes, and all disposables. This was followed up with the order that if these marked drugs and material were found at any point of retail, the retailer would be arrested and punished. This was intended to stop the leakage of government medicines into the public market. Initially, the manufacturers protested and refused. They were then told[12] that payments would be directly from the corporation, and periodic—monthly or quarterly, according to indents. This proved a great sweetener, as hitherto the suppliers had to get their payments from individual hospitals scattered across the state. Once the purchases, orders, and invoices were computerized, it was easy to ensure payment. It is important to recollect that these efforts were made at a time when computers, IT, and digital communication were still in their infancy in India.

Other systems were put in place. Budget allocations for each of the hospitals and dispensaries along with details of drugs that they would be needing were to be supplied to the corporation to enable adequate purchase and stocking. A passbook was given to medical institutions indicating their financial allocations. The allocations were worked out on the basis of past consumption and some norms. There was a system for dealing with surplus stock at the end of the year as well as expiry dates. There were systems for O&M of equipment as well as regimes for indents, purchase, and installations of new equipment. There were regular inspections by the staff of the Tamil Nadu Medical Services Corporation.

The staff had to inspect whether all the drugs were properly accounted for, whether the storage was proper, whether there were any unnecessary drugs, as well as whether the register of local purchases as well as all the drug accounts.

Every one of the steps was intended to make processes and outcomes transparent and insulate the activities from rent seeking people. At the cost of repetition, that this was possible when there were allegations of misdeeds in several departments, was an example of the resilience of administration in Tamil Nadu even in difficult times.

Even after two decades in existences, this system still functions efficiently and effectively in Tamil Nadu. Not that there are no complaints, but the levels of transparency and effectiveness have caught the attention of multilateral agencies and Government of India. Tamil Nadu has been asked to help other states to set up similar mechanisms. Poornalingam is involved in assisting some other states. There is considerable academic literature now on this initiative.

Prabal Vikram Singh and others have noted that the Tamil Nadu Medical Services Corporation (TNMSC) was incorporated in the wake of the massive drug scandal, and the new system incorporated multiple reforms in drug purchase, storage, and distribution systems. He comments that most states are attempting to copy the Tamil Nadu model of centralized tendering and purchase of drugs.

'A study of the Kerala Medical Services Corporation and Odisha's State Drug Manufacturing Unit shows that imitating the original model without factoring the local context and building up the processes does not lead to success.'[13] Kerala's experiment is modestly successful, while in Odisha, it has not worked.[14] The Drug and Food Regulation Authority has reported (2011) that all the patients visiting government health facilities have received all their medicines. An article in *Forbes India* by Dinesh Narayanan lauds Tamil Nadu on having the best pubic healthcare system in the country.[15] In 2006–07, its per capita drug allocation expenditure was Rs 27, as against Rs 2 in Rajasthan and Rs 3 in Uttar Pradesh. The article calls the TNMSC one of the pillars of this successful system. According to the National Sample Survey Organisation (NSSO) 60th round in 2004, the improvements brought down the drug costs for patients in Tamil Nadu hospitals substantially. In comparison, the costs were Rs 3,268 in Haryana, Rs 2,166 in Himachal, and Rs 3,187 in Rajasthan. The total cost of a patient's stay in Tamil Nadu was the lowest at Rs 255 per day. Padmanaban, Raman, and Mavalankar attribute the reduction of maternal mortality in Tamil Nadu to the setting up of the TNMSC.[16]

It is true that in spite of all efforts, these successes have not been replicated in other states. In Bihar, while a corporation has been set up, the systems are not working in a similar manner. There are apocryphal stories that drugs purchased centrally, intended for the districts, are not able to cross even the headquarters before they are diverted and pilfered. In Orissa, though there is a corporation in place, headed by the chief secretary, the co-operation from field officers is missing. Indents do not come on time, nor is the drawal regular for dispensing to the hospitals and clinics. Even the Government of India has noted this. Poornalingam feels that the bureaucracy is much more laidback and does not have the keenness to change. There is also the factor that the public is less aware, when compared with Tamil Nadu, about the services that can be obtained from the government, and hence the ability of the public to mobilize is also lower than in Tamil Nadu.

The PDS is yet another example. During the Second World War, serious shortages of food grains developed in India, and in 1942, the Government of India issued rules under the Defence of India Rules which empowered the provincial governments to regulate the shops dealing in food grains and even take over their businesses, if necessary. The Government of India also set up the Food Department in the same year and entrusted to it the responsibility of procurement, movement, and distribution of food grains as well as of regulation of prices. There were fixed targets for procurement of food grains from surplus states. Several food policy committees reviewed the situation from time to time, and there was a need, after independence, to maintain a buffer stock of food grains. The Food Corporation of India was established in 1965 with this objective in view. After the abolition of statutory rationing in 1953, there was no large-scale distribution of food grains in Tamil Nadu, and District Collectors were left to deal with seasonal conditions as they deemed fit. The next crisis arose in 1964.

It has been pointed out that the system of family cards for rice was an important measure for tackling the rice shortages of 1964, and that Annadurai introduced the one rupee per kilogram rice scheme in 1967, albeit only in Madras and Coimbatore. Over the years, the PDS expanded, covered the entire population, rural areas as well as urban, in the state. In addition to rice, the family cards entitled access to sugar, kerosene, and other goods. Kerosene was available to lower income groups only. The prices of supply varied, and currently rice is given away for free to the poor, and at Rs 5 per kilogram for other cards, up to 20 kilograms a month. The number of cards under the PDS grew from around 120 lakhs in 1985 to nearly 190 lakhs in 2003.

Over this period, the distribution outlets also grew from about 20,000 to over 29,000. The distribution system also developed over the years. A unique feature of the Tamil Nadu system has been that the private sector is not allowed to run ration shops, unlike the situation in Leftist states like Kerala and West Bengal. Initially the cards were attached to local consumer co-operative societies and outlets. Some of these went into default over time, and the TNCSC opened its own retail outlets where the co-operatives had failed, and also in urban areas where there were no co-operative outlets. There was positive response for these, as they were better managed and better stocked, and there was continuous public pressure for opening more of the TNCSC outlets. For the Corporation, this was a losing proposition, given public sector wage scales and overheads, but public and political pressure soon expanded the numbers of these outlets across the state. This was yet one more example of public pressure for services from the state. The TNCSC was also responsible for procurement of rice from farmers during harvest season, and it has been pointed out that Tamil Nadu, as a marginal state, had to depend on rice from outside the state during the years of poor harvest. The TNCSC became a large organization, vital to ensuring supplies to the PDS, and also a place of political patronage for employment, logistics, and warehousing. Over the years starting 1964, the Food and Civil Supplies department, as it was called, became one of the more important and sensitive departments of the government, and the food minister was an important member of the Cabinet.

The PDS distribution reached government services into villages, and it was but natural that it felt the political pressures of the changes in government. Some of the measures included the opening of one shop for every village, universal issue of family cards, and increase in entitlements and reductions in issue prices. There was a brief attempt in the DMK regime of 1989 to 1991 to judge the affordability of the card holders to determine entitlements for these benefits, but this had to be given up in the face of steep opposition.

The Jayalalithaa regime of 1991 to 1996 made some significant changes. In 1991, Viswanathan was the minister for Food and Civil Supplies. An alumnus of the prestigious Loyola College of Chennai, he was one of our contemporaries at University, later joining the DMK and then the AIADMK. He parted ways with Jayalalithaa after only two years as Minister, and went into education. Today, the Vellore Institute of Technology established by him in Vellore is one of the premier educational institutions in the state. It has been accorded the status of a university, and has international recognition and reach.

In 1993, R.M. Veerappan, a close confidante of MGR, became the food minister. A.M. Swaminathan[17] was the Civil Supplies Commissioner between 1991 and 1993 and later food secretary between 1993 and 1995. A number of innovative changes were brought in during this period. Swaminathan, with over three and a half decades of experience in administration, said during discussions that an enlightened minister is a great asset to the administrator. His point was that even if the minister was not very knowledgeable, as long as he was convinced that the action was in his interest and that it was in no way injurious to him politically, but would result in his stock going up, he could be persuaded to take the right step.

On the important question of why programmes work in Tamil Nadu, his view was that the state was unique in many respects. It was one of the earliest to abolish landed gentry, and the communist and the DK movements removed the domination of upper castes from society. The landlord and serf culture was absent in the state, unlike even pockets of Kerala and Andhra. High literacy rates in the state ensured that public awareness about government services was very high. Consumer movements had sprung up even in 1939, and there was a consumer protection forum in the early 1940s. This awareness of rights ensured that the government machinery performed its tasks efficiently.

The revenue department, stretching down from the Board of Revenue in Madras, through the Collector, down to the village revenue inspector and village officers, was a time tested and reliable system in Madras with which the rural population was in constant contact and related to. The hierarchical structure of the department enabled large policies to be planned meticulously for implementation, broken down into elements, and tasks assigned specifically to each member of the structure. The intense social and political activity that was going right through the years of the SRM and later DK and DMK period ensured that there was a close relationship between political developments and the administrative activities even at the village level. Swaminathan feels that, in comparison, rural areas in north India were not as influenced by local politics. In Tamil Nadu the PDS had been entrusted to the management of District Collectors, and it was the revenue hierarchy that controlled the civil supplies set up.

Viswanathan was minister for two years and is even now happy to talk about what could be achieved. The levy system of procurement from farmers, which was an irritant to paddy producers, was abolished, and inter district movement was permitted, with controls over movement only at state borders. These measures had the salutary effect of bringing down the open market prices of rice. There was an attempt to restrict supply of rice to the poorer sections of the population, but this measure had to be withdrawn in a day. The annual issue of family cards was replaced with a system where the cards would be valid for five years. The total number of cards exceeded the number of families as per the national census, and a drive was launched to weed out excess and bogus cards. These bogus cards were a source of leakages benefiting the shopkeeper and local level politician, and again, the cleaning up process removed some political patronage.

After Viswanathan came R.M. Veerappan. Until that time, opening a rice mill required a licence from the state government, after assessing the paddy grown in the area, the number of rice mills already in existence, and other parameters. In fact, it was only a source of patronage for local politicians to recommend or obtain milling licences.

Swaminathan sought to abolish this system, arguing that in a period of economic liberalization, it was up to the investor to decide whether the rice mill would be an economic venture, and that continuing the licencing policy was anti-deluvian. For the minister, it was a source of patronage for the local politicians that was being removed, and it was with great reluctance that he agreed.

Development of the PDS and the services that the system offered to the public evolved over the years. Starting from need-based supply in times of shortage, it developed into a welfare amenity given to every citizen of the state, with increasing subsidies and wider range of products. From the point of view of the citizen, each election campaign offered further concessions in terms of price, quantity, and range of goods. It is interesting to note that because of public appeal and the continuous delivery of services over the decades, every government, whether the DMK or the AIADMK, only sought to enlarge, strengthen, and deepen the services provided. There was never a question of taking away benefits that had been granted in earlier regimes. The public was also fully aware of the services and the political mileage that these services commanded, and has been vigilant and vociferous in demanding that the services be uninterrupted, of quality, and timely. It is in these spheres that the administration, especially the time-tested district administration under the collector, has responded over the decades to deliver on PDS promises. The PDS in Tamil Nadu is an excellent example of synergy between demand for public services, public and political policy, and administrative will and capacity. Tamil Nadu is among the top states in PDS delivery and satisfaction. Long before the Food Security Act was enacted at the Government of India level, all the features of the system were well and truly in place in Tamil Nadu and had indeed been functioning for several years.

At the political level, the Jayalalithaa regime soon lost its popularity. In 1993, there was a strike of the employees of the Chennai Secretariat for greater pay and better service conditions that was put down firmly, with perpetrators being punished, and in some cases, dismissed. The Secretariat staff in Tamil Nadu wield considerable influence, as service matters of all the department personnel all over the state are dealt with there, as also recruitments, postings, and promotions of all senior staff. Further, as pointed out in Chapter 2, most of the seasoned staff were those from the first decade of DMK rule, and in general, the Secretariat staff at that time had an association that was linked to the DMK. This was the first of the Jayalalithaa regimes, and the association took advantage of the situation to mount a protest against actions taken.[18]

There is also a parallel narrative of development and growth. The economic liberalization agenda had unfurled, and there was considerable interest in investing in India. The growth of technical education in Tamil Nadu, albeit a political largesse to those with access, provided a large educated manpower that was suited ideally for the IT industry. Net State Domestic Product (NSDP) grew from 12,633 crores in 1990 to 66,754 crores in 1997.[19] Per capita incomes grew from Rs 2,311 in 1990 to Rs 11,320 in 1997, a five-fold increase. Tamil Nadu has not witnessed such a big boom in incomes and growth in such a short period. There was no significant investment in industry or infrastructure from the state government, but economic liberalization enabled industries like textiles and leather as well as automotive ancillaries and light engineering to grow, quite apart from service industries like IT and financial services. This employment growth led to improvement in incomes and greater urbanization, and took people's attention away to some extent from what was happening to governance. Tamil Nadu in 1996 was a coveted destination for the manufacturing as well as the services sector, a position it maintained until 2011.

There is also recognition[20] of the social change introduced in Tamil Nadu by the Dravidian parties through the implementation of reservation of seats for higher education, which has enabled higher professional education to be available to those belonging to middle castes and classes from district towns. A cadre of officers had thus been created that have roots in small towns and that are willing to work in primary health centres located in rural areas. There was also an effort from the 1970s to train and deploy village health nurses to serve rural communities more rapidly than other parts of India. This led to a steady increase in primary health services. Muraleedharan[21] and others have contended that the slow and steady social change introduced in the state has much to do with improvements in overall health care delivery systems. Even by 1991, Tamil Nadu public service examination placements for different services indicate that the needle had moved significantly towards appointments of the backward classes and the SCs. In 1990–1, in the Tamil Nadu medical service, out of 591 appointments, 106 belonged to the SCs and STs, 119 to most backward classes, 278 to backward classes, and only 88 to forward classes. In various engineering services, the pattern was similar. In the Highways and Rural Works department, for example, out of 47 positions of assistant engineers, there were 10 SC and ST candidates selected, 11 from most backward classes, 26 from backward classes, and none from the forward classes.[22] This is indeed a far cry from where this story started—21 out of 27 engineers selected in the early 1900s belonging to the Brahmin community. Quite apart from the opportunities offered in government positions by a social justice and equal opportunity platform that the Dravidian parties strove to introduce, there was another narrative. Privatization of education and opening up of secondary and tertiary education in the 1980s gave rise to a very large pool of educated youth from rural areas, who belonged to the disadvantaged communities. Far from the hegemony of a small group of forward caste students, education, and hence opportunities were available for all. By 1996, the state had a new development narrative. This is unlike in other states in the Hindi belt, where higher education penetrated rural areas well after 2000, and hence the social imbalances are still to be corrected. Jean Drèze and Amartya Sen[23] argue that struggles for equality by underprivileged groups and the power of public reasoning and social action elevated the visibility for the need for public services, and cite examples of social action by groups independent of the SRM ideology.

It is also true that there was long-term commitment, even before 1967, to the improvement of primary care in rural areas. Muraleedharan feels that the state is unique in India in developing a strong public health management cadre at district level, and that the state bureaucracy has ensured continuity and have formulated, implemented, and adapted government policies to improve health outcomes and equity. Again, there is evidence to show that medical personnel belonging to the backward communities and coming from rural backgrounds had greater understanding of the needs of the poor and of the rural areas, and integrated sympathetically with government policies of that time.

Finally, the welfare programmes contributed to improvements in overall development parameters. It was argued that the origins of focus on nutrition as an overwhelming initiative arose out of the noon meal and the TINP programmes, but the benefits over time were quite measurable and apparent. Noon meals improved nutrition, health, and school attendance. The programmes for women ensured livelihoods as well as healthcare. The welfare schemes of textbooks, notebooks, cycles, and the like encouraged students and reduced drop outs. Privatization of education was the final benefit, ensuring access. In the period 1967 to 1997, Tamil Nadu evolved into a developed state, leading in several areas when compared to the other states. By 2000, in many ways the original SRM agenda had been achieved to a large measure.[24]

At the core of the above narrative is the argument that while the motives of the programmes may have had to do with political or commercial intent, the bureaucracy put in place implementation systems that have stood the test of time. No doubt there was good leadership at the level of the health secretary, but system performance requires the participation and involvement of many people at different levels. Further, over a period of over twenty years, the Health Department has seen many secretaries, and the Tamil Nadu Medical Services Corporation several managing directors. It is impossible to contend that all of them had similar commitment or objectives as those who initially started the programme. Staff has also changed over the years. It is common knowledge that administrative processes have become venal and that standards of two decades ago do not permeate today's staff. The fact that the organization has stood the test of time and that systems are still functional speaks of the capacity and capability of Tamil Nadu administrative machinery. It is also possible to say that at the client level, there is awareness and mobilization that government programmes reach the rural areas, and media and other dissemination modes ensure that everyone is aware of the services available. Local newspapers and pulp journals in Tamil are ready to highlight the shortcomings in government departments and the political class at the village level as well as the district administration is sensitive to public comments and responds. The existence of two strong political parties contending for electoral space also makes for better programme delivery. In a state with higher than average literacy and awareness, with good rural connectivity and infrastructure, any shortfalls in performance can be immediately noticed and highlighted by the opposition. Those in power are aware, since 1991, that they would have to sit in the opposition five years later, and any shortcomings in performance would be waiting to sting them when they are out of power. The people of Tamil Nadu have also become conscious of their rights and responsibilities and are ready to claim the public services due.

The years 1991 to 1996 was also the period when there were complaints of rampant corruption in the administration. The 1996 election results which brought the DMK back to power were in part the result of public revulsion against corruption and high handedness of the earlier AIADMK politicians while in power. In 1996, the DMK started a series of enquiries against the misdemeanours of the past regime, even incarcerating Jayalalithaa in the Chennai jail for a brief period.

There were a number of allegations from different departments. In the noon meal programme department, there were allegations of collusion between suppliers, the government staff, and the politicians to inflate costs of goods supplied, and to supply sub-standard goods. A minister in charge of this department was later (after 1996) arraigned for several improprieties, but the case did not succeed because her personal culpability could not be established in evidence. In another case, two senior officers and the minister were charged with corruption and misuse of government money. The officers faced disciplinary action and were dismissed. The largest of the cases was against the chief minister and her companion, Sasikala, and the latter's relatives, for acquisition of assets were far in excess of known sources of income. This matter that dragged on for over eighteen years, with the final verdict from the Supreme Court being pronounced only in January 2017, sentencing all the accused to terms in prison, forfeiture of properties, and fine. The matter against Jayalalithaa abated as she was no longer alive. The judgement[25] clearly articulates the anguish of the judges and their strong views against the actions perpetrated during this period by the accused.

The question which arises is how these two streams of administration and governance could co-exist. On the one hand, there is evidence of ministers and secretaries pushing for better programmes, better and more efficient administration, while on the other hand, there were departments, officers, and ministers who, apparently, were indulging in corrupt practices. A related question is about the views from the top, from the Chief Minister's Office, about these parallel streams. This question is relevant in Tamil Nadu administration even today, as these trends only accentuated in succeeding administrations.

The hypothesis below is from intimate knowledge of Tamil Nadu and its administration for several decades, though still lacking evidence from an academic point of view. The narratives of the earlier chapters seem to indicate that the administrative hierarchy of Tamil Nadu is still intact. It revolves around the District Collector, a colonial era position, and this functionary oversees almost everything that is happening in his jurisdiction. His direct hierarchy include the revenue and the rural development functions, both of which have been in existence for decades and have clearly identified functions, roles, and responsibilities. He is also responsible for welfare schemes such as noon meals and for the PDS. The collector is assisted by a number of senior officers at the district and the sub-district level, who have their own hierarchies and well set processes. The collector is also supervising and monitoring the programmes of a number of departments including agriculture, public health, irrigation, and other departments. There are departmental supervision personnel who perform the specialized functions related to that department, in a clearly defined hierarchy of their own.

Perhaps the first point to note is that these structures have remained intact over time and over regimes, and all the political parties have used the same machinery over the years to articulate their policies and their programmes. This is, in a way, unique, as in several other states in the country, systems and structures have been overhauled by succeeding governments. It has been discussed in earlier chapters that the social structure of this bureaucracy has changed over the period of the Dravidian rule of fifty years. At the beginning, it comprised predominantly of the forward classes, followed by those castes and classes that were still upper middle class, and over the decades, extending to the incorporation of all the backward classes, most backward classes, and SCs and STs. The current composition of the administrative structure is therefore representative of the diverse class and community structure of Tamil Nadu. It is thus representative of the aspirations and expectations of the different sections of the people. The selection process of the Tamil Nadu Public Service Commission ensures that the allocation of vacancies is within the overall mandate of reservations for the backward classes, most backward classes, and SCs and STs.

Second, social reforms introduced from the 1960s, and indeed, the changes in administration that were brought in early in the Karunanidhi years, enabled close interactions between political officials and the bureaucracy to happen at all levels, whether district, sub-district, or village level. This has meant that at every point, the political expectations of the ruling party are to be kept in mind during the implementation of the programmes. At one level, the political expectations are that government programmes enhance the image of the party in power, and therefore need to be administered and delivered in a manner that satisfies the demands for public services from the people. In a state where there is a close contest every five years between two major parties, it is clear that programmes that are part of the ruling party's agenda need to be delivered right down to the rural levels.

Third, it is also clear that increased literacy, media awareness, and information outreach has made the citizen in Tamil Nadu quite aware of the services that he is to receive from the state, and clever enough to distinguish between the benefits that are promised and those that are finally available. It is difficult for a PDS outlet not to supply free rice that has been promised, or for an NMC not to issue eggs or to supply special food on festive occasions. The citizens would demand and protest, not only with the authorities, but also with the local politicians.

This close interaction between officialdom, the people, and politicians at all levels could perhaps also be the origin of misdemeanours. If at the local level, the official and the politician are in league, then every service can become a charged service, with benefits to be shared. It is easy to project this thought upward, right to the minister and secretary level. It is also possible to presume that this nexus would require close co-operation between the political and the administrative streams.

At the same time, there are services that are politically prestige enhancing, which reach a large number of people, and which could provide a vote enhancing benefit. It is obvious that the politician would ensure that services are not disturbed, and function effectively, and also ensure that the administrative machinery is efficient enough to ensure this. Clearly, selection of personnel posted to operate these programmes would have a track record of implementation ability. The case studies of noon meal schemes, TINP, medical services corporation, and PDS are some of the examples of these programmes.

This argument is capable of verification. It is possible to examine files in the Tamil Nadu archives of the different periods and to look at those files that have subsequently been subject of enquiry and doubt. It is also possible to look at files that have articulated policy and clear implementation and see how these have come about. Some of these have been described in this and preceding chapters. It is not the purpose here to find fault. On the contrary, one can argue that it has been possible to deliver welfare and public good through public policy in a manner that benefits public policy, public good, and political goodwill.

Even anecdotally, this is evident. Amma Canteens, which serve food at highly subsidized rates, function well because it is in the interest of the local politician that this be so, as it serves the common voter. Storm water drains and sewage laying schemes are prone for corruption because the benefits are not individualized, but common in nature. Every programme that benefits individual beneficiaries across all geography and communities, are likely to be well implemented and relatively corruption free. Others, like infrastructure schemes, are likely to suffer.

It is also possible to conclude that this is a unique feature of Tamil Nadu. In the northern, Hindi-speaking states, there has not been such a close correlation between the politicians and the administration, and where it has happened, it has been more for personal gains than for service delivery. In Tamil Nadu, the ideologies of the Dravidian parties to deliver social justice and social welfare have given rise to a large number of programmes over the years, which succeed because of public pressure, political will, and administrative capability. It is difficult to replicate this in a different social milieu.

Notes

1 *Amma: Journey from Movie Star to Political Queen* (Delhi: Juggernaut Books, 2016).

2. It surprisingly resurfaced in 2017.

3. T.N. Ninan and S.H. Venkatramani, 'Tamil Nadu: An Uncertain Future', *India Today*, 15 November 1984.

4. Accessed from Tamil Nadu government archives, G.O.Ms no. 408, Health Department, 1 June 1994.

5. The newspapers reported it as a massive scandal in drug procurement.

6. Accessed in Tamil Nadu government archives, G.O. Ms 446, Health Department, 12 April 1993.

7. He is a serving officer even today.

8. Accessed in Tamil Nadu government archives, G.O. Ms 358, Health Department, 6 May 1994.

9. Interview with R. Poornalingam, June 2017.

10. Accessed from the Tamil Nadu archives, G.O.Ms 349, Health Department, 7 March 1995, 29 May 1995.

11. He has recently (2017) written and privately published a book entitled *Change* about these experiences.

12. Poornalingam in conversation.

13. Prabal Vikram Singh 'Replicating Tamil Nadu's Drug Procurement Model', *Economic and Political Weekly*, 47(39).

14. In August 2017, Rahul Gandhi of the Congress inaugurated Indira Canteens in Karnataka, a copy of Amma Canteens innovated by Jayalalithaaa in Tamil Nadu—it remains to be seen how well it will succeed.

15 http://www.forbesindia.com/article/on-assignment/tamil-nadu-medical-services-corporation-a-success-story/15562/1.

16. P. Padmanabha, Parvathy Sankara Raman, and Dileep V. Mavalankar, 'Innovations and Challenges in Reducing Maternal Mortality in Tamil Nadu, India', *Journal of Health, Population and Nutrition*, 27(2).

17. A.M. Swaminathan, *Food Security—Policy Options for Tamil Nadu* (Academic Foundation, 2009).

18. During later periods that AIADMK was in power, it kept away from meddling with secretariat staff.

19. Commissioner of statistics, Government of Tamil Nadu.

20. 'Innovations in Tamil Nadu', India Seminar.

21. Karthik Muraleedharan, University of Sand Diego, California, 2011.

22. TNPSC placement staff selection commission, Table 22.4, 1990–1.

23. Jean Drèze and Amartya Sen, *An Uncertain Glory: India and Its Contradictions* (Penguin Books, 2013), pp. 79 and 175.

24. With everyone having an opportunity, there are now demands for differentiation, and knowledge that such a measure exists, and the public is knowledgeable about the availability of these public services and therefore in a position to demand the services. It is perhaps a unique element of public awareness and demands for further segmentation in access to facilities and jobs, leading to further political polarization into caste based political parties.

25. Supreme Court, January 2017.

7

WELFARE AS POLITICS
The Post-1996 Scenario

———

By 1996, THE ELECTORATE HAD TIRED OF JAYALALITHAA'S government. In part it was due to perceptions of the excesses of the government. The displays of wealth during the Sudhakaran wedding did not go down well with the media, and Karunanidhi was constantly snapping at the infirmities of the governance. The handling of the strike in the Secretariat, and in general, the handling of government staff had created resentment among them. It is to be remembered that by this time, staff paid for by the government at the rural and village levels was quite substantial. Apart from staff engaged in the noon meal, nutrition, and public health programmes, there were revenue staff, panchayat staff, PDS staff, and staff from a myriad number of government departments. The total staff costs of the Tamil Nadu government are among the highest as a proportion to government expenditure, in the country, and the numbers as a percentage of population, the highest. Over the years, as narrated in earlier chapters, this was a clear policy of the government to provide employment and government salaries to a large number of people at the village and rural levels. In the case of MGR's AIADMK, this was achieved on the shoulders of major social sector programmes, the noon meal programme, a nutrition programme, the enlargement of the PDS, and initiatives in public health. In the case of the DMK, the attempt was initially to recruit volunteers like the prosperity brigade, and subsequently the Makkal Nala Paniyalargar. The difference in the two approaches, as pointed out, was that there were clear public benefits to the programmes announced by MGR, while in the case of the DMK initiatives, they were not well thought out in terms of public service delivery, and hence were not sustainable.

The large numbers of government staff at various levels constituted a large electoral base as well as political patronage points, and the political class at the village level were quite conscious of the electoral consequences of having these groups on their side. The 1996 electoral contest clearly belonged to the influence of the government functionaries.

Apart from public anger at governance, there was also some disquiet within the party. During these five years, the earlier stalwarts, those that had been associated with MGR and had experience in administration, were marginalized, and some of them removed from senior party positions. It is not appropriate to mention names, but several of those leaders who were instrumental in projecting Jayalalithaa as the leader of the AIADMK and the successor to MGR, were no longer there. It is generally believed that the replacements had more to do with their loyalties to her companion, Sasikala, who had by then emerged as an important political figure, albeit not in the public eye.

There was also the support of the mega actor Rajnikant for the DMK-Congress combine in these elections, which, in a film-besotted state, made a lot of difference.

In the Tamil Nadu assembly elections of 1996, the AIADMK lost by a large margin. The DMK secured 221 seats against the AIADMK's four. Several AIADMK bastions crumbled, and Jayalalithaa lost the elections from the Bargur constituency.

On returning to power, Karunanidhi again attempted to do what he had tried in 1989—to stabilize administration, to focus on development, and to initiate change. In the initial months, there was an attempt to redress the wrongdoings of the earlier regime. A large number of criminal cases were filed against ministers and officers, and the police machinery was involved deeply in investigating the misdeeds of the earlier regime. Those at the helm of administration also overreacted, opening up case after case for investigation. The case of ownership of assets beyond the stated income was investigated and filed at this time, which took a long eighteen years to be completed, and ended in conviction. The problem with this approach was that those in administration turned cautious about taking decisions, and the top levels of bureaucracy clearly had two streams now, those that had supported the earlier regime, and those that were in favour with the present one. Over the years, this cleavage has become more permanent and marked, affecting programmes, administration, and delivery in the next two decades.

Given the concern for development and growth, a number of programmes were initiated. One of the most important steps taken in 1996 was to hold the elections for the local bodies, both rural and urban. Rajiv Gandhi had been a strong advocate of the Panchayati Raj system of government, but it was only in 1992, under Narasimha Rao, that constitutional amendments were enacted. The Tamil Nadu Acts were changed to be in conformity with the constitutional amendments in 1994. This was during the AIADMK regime, but for two years afterwards, there was no attempt to hold the local body elections under the new Act.

There were perhaps two reasons for this. As mentioned earlier, the ministry in charge of panchayats and municipalities during the period 1991 to 1996 had suffered from a series of decisions that proved to be totally incorrect and venal. The officers and the minister involved were later arraigned for these decisions, and there are a number of files in the Tamil Nadu Archives that bear witness to these misdemeanours. Bringing in elected local bodies would have diluted the ability of these functionaries to handle the finances of the local bodies in the manner that they were doing. There were substantial funds that were being devolved on local bodies as central grants for programmes, and it did not make sense for this dispensation to part with control over the spending of these allocations to elected local bodies. They saw the advantage in keeping the decision making centralized to the Secretariat.

A second, equally important reason was that the new dispensation required reservation of one third of the positions for women, and also classification of local bodies, based on population, to be reserved for the SCs as well as for tribal people. This was an exercise that the government was not willing to do, for fear of disturbing existing caste and gender configurations in the rural areas. In fact, Jayalalithaa's political management was more in the realm of selecting candidates for winnability based on local considerations, rather than an understanding of the class and caste equations in the rural areas. Therefore, a dispute about criteria for reservations and categorization of local bodies was engineered, and as the dispute dragged on in the High Court, it gave an opportunity for the government to postpone local body elections.

There was a third, more important reason as well. The structure of the rural local body administration, which had been established in 1958, envisaged a two-tier system where the elected heads of panchayats would be members of the Panchayat Union, which was integrated geographically with the Development Block. The new act envisaged a three-tier structure, at the panchayat, block, and the district levels, all separately elected, and with no interlinkages. The new act created three different political powers and patronage centres over the same geography—the panchayat president, the block level elected functionary, and the district level person, all this in addition to the MLAs and MPs. It was felt that there would be disputes, ego clashes, and disturbance to the administration if elections were held on the basis of the new legislation.

In 1996, one of the first tasks of the Karunanidhi government was to find a resolution to this. In hastening the local body elections, there was another political motive that became apparent. Karunandhi wanted his son Stalin to become the Mayor of Chennai Corporation, obviously giving a signal that he was grooming him for later succession.[1]

I was involved with the process for rural local bodies, and another colleague, Ms Malathi, who went on to become the chief secretary, with the urban local bodies. The task was complex. There was a need to define the role and responsibilities of the new bodies. It was also important to make budgetary provisions, not only for their revenue expenditure, but also for the development tasks for which each tier would be responsible. There was need to allocate resources on the pattern of the Finance Commission devolutions as well as mandated state grants. The organization of the administrative structure was in line with the earlier Panchayat Act, and needed to be completely changed. And Karunanidhi was particular that the elections should be held as soon as possible. We worked very hard to achieve all this, and the government orders in the archives bear witness to the detailed exercises that were carried out to make these significant structural changes happen. The local body elections were held in October 1996, and the implementation of the new rules, administration, as well as financial devolution happened smoothly, without a hitch.

The above narrative is only to illustrate the resilience of the administrative hierarchy. The same department, a year earlier, had been the subject of a number of investigations for wrong doing, and yet within a year, was able to transform itself into a task based structure, focusing on the implementation of new guidelines and development initiatives. It is fascinating to examine the documents in the archives for the periods 1995, 1996, and 1997 for this department, and to note the change in approach from one which was totally wilful, to another that was policy and development driven, and yet without much change in the personnel.[2] Once again, it strengthens the hypothesis that the implementation structure of the bureaucracy is resilient enough to adapt quickly to changes in the political directions, and politicized enough to sail with the wind.

I left the state in 1997 to work in the central government in Delhi. Narrative for the subsequent years is based on reports, archival information, and conversations with peers and colleagues.

Apart from the initiative to bring in local body elections, there were several other measures taken by Karunanidhi in the period 1996 to 2001. Some ideas emanated from him. The Uzhavar Sandhai (or the farmers' market) was an establishment of markets for farmers to bring their produce for sale without any intermediation by middlemen. Samathuvapuram (or equality town) was an attempt to bring people of different castes together into a single community living project, with common access to water, education, and public amenities. There were programmes for desilting of irrigation tanks for improving storage of water during rains. There were also schemes for enlargement of benefits under the PDS as well as the noon meals programme. District Collectors rose to the occasion, and programmes that had the chief minister's attention were executed with speed and efficiency.

There was a curious shadow battle going on between the DMK and the AIADMK for influence at the central level. DMK remained associated with the governments at the Centre between 1996 and 1998, and when the Bharatiya Janata Party (BJP) alliance came to power in 1998, it was the AIADMK that allied themselves to the

National Democratic Alliance (NDA). The association of AIADMK with the BJP was short lived, from 1998 to 1999, and Jayalalithaa made demands of the NDA which couldn't be fulfilled. DMK was associated with the government at the centre, from 1999 to 2004 and Murasoli Maran was an important minister in Delhi. DMK remained associated with them throughout this period, breaking away only at the end to re-join the Congress. From 2001, the AIADMK was back in power in the state, and the DMK at the centre was important as a protection for itself against vindictive action at the state level. Remaining with the NDA and the BJP was more to ensure that they were protected against wilful action by the Jayalalithaa regime at the state level. The DMK was clearly more adept at adjusting to political changes at the central level. It associated with the NDA up to 2004, and then changed over to the Congress. In the state, it was clear that the NDA agenda did not cut any ice in 2004—the AIADMK lost all seats in 2004. Once again, the DMK was in power from 2004 to 2014 at the centre, and this time with much greater muscle, with three cabinet ministers, and ministers of state rank in powerful ministries.

There was another internal problem that was emerging. Karunanidhi's family members started intervening in decisions, both overtly as well as covertly. It was clear to the administration that a number of power centres had emerged, and that they needed to tread warily.

Going into the campaign in 2001, the DMK emphasized two themes: good governance and achievements since 1996. Karunanidhi was portrayed as the leader of a party interested in development and good government. Opinion poll evidence suggests that the development achievements

of the DMK administration were widely acknowledged by
the voters. Karunanidhi was the public face of the party in
government, and in spite of advancing years campaigned
widely during the elections in 2001. It appeared that he
would pass on the mantle to his son Stalin who had been
the Mayor of Chennai and had been given important
responsibilities. It was also apparent that not all of the
family members of Karunanidhi, including Alagiri and
Kanimozhi, accepted this succession line as granted.

Jayalalithaa and the AIADMK seized on this issue and
mocked the DMK for succumbing to 'family rule', putting
Karunanidhi on the defensive. In the public perception,
the issue of succession was much more relevant in the
DMK than the AIADMK, where Jayalalithaa was firmly in
control. She had just sacked several senior leaders in 2000,
and made it clear that she was solely in command.

For the first time, the contest between the two parties
was disjointed. The Dravidian ideals were very much
in the background, but the allies of the two parties
identified different enemies and issues. The AIADMK did
not criticize the BJP, which was in power at the centre.
The Trinamool Congress (TMC) had allied with the
AIADMK, ostensibly to counter the threat to secularism
posed by the BJP. However, the TMC was reluctant to
criticize the DMK. It was clear that all the parties were
hedging their future options and keeping opportunities
for change open.

At the polls, the AIADMK and its allies secured a
convincing mandate, winning 195 of the 234 seats in
the assembly. The AIADMK won 132 of the 141 seats
it contested, and did not need support from its alliance
partners to form a government.

This election made it clear that the structural advantages derived from the Dravidian ideology in the state would remain with the Dravidian parties,[3] namely the DMK and the AIADMK, and the allies would be able to make a difference only in areas where they had some numerical or caste based advantage. The poor performance of the Marumalarchi Dravida Munnetra Kazhagam (MDMK), standing alone, made it clear that Tamil Nadu was not ready for a third front. The everyday vocabulary of politics is biased towards the Dravidian parties. In both parties, there was an increased emphasis on the importance of caste identity. During the late 1990s, the DMK faced rising caste violence in the state. The AIADMK, with its links to the Thevars, has been more adept at riding this trend of caste-based political identification.

A further point to note is that the 2001 elections proved that good governance and development delivery alone would not be adequate to sway the voter. It was clear that he would take service delivery for granted and expect that electoral promises would be delivered. These acts alone would not be enough to ensure loyalty of the voter to a party during the next polls. There was no particular reason for the voter to reject the performance of the DMK regime, even though Jayalalithaa on return to power, attempted to file a number of cases against Karunanidhi, had him arrested, and included several officers in the charge sheets. These cases subsequently lapsed due to lack of evidence. By this time, officers had been clearly allocated into the DMK and the AIADMK camps, even though several of them were not politically inclined, but just happened to be in particular posts in particular regimes. The labels stuck, and to this day,

Tamil Nadu officers are wary of being categorized in this manner.

By the time of the parliamentary elections of 2004, the equations had changed again. I was with Prime Minister Atal Behari Vajpayee when the DMK announced that it was parting with the NDA alliance and going ahead in the state with the Congress. The Prime Minister recognized the need for the DMK to do so, and was gracious in the parting. It was clear by then that the AIADMK could not deliver much for the NDA. In the 2004 national elections, it was the poor performance of the Telugu Desam Party (TDP) in Andhra and the AIADMK wipe out in Tamil Nadu that finally cost the NDA their numbers.

The DMK delivered stellar results in the parliamentary elections, winning sixteen seats and delivering ten for the Congress. Its ally PMK won five seats. Given that the United Progressive Alliance (UPA) was a coalition of several parties, the DMK was able to secure two important cabinet berths and three equally powerful seats for the ministers of state; the PMK secured the Health Ministry. Between 2004 and 2009, the focus of the DMK leadership was much more on the central ministries. They had secured important ministries with enormous patronage, and it was clear that the family members of Karunanidhi had an advantage. Reports of the Comptroller and Auditor General on malfeasance in the telecom department, headed by first one and then another of the DMK party men, have resulted in criminal cases against both, as well as against some businessmen and officers, which are still under trial.

The DMK carried the advantages to the 2006 elections, but lost to the AIADMK in 2011. The consequences can be seen in the 2006 and 2011 polls, with the DMK winning one, and the AIADMK the other. The shift in loyalties every five years reflected the maturing of the voter and his clarity of expectations of public services from the system. In fact, the voter by now had put both the parties on notice. The parties responded with more innovative schemes of giveaways. It was no longer a theme of social justice, social equality, or social welfare. It was merely providing schemes of attractive giveaways that would sway the voter.

The Dravidian and the SRM ideology had diluted itself to a level where voter appeasement was the single point agenda in the elections. There is an important lesson here for the future. Space in the Dravidian political milieu has to be created either on the basis of caste or on the basis of a new ideology, or perhaps, by an overarching leadership that can reach directly to the people to address their grievances and promise opportunities that these parties have not been able to do. The BJP, which is interested in spreading its wings in Tamil Nadu, needs to take these factors into account, and some of these issues will be discussed in the final chapter.

Notes

1. It was only in the next period, 2006–11, that the competition between the siblings Alagiri, Kanimozhi, and Stalin intensified. In 1996, we thought of Stalin as the only heir to the DMK leadership mantle.
2. In the RD and MAWS departments, the changes happened at the top levels, and numbered less than half a dozen. Yet the performance orientation was totally different between 1995 and 1997.
3. A.K.J. Wyatt, 'New Alignments in South Indian Politics— The 2001 elections in Tamil Nadu', *Asian Survey*, 42(5): 733–53.

8

Freebies for Votes

2006 to 2016

———

The DMK ruled the state from 2006 to 2011 and the AIADMK from 2011 to 2016. In 2016, the AIADMK sprang a surprise and won a mandate for the second time, something that had not happened since 1984. In December 2016, Jayalalithaa died, and the current government is the remnant of the AIADMK, which seems to have several contenders for the top slot, and yet, as an entity, is unwilling to give up the right of governance. In governance, the policy of the parties is far removed from what the Dravidian parties started off with in 1967, and even further removed from the ideologies of the SRM of Periyar that started the process of Dravidian rule and brought to the forefront these regional parties.

In the period from 2001 to 2006, the AIADMK was in power, but there were no excesses of the kind that had occurred during the first regime of 1991. Jayalalithaa appeared to have matured. She did not take on an adversarial stance with government staff, rather appearing to accede to their demands. Welfare schemes were enlarged, with more being given under the midday meals scheme and greater benefits made available to women, the aged, and pregnant women.

The 2006 election was a closely fought one. It appeared that there was acceptance of the existing Jayalalithaa regime, and people were satisfied with the government and the development activities undertaken. Until April 2006, barely a month before the elections, AIADMK leaders were confident of victory. The opinion polls in the first week of April—after Jayalalithaa kicked off her election campaign—also predicted a clear victory for the AIADMK. Her approval rating was 67 per cent, and people did not have anything bad to say about her. Her handling of the relief work after the tsunami of 2004 was widely appreciated. What changed in the four weeks that followed? Just before campaigning started in Tamil Nadu for the assembly election, it appeared a foregone conclusion that Jayalalithaa would return to power, a feat achieved only by MGR in the past.

This changed suddenly when Karunanidhi released the DMK election manifesto. He announced that ration rice would be made available at Rs 2 per kilogram for all card holders and a free colour television would be given to women of every family. In addition, a free gas stove would be provided to all poor women. Free electricity would be provided to all farmers and weavers, and co-operative societies would waive off all farm loans. Further, maternity assistance would be given to all mothers-to-be for six months at the rate of Rs 1,000. The manifesto says, 'We will implement the recommendations of the Sixth Pay Commission as and when they are announced.'

The wide-ranging poll pledges included reinstallation of the Kannagi statue at the same place from where it was removed by the AIADMK government, re-establishing MGR Film City, and implementation of all DMK schemes, which were discontinued by the current AIADMK administration.

Addressing a press conference after releasing the manifesto, Karunanidhi said free colour televisions would be given to families after ascertaining whether they had a television or not. On the Rs 2 per kilogram rice, he said all family card holders drawing it under the public distribution system would be eligible.

While educated urban Tamil voters and the media initially scoffed at the manifesto, the DMK's offer of freebies made rural Tamil Nadu look at it with keener interest. Finance Minister P. Chidambaram said the DMK's election manifesto seemed to be the hero of the 2006 election in Tamil Nadu. Perhaps this manifesto was Karunanidhi's winning script. He understood the pulse of the poor people of Tamil Nadu much better than anybody. There was also a promise of giving two acres of land free to all landless agriculturists—clearly an impossible promise.

He also explained the economics behind his promises saying that the total amount spent on these could be absorbed easily in a budget of Rs 30,000 crore. He said there were 1.5 crore ration card holders in the state.

Each cardholder was entitled to 20 kilograms rice a month. At present, it was being sold at Rs 3.50 per kilogram. If the price were reduced to Rs 2, the additional subsidy burden would be Rs 1.50 per kilogram. For the 30 crore kilograms that would be dispensed through the PDS, the additional subsidy would be Rs 45 crore. This would come to Rs 540 crore annually. Also, the state had 55 lakh acres of wasteland. There were attempts by the AIADMK government to give this to the rich and land sharks, he said. As these attempts were on, the elections were announced. If the DMK came to power, this land would be given to landless farm labourers. Refuting the claim that the free television scheme would cost Rs 15,000 crore, he said it would cost Rs 1,060 crore. Television was an important medium to educate and inform people about various developments. Explaining how the DMK would implement the scheme if it came to power, he said there was a total of 156 lakh families in the state. Of this, 53 lakh were below the poverty line. At Rs 2,000 a television set, and assuming that all those under the poverty line needed to be given one, this scheme would cost only Rs 1,060 crore. If the DMK came to power, it would implement the programme over two years. The government needed to spend Rs 530 crore a year.

Till Karunanidhi released his party manifesto, Jayalalithaa spoke only about the achievements of her government—how she handled disasters, how she helped the poor students of Tamil Nadu by distributing books and bicycles, and so on. But she saw that from the moment Karunanidhi offered them free colour television sets, a cable connection and rice for Rs 2 per kilogram, there was a change in the mindset of the people. Immediately,

Jayalalithaa pressed the panic button and started announcing freebies one after another.

As the media put it, there was a battle between chemistry and arithmetic in the minds of the people, and arithmetic won. In the event, the DMK did not get an absolute majority in the assembly, winning only 96 seats against 61 for the AIADMK. The Congress won 34 seats—in the alliance, Karunanidhi had given away over 100 seats to the allies, contesting only 130 seats. The freebie announcements came after opinion polls indicated a clear win for the AIADMK, shifting voter preferences markedly in the last few weeks before the polls.

This election is important from the point of view of our narrative so far. It marked a decisive shift away from policies of welfare and of social justice, empowerment, and opportunities. It marked the beginning of fairly reckless promises of free gifts and benefits paid for from the exchequer. There was no Dravidian agenda here, or any attempt to target the weaker sections—the freebies promised would be available to all. There were also unsustainable promises like the grant of free land to every person who did not have land, which was clearly impossible to implement. Yet, Karunanidhi saw this as a last desperate attempt to come back to power. Interestingly, the people had also become wise and somewhat cynical and were ready to accept whoever gave them the most, and that defines the Tamil Nadu voter even today, a far cry from the principled demands for equality and social justice. There was also the growing feeling that the politician was venal and in the political game only for personal gains, hence the total disenchantment with ideological promises and focus on individual gains.

In the elections of 2006, 2011, and 2016 we see no mention of the original ideological agenda of the Dravidian movement. It must be recognized that this trend had started even earlier, with Jayalalithaa in 1991, but it was blatant and responsible for changing electoral outcomes only by 2006. In the event, it did not give Karunanidhi a majority in the assembly, and he ruled only with the outside support of the Congress, a fact the AIADMK was always pointing out, calling it a 'minority DMK' government.

In a substantial measure, this was also due to the maturing of the voter, and the improvements in livelihoods and infrastructure that were clearly visible in Tamil Nadu. The economic developments in Tamil Nadu were making it the second most developed state in the country. Between 2003 and 2013, the GDP of the state grew at an annual compounded growth rate of 9 per cent, and by 2013–14 was at USD 80 billion.[1] Per capita incomes had also grown apace, and population growth between 1991 and 2001 was 11.1 per cent, among the lowest in the country. Literacy rates were at 80 per cent, and per capita incomes at around Rs 114,000. There were 8.5 lakh medium and small industries in Tamil Nadu by 2011, with an investment of over USD 8 billion. Between 1993 and 2005, Tamil Nadu's GSDP (at constant prices) grew at 5.46 per cent per annum, and the poverty ratio declined by 3.31 per cent per annum.[2] Incomes were supplemented by a number of welfare schemes like midday meals in schools, free education, textbooks, highly subsidized rations, free electricity for farmers, and several schemes for expectant mothers, destitute women, and the poor. The total percentage of the population below the poverty line declined from 56.4 per cent of the population to 26.1 per cent between 1973–74 and 1999– 2000.[3]

Therefore, the electorate was literate, employed, and better off than in most other states. Consequently, the voter had a clear idea of the kind of benefits that each of the two parties offered and was clearly capable of making a reasoned, personally beneficial, choice. The two parties, the DMK and the AIADMK, seemed to have also realized that it was no longer Dravidian sentiments that swayed the voter, but more reasoned economic benefit considerations.

This was apparent in 2011, for it was now Jayalalithaa's turn. Not to be caught off guard, she was the first to unveil her electoral promises. Rice to cardholders below a specified income level was made totally free from the PDS scheme. For others, 20 kilograms of rice were provided at Rs 2 per kilogram.

The other major announcement was that free laptops would be given to every girl child in the twelfth grade. The state government's ambitious free laptop scheme, under which 68 lakh laptops would be distributed to students started on 15 September 2011. The scheme was widened to include students of government aided higher secondary schools, arts and science colleges, engineering colleges, and polytechnic colleges. The whole project was budgeted at a cost of Rs 10,200 crore.

There were also announcements of free goats (four per family), milch cows, and even fans and rice cookers. The principled programmes of the MGR years targeting the poor and the underprivileged, had morphed into a freebies-for-votes approach.

The AIADMK swept the polls, winning 150 seats against the DMK's 23.

To keep the public engaged, Jayalalithaa this time adopted a further strategy of periodically announcing programme after another. She made a suo motu statement in the assembly announcing a new expanded social security scheme for farmers and agriculture workers, which included a monthly pension of Rs 1,000 for those over 60 years of age, educational assistance for their children, and marriage and maternity assistance. This Chief Minister's Farmers' Security Scheme would cover small and medium farmers in the age group of 18–65 years, who owned 2.5 acres of wetland or 5 acres of dry land. Agriculture workers and lease holders in the same age group were also eligible for the benefits.

On yet another occasion, speaking on educational assistance, she said the children of beneficiaries studying in Industrial Training Institutes (ITIs) would get Rs 1,250 to Rs 1,950 per year. Undergraduate students would be given Rs 1,750 to Rs 2,500 and postgraduate students, Rs 2,250 to Rs 3,750. Students on undergraduate professional courses would get Rs 2,250 to Rs 4,750 and postgraduate students, Rs 4,250 to Rs 6,750.

She also took pains to point out, in several forums, that schemes being announced by the centre were but replicas of schemes under implementation in Tamil Nadu. Some of its schemes were 'belated attempts by Centre to replicate State schemes,' she said. For instance, the Indira Gandhi Matritva Suraksha Yojana 'draws inspiration' from Tamil Nadu's Dr Muthulakshmi Reddy Scheme, under which government provided a much higher benefit of Rs 12,000 and wider coverage, she said. She also prided herself on fiscal management, and the Planning Commission complimented the state government in 2013 for its sound fiscal position arising from significant increase in mobilization of resources, especially the state's own tax revenue for the

State Plan. 'The State's Tax-GSDP ratio is likely to cross 10 per cent during 2013–14 making it as one of the leading States in the country in terms of tax mobilisation. The outstanding liabilities as a percentage of GSDP are well within the fiscal consolidation requirements as per the 13th Finance Commission.' It noted that state continued to maintain favourable social indicators, especially health indicators such as birth rate, infant mortality rate (IMR), maternal mortality rate (MMR), total fertility rate (TFR), and neonatal mortality rate (NMR). 'The State also ranks better than the national average in most of education indicators.'

The most innovative scheme that was introduced was the 'Amma Canteen', first in Chennai, and then in other Corporations. In the Amma Canteens, a breakfast of *idlis* (savoury rice cake) and *sambar* was available at Re 1 per idli, and a lunch of tamarind rice or curd rice at Rs 5. It was manned by women, nominally paid, who cooked and served the food. Over a period of time, over 500 Amma Canteens opened up in Chennai, and the total number in the state was close to 1,500. There was a large picture of Jayalalithaa at the entrance to every canteen, and the place was hygienically maintained and the food quality was satisfactory. Local bodies, corporations, and municipalities were expected to maintain the canteens and to subsidize the expenditure. Another initiative was 'Amma Neer' which was bottled water at Rs 5 per litre at bus stands and railway stations.

The government's stance towards the central government, the period 2011 onwards can be considered to be adversarial. In the campaign for the 2014 elections, Jayalalithaa was vituperative against the Congress, to the extent that several prominent Congress leaders in Tamil Nadu did not even contest in the elections. Even after 2014, with the BJP in power at the centre, even though AIADMK had 38 members in the Lok Sabha and 16 in the Rajya Sabha, the party did not leverage its strength in national politics in any manner—a clear difference between Jayalalithaa and Karunanidhi, as the latter had always been particular to be on the right side of the central government, and had been able to benefit from this association at all times, as had MGR. But, somehow, Jayalalithaa chose to stand up to the central government, refusing to be on board with national schemes like the UDAY scheme or the Goods and Services Tax (GST). During this period, it was difficult to get access to her as she chose to remain aloof and ruled by fiat rather than consensus.

An interesting feature of this period was that Jayalalithaa was not as accessible as she had been in her earlier terms. In the first tenure between 1991 and 1996, she had taken considerable interest in some selected programmes, and in others, had obviously allowed her ministers a free hand. The period 2011 onwards was very different. She kept aloof from officers and her own party functionaries, going away for long intervals to her mansion in the hills at Kodanadu in the Nilgiri Hills. The announcements for different programmes emanated from suo motu statements in the legislative assembly, rather from examination of alternatives.

There are several possible explanations for this. First, it is true that her health was indifferent in these later years, and she was not able to spend long hours at work. Second, it was quite clear that she no longer believed in social reform or the Dravidian ideology as before, and viewed each action as an opportunity to win elections. Third, from her own experience, she had discovered that there was little political or economic advantage in going against her rivals, including those in the media like the Sun TV group. Confronting them with criminal cases and regulatory controls was not an approach she seemed to favour, perhaps concluding that these would only be effective as long as she was in power. She focused on programmes of direct benefit to the largest sections of the electorate, like the Amma Canteens or the free rice programme. The grant of free rice was the eventual culmination of the freebies that were being granted, in ever-increasing measure, for over thirty years. However, it is not clear where the ideas for some of the other programmes like Amma Neer and Canteens emerged from. It must also be recognized that she maintained tight control over her party, removing and adding senior party functionaries at will. That she was well briefed by her inner coterie of advisers is clear, and this included the intelligence chiefs of police as well as Sasikala and her relatives. However, working out details of the programmes was probably left to two or three officers in her secretariat, in whom she had absolute trust.

This is again a feature of Tamil Nadu. Between 1984 and 1987, with MGR incapacitated, administration was very much in the hands of the bureaucracy. This was largely true of the recent period as well. Even at present, with AIADMK party in internal flux, day-to-day administration is being managed with reasonable success by the bureaucracy. Officers still report to work on time— there are several states in the north, where the secretariat sees footfalls only around midday.

Three things are to be noted at this point. First, schemes like the Amma Canteens, the provision of mixies and grinders, focusing very much on the persona of the chief minister, ensured that her image and that of her government was visible to everyone on a daily basis, and served to strengthen the political base of the party. In this, she had a taken a leaf out of MGR's book, whose nutritious midday meal programme was intended for just this purpose. Recognizing the growing urbanization of the state and the large number of unorganized service sector employees, this scheme focused on urban areas, again a clever political move.

Second, it was quite clear to her that the electorate weighed the two parties on the basis of giveaways and that election promises once in five years were not enough and that she had to keep the flow of goodies coming. Therefore, she saw to it that there were announcements every year about some scheme or the other. This policy gave her the dividends of a repeat victory in 2016, as the populace had very little to complain about.

Third, in the chronology of this narrative, it can be noted that the Karunanidhi announcements of 2001 and even some of the 2006 announcements left little room for the administration to show its mettle. In the Amma Canteen and water schemes, once again there was an opportunity for the administrative hierarchies to demonstrate the skills of organization, logistics, and supervision that had been such an important feature of the performance of the midday meal schemes. To ensure that in over 1,000 locations, 2,000–3,000 idlis are prepared every morning and sold without complaint of quality or quantity is a very big task. It is a tribute not only to the higher ups who organize the entire programme, but even for the last level cook, server, and cleaner who maintain the system day after day without fail—this is again a tribute to the strength of Tamil Nadu's administrative capability.

Once again, in the same manner as in the midday meal programme, it was a programme initiated by the leader, but the lowest level political worker benefitted from the political advantage that the smooth running of the scheme provided him, and therefore it was in his interest as well that the scheme ran smoothly.

There is an interesting corollary to the decision-making process. Unlike the period 1993 to 1996, during which administrative processes were all documented and are available in the form of Government Orders in which the notes are open to scrutiny in the archives, the later period of Jayalalithaa totally eschewed this. Perhaps she was aware that a paper trail of reasoning and orders might at some stage be used against her, and so the entire process became much more ad-hoc. There would be an announcement in the assembly that would be followed by orders. Or there would be discussions in the Cabinet, without any paper trail, that would end up in decisions being communicated. The responsibility of decision making became much more opaque and it remains so to this day. The archives do not contain any orders on the reasons for the Amma Canteens. After the announcements, the Chennai Corporation was asked to set up these canteens, and to meet the expenditure from their own budgets. This dispersal of decision making, although directed from the top, was probably an attempt to avoid any detailed scrutiny of decision-making processes in later times.

During the period 2011 to 2017, state finances suffered as a result of these decisions. There was no investment in infrastructure or in industry. A number of projects that started during the earlier DMK regime were stalled. The DMK had built a huge complex in Chennai, in the centre of the town, in Anna Salai, to house the Secretariat and the assembly. The work could not be completed by 2016, and as soon as Jayalalithaa returned to power, she overturned this decision, and converted these buildings into a hospital, preferring to retain the Secretariat at the existing location. Not much can be read into this decision except political pique and rivalry, and some personal animosity towards Karunanidhi.

The budget for 2017–18 revealed that the fiscal deficit for the previous year, at Rs 61,341.23 crores, was 4.58 per cent of the state GSDP, among the highest as compared to other states. This was far in excess of the budget estimates made the previous year of Rs 40,533.84, although some of the increase could be attributed to the taking over of the loans of the power distribution utility. The revenue deficit projected for 2017–18 was Rs 15,930 crores. The net outstanding debt of the state government in 2017 was Rs 314,356 crores, amounting to 20.90 per cent of the state domestic product, one of the highest among the states. The RBI, in its report on state finances, has expressed concern at the fiscal stress in Tamil Nadu.[4] The fiscal deterioration is noticeable from 2014 and a steady stream of welfare giveaways without matching revenues has eaten into budgetary margins. The government of 2011 onwards appeared to have given up all considerations other than free gifts in its effort to retain the interest of the voter. This development is a far cry from the initial years of the DMK and the AIADMK, where programmes were intended to address and remove existing social imbalances, and to offer equal opportunities and a platform for all.

Notes

1. Estimated to be 210 billion in 2017.
2. Girija Vaidyanathan, Atul Anand, and R. Srinivasan; *Dimensions of Rural Poverty in Tamil Nadu.*
3. www.tamilselvi.com/poverty.html (accessed on 14 August 2017).
4. RBI report on State finances, RBI, 12 May, 2017.

9

Looking at the Future

————

Throughout this narrative, continuity of ideology, policy and implementation is seen in programme after programme. After the initial structure was created during the first decade of the DMK regime, and the earlier colonial as well as Congress hierarchies had been dismantled, the transitions have been seamless. Whether this is attributed to the politicization or the social change in the structure of the bureaucracy, or to the mere ability of the administration to execute policy in an efficient manner, there is evidence of performance and delivery in case after case. The role of District Collector and the district officials remains intact even after 70 years of independence, and the tasks of implementation and problem solving still remains with the district collector. That he was hemmed in by political pressures much more than in earlier decades is a testimony not only to the growing democratic process, but also to public awareness of rights, responsibilities, and demands for services, that express themselves through alternative outlets which include political lobbying. There is definitely greater awareness among the public about programmes and the services that the state had promised. The structure has wobbled, but found a new normal, which is now operational in Tamil Nadu.

There is another thought that surfaces. The willingness of the administrative system to readily execute the political will, even if sometimes the political directions are for the benefit of those in power rather than for the welfare of the people, is perhaps a limitation of the Tamil Nadu system. The willingness to acquiesce to orders, even if they are partisan, is not necessarily an example of good administration. All major schemes have come from the top, not from ideas that have been analysed, examined, and debated. There are programmes that have been wished upon the executive, that have been then executed well. There are a few examples of innovation, experimentation, and fresh thinking that have worked their way up from the administrative hierarchies up into the political realm, but largely, the story has been of efficient, dutiful implementation. Once the administration has become task-oriented, it appears to have focused on efficiency rather than innovation. In the new normal, this moves the administration to performing assigned tasks, not to a thinking role. It is a matter of debate whether this represents a maturing of the democracy, or is a retrograde move where political play determines administrative action.

In the first decade, the focus had been on correcting the wrongs done to the backward classes, to restore societal balance on the basis of strength in the population, and to open up opportunities for everyone to access education, government jobs, and public services. The next decade focused on making these entitlements affordable. It was recognized that availability of education alone did not enable access to it, and that social support, in the form of midday meals, textbooks, and notebooks as well as the PDS, was necessary to provide a level of livelihood that would enable the next generation to aspire to a better standard of living. In a large measure, this has been achieved, and the number of first generation graduates and engineers is close to 35 per cent of those admitted. These first generation educated are aspiring to improve themselves further in society, and appearing for competitive examinations for the civil services and for admissions to the IITs and IIMs and scoring well.

In terms of caste and class composition, the early years saw the dominance of Brahmins in government services give way to a proportionate representation scenario. Initially, this benefitted the classes below the Brahmins, and over time, demands from the more backward classes grew and had to be accommodated in the reservation policies for jobs as well as for education. Rural employment in the PDS, midday meal programme, TINP, public health, and other programmes also benefitted women as well as those of the more backward and disadvantaged classes.

Economic development has ensured that livelihood is not a concern for the majority of the people. There are arguments that show that a very large number of people who are above the poverty line are in danger of slipping below due to calamities, illnesses, or sudden expenditures, but the higher level of urbanization in the state has ensured that there is sufficient resilience in the informal service sector economy to absorb youth migrating from rural areas. The control over growth of the population has also helped ensure that family sizes are small enough to be taken care of by one or at most two breadwinners.

In spite of all this social change, there has not been a significant improvement for the Dalits. Somewhere along the way, the SRM as well as the Dravidian movement left them by the wayside. A further concern has been the number of caste-based organizations that have sprung up, some as political parties, others as pressure groups that are exerting pressure on the elected representatives in separate geographical areas. The schism among castes is as strong as ever, and the electorates are aware of this. Since being backward is no longer a special advantage (almost 95 per cent of the entire state can claim to be among the backward classes—less than 5 per cent of the population is now classified as forward), pressure groups try to leverage local differences for marginal advantage. Even in education, in all streams other than medicine there are enough seats available among private and government colleges. The big debate over the National Eligibility cum Entrance Test (NEET) examinations in Tamil Nadu is because the state education standards are far below The Central Board of Secondary Education (CBSE) and the state board students are not getting placements even in medical colleges in the state.

It is also clear that the freebies programme has reached its peak. In the PDS, there are restrictions on subsidies for food grains from PDS stores for those earning 1 lakh or more per year, which accounts for most of Tamil Nadu. If the state has to continue this programme, central grants will not be available and all expenditure will have to be from state funds. The introduction of GST is also likely to impact the state, as it is a manufacturing and exporting state, and GST is levied at the point of sale. The lack of rainfall has reduced food grains output by 40 per cent in 2017, and farmers are in distress. Encouragement for industry from other states, notably adjacent Andhra Pradesh is leading to investment moving away from Tamil Nadu. There is also a slowing down of the growth of the IT industry, which has been a mainstay of employment for a large number of engineering students from the state.

Unfortunately, this is also a period in which there appears to be a vacuum in the political leadership. With the death of Jayalalithaa, a clear hierarchy in the AIADMK is yet to emerge, and in the DMK, with Karunanidhi totally incapacitated, Stalin has now to assert his authority and leadership. The BJP was not able to make inroads in the state during the 2014 elections, and though they are trying very hard to make a mark, it may be some more time before they are visible in any significant manner on the electoral scene.

To go back to the origins, what of the SRM and the Dravidian ideals? Are Tamil sentiments totally gone?

Surprisingly, some events in 2017 indicate that the origins of the movement are still alive and active in Tamil Nadu. After 2014, Tamil Nadu has not really felt integrated into the new national politics of the NDA. There has been a feeling of neglect by the central government, accentuated by the fact that Jayalilathaa was never able to get close to the new dispensation. There is a feeling that Tamil Nadu and Tamils are not getting their due from the centre. There was a huge social media-based protest in February 2017 over *jallikattu*. This is a social cum religious festival prevalent in a few districts in Tamil Nadu, notably in Madurai and Alanganallur, and resembles festivals in other parts of the world where specially grown bulls are let loose in an arena to be chased and subdued by youth. It is a festival that celebrates a particular kind of masculinity, and suddenly, in 2013, the Supreme Court, on a petition against cruelty to animals, banned the festival. Though this is not a major festival in most parts of the state, there was a sudden upsurge of sentiment and thousands of youth congregated on the Marina Beach in Chennai demanding restoration of the festival. The state government had to hurriedly pass an enabling legislation, for which they had to get the assent of the President of India, and then announce the resumption of jallikattu. The youth were, however, not satisfied, as they consider it a temporary measure and not a permanent solution.

There have been other outpourings since then. There has been discourse in the digital media for reviving a demand for Dravidian state, and the map of the new Dravida Nadu encompasses parts of Kerala, Karnataka, Telengana, and Andhra Pradesh. Academics have been vociferous in seminars about the reversion to the earlier days of neglect of the south and the development of the north. The political parties in the state have understandably kept away from the sentiments, as they are not sure how deep the feelings run. It is clear that they would be happy to capitalize on the sentiments, once they see that it is to their advantage. There is also a decline in central investments and central projects in the state in the last few years that has been noticeable, and the government has let it be known that several major proposals are held up by the central government. There is an undercurrent of resentment against the neglect, and at a time when the BJP is seeking to expand its presence in the state, either directly or in association with those that are currently in power, it appears important that there is no room for misapprehensions.

An example of an issue that has agitated Tamil Nadu recently, namely NEET examinations for admission into medical colleges. The Supreme Court directed in 2014 that there should be a common platform for admission to medical colleges and that there should be a common entrance examination to determine eligibility for admissions to medical colleges after class 12. The mandate was opposed by the Tamil Nadu government, who after failing in appeal to the Supreme Court as well as to the central government, tried to bring in legislation to get the state exempted from this requirement. It is surprising that Tamil Nadu has taken this position, which none of the other states have.

There appear to be three reasons which strengthen the arguments in this whole narrative. First, Tamil Nadu has a large number of medical colleges, both private and government. Private colleges have some political backing, and therefore there is the apprehension that selection according to NEET results will remove political patronage in allocating seats, as well as reduce commercial benefits of admission and fees to the promoters.

Second, in a state where tertiary education has been a matter of pride ever since MGR's time, there is an apprehension that the results would weigh against the

Tamil Nadu students, if only for the reason that the curriculum of the state board schools has been neglected, and is quite behind the curriculum of the central board of school education. Very high marks in the state board exams does not necessarily translate into ability to perform well in the NEET examinations. For the state administration, it would be a clear signal that they have neglected curriculum in favour of more privatization at the school level. If the NEET examinations were not there, the students would be admitted on the basis of their school examination results, which are now apparently below central board standards.

Third, there is genuine apprehension that parents of children, especially from rural areas, who have striven hard to make opportunities available to the next generation, at some sacrifice, would be dissatisfied by the government's and political parties' attempts to find a solution and have a grievance against them. The complaint is that the government did nothing to prepare students for the NEET examinations by offering coaching, changing curriculum, improving teaching, and other means. There is an apprehension of a political backlash from the voters, especially if the NEET results in a large number of students from other states finding seats in medical colleges in Tamil Nadu, while Tamil Nadu students are left out.

It is interesting that this issue has become so important in Tamil Nadu and not in the other states. One can go back to the narrative and find that the gradual progression of social upliftment opportunities have over the last fifty years created a society that is now aspirational, capable, and also demanding, and governments have to be sensitive about their demands. In fact, the NEET controversy exemplifies all that this entire narrative has been about—that social transformation has now put power in the hands of the people, not just the forward communities, but all classes, and in future, they are likely to be the arbiters of what they want from the state. This is a position quite unique. In no other state is there so much synergy between the demand for public services and the sensitivity of the political parties to respond to it. At a time when parts of the AIADMK are moving towards some understanding with the BJP, there is a fear that this issue may raise public feelings against the central government and accentuate nascent Dravidian feelings once more.

The future of politics and administration in Tamil Nadu is at crossroads. In politics, there is lack of clarity on the succession in the AIADMK, with rival factions staking claim to legitimacy of control over the party. In the economy, there is a slowing down of investments, and a slowdown in the services sector, including IT. The fiscal position is stressed, with most of the expenditure on the revenue and social welfare side, not on capital projects. Revenues are likely to be impacted by GST, as Tamil Nadu is a major manufacturing state. Agriculture has been affected by poor rainfall and farmers are in distress.

A major worry is that there does not appear to be any charismatic leader in the horizon who can take the state forward. Tamil Nadu has been fortunate in having a succession of leaders who, by their stature, were able to guide their parties and policies, starting from Kamaraj and including Annadurai, Karunanidhi, MGR, and Jayalalithaa. Caste continues to be an important factor. An interesting fallout of fifty years of striving for self-respect among the backward classes is that now over 95 per cent of the state population claims backward class status. This has resulted in the demands for further segmentation to have stratified access to the facilities that the backward classes command. This has exacerbated feelings of caste and community differences. The worry is that in the absence of such a towering personality, how will Tamil Nadu politics develop? Recently, film star Rajnikanth and Kamal Haasan have separately announced their entry into politics.

It has been argued that the administration is excellent at implementing programmes efficiently and within the parameters of political policy, also that it will wait for policy to be formulated. The very success of Tamil Nadu is based on charismatic leadership with a social justice and welfare agenda, a pliant administration, and at the other end is public well aware of its rights to public services.

The future is now a question mark, waiting for a new paradigm to emerge.

BIBLIOGRAPHY

Books and Journal Articles

Abraham, Joseph, 1995, 'Impact of Prohibition on State Excise: Study of Four Southern States', *Economic and Political Weekly*, 30(48): 3051–53.

Adiseshiah, Malcolm S., 1974, 'A Learning System in Tamil Nadu', *International Review of Education*, 20(4).

Afridi, Farzana, 2005, 'Midday Meals in Two States: Comparing the Financial and Institutional Organisation of the Programme', *Economic and Political Weekly*, 40(15): 1528–29.

———, 2007, 'The Impact of School Meals on School Participation: Evidence from Rural India', *Journal of Development Studies*, 47(11): 1636–56.

Ahluwalia, Deepak, 1993, 'Public Distribution of Food in India. Coverage, Targeting and Leakages', *Food Policy*, 18(1): 33–54.

Aiyar, Mani Shankar, 2010, 'Local Government in India and China', *Brown Journal of World Affair*, xvii(i): 221–33.

Akhila, R., 2004, 'Reaching Global Goals in Primary Education', *Economic and Political Weekly*, 39(25): 2617–22.

Ambirajan, S., 1999, 'State Government Subsidies: The Case of Tamil Nadu', *Economic and Political Weekly*, 34(14).

Ananth, Krishna, 2006, 'Changing Dynamics in Tamil Nadu', *Economic and Political Weekly* 46(2): 1232–33.

———, 2014, 'Fragmented Politics in Tamil Nadu', *Economic and Political Weekly*, XLIX(15): 1–4.

Andersen, L.T., S.H. Thilsted, B.B. Nielsen, and Suguna Rangasamy, 2002, 'Food and Nutrient Intakes among Pregnant Women in Rural Tamil Nadu, South India', *Public Health Nutrition*, 6(2): 131–37.

Arabindoo, Pushpa, 2011, 'Beyond the Return of the "Slum"', *City*, 15(6): 631–35.

———, 2009, 'Falling Apart at the Margins? Neighbourhood Transformations in Peri-Urban Chennai', *Development and Change*, 40(5): 879–901.

Aruna, R., 1999. '"Learn Thoroughly": Primary Schooling in Tamil Nadu', *Economic and Political Weekly*, 34(18): 1011–14.

Ayres, Ron and Manuela Torrijos Simon, 2003, 'Education, Poverty and Sustainable Livelihoods in Tamil Nadu: Inequalities, Opportunities and Constraints', *Review of Political Economy*, 15(2): 211–29.

Babu, Suresh Chandra and J. Arne Hallam, 1989, 'Socioeconomic Impacts of School Feeding Programmes Empirical Evidence from a South Indian Village', *Food Policy*, 14(1): 58–66.

Bahl, R., G. Sethi, and S. Wallace, 2010, 'Fiscal Decentralization to Rural Local Governments in India: A Case Study of West Bengal State', *Publius: The Journal of Federalism*, 40(2): 312–31.

Bajaj, Monisha, 2012, 'From "Time Pass" to Transformative Force: School-Based Human Rights Education in Tamil Nadu, India', *International Journal of Educational Development*, 32(1): 72–80.

Bajpai, Nirupam, Jayanthi Srilekha, and Anjali Chowfla, 2013, 'Inequality: A China and India Perspective', Columbia Global Centers—South Asia Working Papers no. 7.

Basu, Raj Sekhar, 2011, 'The Making of Adi Dravida Politics in Early Twentieth Century Tamil Nadu', *Social Scientist*, 39(7): 9–41.

Besley, Timothy, Rohini Pande, Lupin Rahman, and Vijayendra Rao, 2004, 'The Politics of Public Good Provision: Evidence from Indian Local Governments', *Journal of the European Economic Association*, 2(2–3): 416–26.

Bird, Richard M., 2010, 'Subnational Taxation in Developing Countries: A Review of the Literature', University of Toronto.

Biswas, Rongili, Sugata Marjit, and Velayoudom Marimoutou, 2010, 'Fiscal Federalism, State Lobbying and Discretionary Finance: Evidence from India', *Economics and Politics*, 22(1): 68–91.

Blomkvist, Hans, 1989, 'Housing and the State in the Third World: Misperceptions and Non-Perceptions in the International Debate', *Scandinavian Housing and Planning Research*, 6(3): 129–41.

Bohlken, Anjali Thomas, and Ernest John Sergenti, 2010, 'Economic Growth and Ethnic Violence: An Empirical Investigation of Hindu-Muslim Riots in India', *Journal of Peace Research*, 47(5): 589–600.

Chakravarthy, Venkatesh, 2000, 'A Letter to the Editor: Hindutva in Tamil Nadu', *Economic and Political Weekly*, 35(30): 22–24.

Chidambaram, Soundarya, 2012, 'The "Right" Kind of Welfare in South India's Urban Slums Seva vs. Patronage and the Success of Hindu Nationalist Organizations', *Asian Survey*, 52(2): 298–320.

Chima, Jugdep S., 2012, 'Changing Patterns of Democracy and Political Representation in India: An Introduction', *Asian Survey*, 52(2): 239–46.

Chopra, Surabhi, 2009, 'Holding the State Accountable for Hunger', *Economic and Political Weekly*, 44(33): 8–12.

Clay, Edward J., 1986, 'Rural Public Works and Food-for-Work: A Survey', *World Development*, 14(10–11): 1237–52.

Cornia, Giovanni Andrea, and Frances Stewart, 1993, 'Two Errors of Targeting', *Journal of International Development*, 5(5): 459–96.

Datt, Gaurav and Martin Ravallion, 1998, 'Why Have Some Indian States Done Better than Others at Reducing Rural Poverty?' World Bank Working Paper No. 1594.

Deodhar, Satish Y., Sweta Mahandiratta, K.V. Ramani, Dileep V. Mavalankar, Sandip Ghosh, and Vincent Braganza, 2010, 'An Evaluation of Mid Day Meal Scheme', *Journal of Indian School of Political Economy*, 22(1–4): 33–48.

Dev, Mahendra and Jos Mooij, 2002, 'Social Sector Expenditures in the 1990s: Analysis of Central and State Budgets', *Economic and Political Weekly*, 37(9): 853–66.

———, 2003, 'Patterns in Social Sector Expenditures: Pre- and Post-Reform Period', no. August 1947: 1–30.

Dickey, Sara, 1993, 'The Politics of Adulation: Cinema and the Production of Politicians in South India', *The Journal of Asian Studies*, 52(2): 340–72.

———, 2012, 'The Pleasures and Anxieties of Being in the Middle: Emerging Middle-Class Identities in Urban South India', *Modern Asian Studies*, 46(3): 559–99.

Drèze, Jean, 2004, 'Mid-Day Meals and Children's Rights', *Economic and Political Weekly*, 39(19): 1937–38.

Drèze, Jean and Aparajita Goyal, 2003, 'Future of Mid-Day Meals', *Economic and Political Weekly*, 38(44): 4673–83.

Drèze, Jean and Geeta Gandhi Kingdon, 1999, 'School Participation in Rural India', http://citeseerx.ist.psu.edu/viewdoc/download?

Duraisamy, P., Estelle James, Julia Lane, and Jee Peng Tan, 1998, 'Is There a Quantity-Quality Trade-off as Pupil-Teacher Ratios Increase? Evidence from Tamil Nadu, India', *International Journal of Educational Development*, 18(5): 367–83.

Forrester, D., 1976, 'Factions and Filmstars: Tamil Nadu Politics since 1971', *Asian Survey*, 16(3): 283–96.

Gaiha, Raghav, Katsushi Imai, and P.D. Kaushik, 2001, 'On the Targeting and Cost-Effectiveness of Anti-Poverty Programmes in Rural India', *Development and Change*, 32(2): 309–42.

Gaiha, Raghav, 1996, 'The Employment Guarantee Scheme in India The EGS Scheme: Is It Mistargeted?' *Asian Survey*, 36(12): 1201–12.

Gaiha, Raghav, V.S. Kulkarni, M.K. Pandey, and Katsushi Imai, 2010, 'National Rural Employment Guarantee Scheme, Poverty and Prices in Rural India', *Journal of Asian and African Studies*, 45(6): 645–69.

Gaitonde, Rakhal, 2012, 'Registration and Monitoring of Pregnant Women in Tamil Nadu, India: A Critique', *Reproductive Health Matters*, 20(39): 118–24.

Gebert, Rita, 1989, 'Poverty Alleviation and Village Politics in Tamil Nadu: Whose Interests First?' *Economic and Political Weekly*, 24(4): 197–99.

Geetha, V. and S.V. Rajadurai, 1993, 'Dalits and Non-Brahmin Consciousness in Colonial Tamil Nadu', *Economic and Political Weekly*, 28(39): 2091–98.

George, S.M., M.C. Latham, E.A. Frongillo, R. Abel, and N. Ethirajan, 1993, 'Evaluation of Effectiveness of Good Growth Monitoring in South Indian Villages', *The Lancet*, 342(8867): 348–52.

George, Sabu M., 1992, 'Female Infanticide in Tamil Nadu, India: From Recognition Back to Denial?', http://womenstudies.in/elib/sex_selection/ss_female_infanticide_in_tamil.pdf

Gopalan, C., 1984, 'Choosing 'Beneficiaries' For Feeding Programmes', *NFI Bulletin*, http://nutritionfoundationofindia.res.in/pdfs/BulletinArticle/Pages_from_nfi_10_84_2.pdf

Gorringe, H., 2012, 'Caste and Politics in Tamil Nadu', India Seminars, retrieved from http://www.india-seminar.com/2012/633/633_hugo_gorringe.htm

Guhan, S., 1994. 'Social Security Options for Developing Countries', *International Labour Review*, 133(1): 35.

Gupta, Monica Das, B.R. Desikachari, T.V. Somanathan, and Padmanaban, 2009, 'How to Improve Public Health Systems: Lessons from Tamil Nadu', Policy Research Working Paper no. WPS 5073, World Bank.

Haan, Arjan de, 2013, 'The Social Policies of Emerging Economies: Growth and Welfare in China and India', Working Papers 110, International Policy Centre for Inclusive Growth.

Hardgrave, Robert L. and Anthon C. Neidhart, 1975, 'Films and Political Consciousness in Tamil Nadu', *Economic and Political Weekly*, 10(1).

Hardgrave, Robert L., 1965, 'The DMK and the Politics of Tamil Nadu', *Pacific Affairs*, 37(4): 396–411.

———, 1973, 'Politics and the Film in Tamil Nadu: The Stars and the DMK', *Asian Survey*, 13(3): 288–305.

Harriss, John, 1983, 'Implementation of Food Distribution Policies a Case Study in South India', *Food Policy*, May.

———, 2001, 'Populism, Tamil Style: Is It Really a Success?', http://www.lse.ac.uk/internationalDevelopment/pdf/WP/WP15.pdf

———, 2002, 'Whatever Happened to Cultural Nationalism in Tamil Nadu? A Reading of Current Events and the Recent Literature on Tamil Politics', *Commonwealth and Comparative Politics*, 40(3): 97–117.

Harriss, John, J. Jeyaranjan, and K. Nagaraj, 2010, 'Land, Labour and Caste Politics in Rural Tamil Nadu in the 20th Century: Iruvelpattu (1916–2008)', *Economic and Political Weekly*, 45: 47–61.

Harriss-White, Barbara, 1986, 'Meals and Noon Meals in South India: Paradoxes of Targeting', *Public Administration and Development*, 6(4): 401–10.

———, 1988, 'Policy Is What It Does: State Trading in Rural South India', *Public Administration and Development*, 8(2): 151–60.

———, 2004, 'Nutrition and Its Politics in Tamil Nadu', *South Asia Research*, 24(1): 51–71.

Harriss-White, Barbara and Philip Payne, 1984, 'Rejoinder—Magic Bullets and the Nutrition Agenda', *Food Policy*, no.: 313–16.

Hasan, Arif and Chetan Vaidya, 1986, 'Two Approaches to the Improvement of Low-Income Urban Areas – Madras and Orangi', *Habitat International*, 10(3): 225–34.

Hasan, Z., 2003, 'Review of Christoph Jaffrelot's book "India's Silent Revolution"', *The Hindu*, retrieved from http://www.thehindu.com/lr/2003/02/02/stories/2003020200180300.htm.

Heaver, Richard, 2002, 'India's Tamil Nadu Nutrition Program—Lessons and Issues in Management and Capacity Development', International Bank for Reconstruction and Development, Washington DC.

Herring, Ronald J. and Rex M. Edwards, 1983, 'Guaranteeing Employment to the Rural Poor: Social Functions and Class Interests in the Employment Guarantee Scheme in Western India', *World Development*, 11(7): 575–92.

Imai, Katsushi, 2007, 'Targeting versus Universalism: An Evaluation of Indirect Effects of the Employment Guarantee Scheme in India', *Journal of Policy Modeling*, 29(1): 99–113.

Integrated Child Development Service, 2017, 'A Coordinated Approach to Children's Health in India', *The Lancet*, 317(8221): 650–53.

Irudayarajan, S. and J. Jayakumar, 1992, 'Impact of Noon Meal Programme on Primary Education: An Exploratory Study in Tamil Nadu', *Economic and Political Weekly*, 27(43/44): 2372–80.

Jaffrelot, Christophe, 2000, 'Sanskritization vs. Ethnicization in India: Changing Identities and Caste Politics before Mandal', *Asian Survey*, 40(5): 756–66.

Jaffrelot, Christophe and Gilles Verniers, 2011, 'Re-Nationalization of India's Political Party System or Continued Prevalence of Regionalism and Ethnicity?' *Asian Survey*, 51(6): 1090–112.

Jairaj, Amrita and Barbara Harriss-White, 2006, 'Social Structure, Tax Culture and the State: The Case of Tamil Nadu', *Economic and Political Weekly*, 41(51): 5247–56.

Jayaraman, Rajshri, Dora Simroth, and Francis D.E.V. Ericourt, n.d., 'The Impact of School Lunches on Primary School Enrollment: Evidence from India's Midday Meal Scheme,' *The Scandinavian Journal of Economics*, 117(4): 1–46.

Jeyaranjan, J., 2011, 'Women and Pro-Poor Policies in Rural Tamil Nadu: An Examination of Practices and Responses', *Economic and Political Weekly*, 46(43): 64–74.

Jha, Raghbendra, Raghav Gaiha, and Manoj K. Pandey, 2012, 'Net Transfer Benefits under India's Rural Employment Guarantee Scheme', *Journal of Policy Modeling*, 34(2): 296–311.

Kailasapathy, K., 1979, 'The Tamil Purist Movement: A Re-Evaluation', *Social Scientist*, 7(10): 23–51.

Kajisa, Kei and N. Venkatesa Palanichamy, 2009, 'Impacts of Organic Farming in a Developing Country: Evidence from Tamil Nadu, India, from 1993 to 2003', Paper presented at International Association of Agricultural Economists Conference, Beijing, China, 16–22 August.

———, 2010, 'Schooling Investments over Three Decades in Rural Tamil Nadu, India: Changing Effects of Income, Gender, and Adult Family Members' Education', *World Development*, 38(3): 298–314.

Kaliappan, T.P., 1991, 'Shelter Programme in Tamil Nadu State', *Building and Environment*, 26(3): 277–87.

Kalirajan, K.P. and R.T. Shand, 1985, 'Types of Education and Agricultural Productivity: A Quantitative Analysis of Tamil Nadu Rice Farming', *The Journal of Development Studies*, 21(2): 232–44.

Kaur, Baljit and Amarjit Singh Sethi, 2007, 'Liberalisation and Social Sector Expenditure: An Inter-State Analysis in India', *Journal of Income and Wealth*, 29: 79–92.

Khera, Reetika, 2006, 'Mid-Day Meals Primary Schools in Achievements and Challenges', *Economic and Political Weekly*, 41(46): 4742–50.

Koteswara Prasad, G., 2009, 'Tamil Nadu: Against Expectations', *Economic and Political Weekly*, 44(39): 121–24.

Kurian, N.J., 2000, 'Widening Regional Disparities in India: Some Indicators', *Economic and Political Weekly*, 35(7): 538–50.

Lakshmi, C.S, 1990, 'Mother, Mother Community and Mother-Politics in Tamil Nadu', *Economic and Political Weekly*, 25(42): WS72–WS83.

M.T, 1988, 'The God That Died the MGR Phenomenon', *Economic and Political Weekly*, 23(1): 21–23.

Ma, Sai, 2008, 'Sustainability of India's Welfare System in the Context of Globalization: A Comparative Study of Maharashtra and Tamil Nadu', *Southeast Review of Asian Studies*.

Mahal, Ajay and Anup K. Karan, 2007, 'Adequacy of Dietary Intakes and Poverty in India: Trends in the 1990s', *Economics and Human Biology*, 6(1): 57–74.

Majumdar, Manabi, 2005, 'Schooling and "Skilling" of Country's Youth', *Economic and Political Weekly*, 40(22): 2351–63.

Mane, R.P., 2006, 'Targeting the Poor or Poor Targeting: A Case for Strengthening the Public Distribution System of India', *Journal of Asian and African Studies*, 41(4): 299–317.

Mangalamurugesan, N.K., 1977, *Self-Respect Movement in Tamil Nadu 1920–1940*, Madurai: Koodal Publishers.

Manivannan, R., 1992, '1991 Tamil Nadu Elections: Issues, Strategies and Performance', *Economic and Political Weekly*, 27(4): 164–70.

Manoharan, Karthick, 2016, 'The Englightened Theology of a Tamil Saivite: Book Review of Religion, Caste and Nation in South India by Ravi Vaithees', *The Wire*, retrieved from https://thewire.in/88351/enlightened-theology-tamil-saivite/

Markussen, Thomas, 2011, 'Inequality and Political Clientelism: Evidence from South India', *Journal of Development Studies*, 47(11): 1721–38.

Mehrotra, Santosh, 2006, 'Reforming Elementary Education in India: A Menu of Options', *International Journal of Educational Development*, 26(3): 261–77.

Mencher, Joan P., 1974. 'Conflicts and Contradictions in the "Green Revolution": The Case of Tamil Nadu', *Economic and Political Weekly*, 9(6/8, Annual Number): 309–23.

Meng, Li, 2012, 'China's Local Government Debt Crisis', *SERI Quarterly*.

Mooij, Jos, 1999, 'Food Policy in India : The Importance of Electoral Politics in Policy', *Journal of International Development*, 11(4): 625–36.

Moses, B.C., 1983, 'Noon Meals Scheme', *Economic and Political Weekly*, 18(4): 101–3.

Muralidharan, Karthik and Kremer, Michael, 2006, 'Public and Private Schools in Rural India', in Rajashri Chakrakbarti and Paul Peterson (eds), *School Choice International: Exploring Public-Private Partnerships*, Cambridge, MA: MIT Press.

Nandha, B. and K. Krishnamoorthy, 2012, 'Impact of Education Campaign on Community-Based Vector Control in Hastening the Process of Elimination of Lymphatic Filariasis in Tamil Nadu, South India', *Health Education Research*, 27(4): 585–94.

Navaneetham, K, and A Dharmalingam, 2000, 'Utilization of Maternal Health Care Services in South India', *Social Science & Medicine*, 55(10): 1–40.

Navaneethan, Palanisamy, Thiagarajan Kalaivani, Chandrasekaran Rajasekaran, and Nautiyal Sunil, 2011, 'Nutritional Status of Children in Rural India: A Case Study from Tamil Nadu, First in the World to Initiate the Mid-Day Meal Scheme', *Health*, 3(10): 647–55.

Niesz, Tricia and Ramchandar Krishnamurthy, 2012, 'Bureaucratic Activism and Radical School Change in Tamil Nadu, India', *Journal of Educational Change*, 14(1): 29–50.

Padmanaban, P., P.S. Raman, D.V. Mavlankar, 2009, 'Innovations and Challenges in Reducing Maternal Mortality in Tamil Nadu, India', *Journal of Health Population and Nutrition*, 27(2): 202–19.

Pal, Sarmistha and Robert Palacios, 2011, 'Understanding Poverty among the Elderly in India: Implications for Social Pension Policy', *Journal of Development Studies*, 47(7): 1017–37.

Palaniswamy, Nethra and Nandini Krishnan, 2012, 'Local Politics, Political Institutions, and Public Resource Allocation', *Economic Development and Cultural Change*, 60(3): 449–73.

Pande, R.P., A. Malhotra, and S. Namy, 2012, 'Fertility Decline and Changes in Women's Lives and Gender Equality in Tamil Nadu, India', International Center for Research on Women.

Pandian, J., 1998, 'Re-Ethnogenesi: The Quest for a Dravidian Identity among the Tamils of India', *Anthropos*, 93(4/6): 545–52.

Pandian, M.S.S., 1988, 'An Election That Was Not', *Economic and Political Weekly*, 23(49): 3–4.

———, 1989, 'DMK' S Miscalculations', *Economic and Political Weekly*, 24(48): 2628–29.

———, 1990, 'From Exclusion to Inclusion Brahminism's New Face in Tamil Nadu', *Economic and Political Weekly*, 25(35): 1938–39.

———, 1994, 'Notes on the Transformation of "Dravidian" Ideology: Tamil Nadu, c. 1900–40', *Social Scientist*, 22(5/6): 84–104.

———, 1996, 'Towards National-Popular: Notes on Self-Respecters' Tamil', *Economic and Political Weekly*, 31(51): 3323–29.

———, 2001, 'On Nationalism and Ethnicity', *Economic and Political Weekly*, 36: 3362–63.

———, 2009, 'Dravidian Politics and Muslims Politics and Muslims of Tamil Nadu by S M Abdul Khader Fakhri', *Economic and Political Weekly*, 44(43): 37–38.

Panneerselvam, O., 2016, 'Policy Note on Planning and Development and Special Initiatives Department', Demand number 36, Minister for Finance, Personnel and Administrative Reforms, Government of Tamil Nadu.

Patnaik, Utsa, 1997, 'Political Economy of State Intervention in Food Economy', *Economic and Political Weekly*, 32(20/21): 1105–12.

Pelletier, D.L. and R. Shrimpton, 1994, 'The Role of Information in the Planning, Management and Evaluation of Community

Nutrition Programmes', *Health Policy and Planning*, 9(2): 171–84.

Phugh, Cedric, 1990, 'The World Bank and Housing Policy in Madras', *Journal of Urban Affairs*, 12(2): 173–96.

Pinto, Ambrose, 1999, 'End of Dravidian Era in Tamil Nadu', *Economic and Political Weekly*, 34(24): 1483–88.

Prabhu, K. Seeta, 1999, 'Social Sectors during Economic Reforms: The Indian Experience', *Oxford Development Studies*, 27(2): 130–53.

Prasad, K.V. Eswara, 1995, 'Social Security for Destitute Widows in Tamil Nadu', *Economic and Political Weekly*, 30(15): 794–96.

Rajan, S. Irudaya and A. Jayakumar, 1992, 'Impact of Noon Meal Programme on Primary Education: An Exploratory Study in Tamil Nadu Impact of Noon Meal Programme on Primary Education an Exploratory Study in Tamil Nadu', *Economic and Political Weekly*, 27(43): 2372–80.

Rajivan, Anuradha, 2005, 'History of Direct Nutrition Schemes in Tamil Nadu', https://pdfs.semanticscholar.org/0587/cbd5d730 05b1ec8bbf12f0f4d43b2bc64cce.pdf

———, 2006, 'ICDS with a Difference', *Economic and Political Weekly*, 41(34): 3684–88.

Ram, N., 1979, '*Dravidian Movement in Its Pre-Independence Phases*', *Economic and Political Weekly*, 14(7/8): 377–402.

Rama V. Baru, Rajib Dasgupta, Mita Deshpande, and Aparna Mohanty, 2008, 'Full Meal or Package Deal?' *Economic and Political Weekly*, 43(24): 20–22.

Raman, C.K., 1983, 'Symbols, Women and Tamil Nadu Politics', *Economic and Political Weekly*, 18(30): 1335–36.

Raman, Nithya, 2011, 'The Board and the Bank: Changing Policies towards Slums in Chennai', *Economic and Political Weekly*, 46(31): 74–80.

Rao, M. Govinda and Richard M. Bird, 2010, 'Urban Governance and Finance in India', http://www.nipfp.org.in/media/medialibrary/ 2013/04/wp_2010_68.pdf

Rukmani, R., 1994, 'Urbanisation and Socio-Economic Change in Tamil Nadu, 1901–91', *Economic and Political Weekly*, 29(51): 3263–72.

Sachs, Jeffrey, Nirupam Bajpai, and Ananthi Ramiah, 2002, 'Understanding Regional Economic Growth in India', Centre for International Development, http://earth.columbia.edu/sitefiles/file/about/director/documents/AEP2002with BajpaiandRamiah-UnderstandingRegionalEconomicGrowthin India.pdf

Sadanandan, Anoop, 2012, 'Bridling Central Tyranny in India: How Regional Parties Restrain the Federal Government', *Asian Survey*, 52(2): 247–69.

Sakthivel, S. and Pinaki Joddar, 2006, 'Sector Unorganised Workforce in Security India Coverage', *Economic and Political Weekly*, 41(21): 2107–14.

Saravanan, S. and A. Joseph Durai, 2012, 'Growth Pattern Disparities: An Inter-State and Intra-State Analysis', *Atlantic Review of Economics*, 21.

Saravanan, Velayutham, 2001, 'Technological Transformation and Water Conflicts in the Bhavani River Basin of Tamil Nadu', *Environment and History*, 7(3): 289–334.

Sastry, K. Ramaswamy, 1974, 'A Chronicle of the DMK Split', *Economic and Political Weekly*, 9(13).

Shah, Anwar (ed.), 2012, 'Local Governance in Developing Countries', http://siteresources.worldbank.org/PSGLP/Resources/LocalGovernanceinDeveloping.pdf

Shankar, Shylashri, Raghav Gaiha, and Raghbendra Jha, 2011, 'Information, Access and Targeting: The National Rural Employment Guarantee Scheme in India', *Oxford Development Studies*, 39(March 2015): 69–95.

Sharma, M.L. and Geetesh Sahni, 2010, 'An Evaluation Study of Mid-Day Meal Programme in Jaipur', http://www.profes sionalpanorama.in/wp-content/uploads/2015/02/15-geetesh-ji.pdf

Sharma, Sushma, Santosh Jain Passi, Salila Thomas, and Hema Gopalan, 2006, 'Evaluation of Mid-day Meal Programme in MCD schools', http://mdm.nic.in/Files/Initiatives%20&%20Case%20Studies/NUTRITION_%20FOUNDATION_%20OF_%20INDIA.pdf

Shekar, Meera, 1991, 'The Tamil Nadu Integrated Nutrition Project: A Review of the Project with Special Emphasis on the Monitoring and Information System', http://www.cfnpp.cornell.edu/images/wp14.pdf

Shekar, Meera and M.C. Latham, 1992, 'Growth Monitoring Can and Does Work! An Example from the Tamil Nadu Integrated Nutrition Project in Rural South India', *The Indian Journal of Pediatrics*, 59(1): 5–15.

Shen, Chunli and Heng Fu Zou, 2014, 'Fiscal Decentralization and Public Services Provision in China', *Annals of Economics and Finance*, 15(1): 135–60.

Sivasakthi, T. and R. Balasubramanian, 2012, 'The Impact of Social Welfare Programmes on Household Food Security—An Economic Analysis', *Indian Journal of Agriculture Economics*, 532.

Sridhar, Devi, 2008, 'Hungry for Change: The World Bank in India', *South Asia Research*, 28(2): 147–68.

Srinivasan, S. and A.S. Bedi, 2009, 'Girl Child Protection Scheme in Tamil Nadu: An Appraisal', *Economic and Political Weekly*, 48(48): 10–12.

Srinivasan, Vivek, 2010, 'Understanding Public Services in Tamil Nadu an Institutional Perspective', *Social Science—Dissertations*. 175, http://surface.syr.edu/socsci_etd/175.

Steer, W.S., 1956, 'The Financing of Local Government', *The Political Quarterly*, 27: 423–33.

Subbiah, A.R., 1992, 'A Letter to the Editor: Caste and Politics in Tamil Nadu', *Economic and Political Weekly*, 27(1): 4–5.

Subramanian, Narendra, 1999, *Ethnicity and Populist Mobilization*, Delhi: Oxford University Press.

Subramanian, Narendra, 2002, 'Identity Politics and Social Pluralism: Political Sociology and Political Change in Tamil Nadu', *Commonwealth & Comparative Politics*, 40(3): 125–39.

———, 2007, 'Populism in India', *SAIS Review of International Affairs*, 27.1: 81–91.

Suresh, V., 1992, 'The DMK Debacle Causes and Portents', *Economic and Political Weekly*, 27(42): 2313–21.

Swaminathan, Madhura, 1990, 'Village Level Implementation of IRDP: Comparison of West Bengal and Tamil Nadu', *Economic and Political Weekly*, 25(13): A17–27.

Swaminathan, Mina, 1991, 'Child Care Services in Tamil Nadu Published by: Economic and Political Weekly Child Care Services in Tamil Nadu', *Economic and Political Weekly*, 26(52): 2988–92.

Swaminathan, Padmini, J. Jeyaranjan, K. Jayashree, and R. Sreenivasan, 2004, 'Tamil Nadu's Midday Meal Scheme Where Assumed Benefits Score over Hard Data', *Economic and Political Weekly*, 39(44): 4811–21.

Swamy, A., 1989, 'Parties, Political Identities and the Absence of Mass Political Violence in South India', *Community Conflicts and the State in India*, no. 1, 993: 108–48.

Swamy, Arun R., 1996, 'Sense, Sentiment and Populist Coalitions: The Strange Career of Cultural Nationalism in Tamil Nadu', in Subrata K. Mitra (ed.), *Subnational Movements in South Asia*, Westview Press.

Tang, Bo-sin, Siu-wai Wong, and S.C. Liu, 2011, 'Institutions, Property Taxation and Local Government Finance in China', *Urban Studies*, 48(5): 847–75.

Venkatachalapathy, A.R., 1995, 'Dravidian Movement and Saivites: 1927–1944', *Economic and Political Weekly*, 30(14): 761–68.

Vijayabaskar, Padmini Swaminathan, S. Anandhi, and Gayatri Balagopal, 2004, 'Human Development in Tamil Nadu Examining Linkages', *Economic and Political Weekly*, 39(8): 797–802.

Viswanathan, Brinda, 2006, 'Access to Nutritious Meal Programmes: Evidence from 1999-2000 NSS Data', *Economic and Political Weekly*, 41(6): 497–506.

Wadhwa, Kiran, 1988, 'Housing Urban Programmes for Shifting Priorities', *Economic and Political Weekly*, 23(34): 1762–67.

Waran, Brenda and Natalie Waran, 1993, 'Release of the Poor through Education in Tamil Nadu, India', *Development in Practice*, 3(2): 124–26.

Wyatt, A.K.J., 2002, 'New Alignments in South Indian Politics', *Asian Survey*.

Wyatt, Andrew, 2013, 'Combining Clientelist and Programmatic Politics in Tamil Nadu, South India', *Commonwealth & Comparative Politics*, 51(1): 27–55.

———, 2013, 'Populism and Politics in Contemporary Tamil Nadu', *Contemporary South Asia*, 21: 1–17.

———, 2013, 'Combining Clientilist and Programmatic Politics in Tamil Nadu, South India', *Commonwealth and Comparative Politics*, 51(1): 27–56.

Newspaper Articles and Other Sources

'1,237 beneficiaries receive four-gram gold for marriage', *The Hindu*, 9 November 2011.

'10 Lakh More Colour TV Sets for Free Distribution', *The Times of India*, January 2011.

'An Excellent Scheme', *The Hindu*, 19 September 2011.

'Behind the success story of universal PDS in Tamil Nadu', *The Hindu*, 11 August 2010.

'BJP's "New Role" Criticised', *The Hindu*, 10 January 2000.

Citizen's Charter (2013). Social Welfare and Noon Meal Programme Department, Government of Tamil Nadu.

'CM Firm on Party Restructure', *The Hindu*, 20 January 2000.

'CM seeks additional funds from Centre', *The Hindu*, 11 June 2013.

Daniel, Sam, and Mohammed Peer. 'Tamil Nadu Polls: Jayalalithaa Trumps DMK Offers of Freebies for Voters', *NDTV*, 24 March 2011.

Daniel, Sam. 'Jayalithaa's one-rupee idlis are a hit', *NDTV*, 17 April 2013.

'DMK Govt. Has Failed on All Fronts: Moopanar', *The Hindu*, 9 May 2001.

'DMK Govt. in a Dilemma', *The Hindu*, 2 June 2000.

'DMK Manifesto Full of Goodies', *The Hindu*, 30 March 2006.

'DMK Manifesto Hero of 2006 Election', 11 May 2006.

'DMK Regime like Kamaraj Rule: CM', *The Hindu*, 15 March 2001.

'DMK's Stand on Constitution Review Unclear, Says CPI', *The Hindu*, 1 February 2000.

'Economics of DMK's Poll Promises', *The Hindu*, 6 April 2006.

'Expanded Social Security Scheme for Farmers', *The Hindu*, 11 September 2011.

'Free hampers given under the watchful eyes of police', *The Hindu*, 12 January 2013.

'Free Laptops given to Govt. School Students Being Sold Online Staff', *The Hindu*, 2 July 2013.

'Free milch cows scheme starts paying dividends', *The Hindu*, 18 April 2013.

Ganapathy, V. 'CM Has Stifled Democracy: Jayalalitha', *The Hindu*, 1 May 2001.

'Govt. Respects Opposition Views', *The Hindu*, 15 March 2000.

'HC Orders Release of AIADMK Leaders, Workers', *The Hindu*, 17 February 2000.

ICR Review on Second Tamil Nadu Integrated Nutrition Project (1998). Operations Evaluation Department.

'Idlis for Re. 1, curd rice for Rs. 3 at new Corporation restaurants', *The Hindu*, 20 February 2013.

'India Approves Ambitious Food Security Program', *The Wall Street Journal*, 4 July 2013.

'Jayalalitha Condemns Ministers "Behaviour"'. *The Hindu*, 2 June 2000.

'Jayalalitha Trial to Be Three Days a Week', *The Hindu*, 29 March 2000.

'Jayalalithaa Shuts the Door on Allies', *The Hindu*, 11 June 2013.

Jayanth, V. 'Tamil Nadu'S Cliffhanger of an Election', *The Hindu*, 8 May 2006.

Joint Review Mission on midday meals scheme in Tamil Nadu. Department of School Education and Literacy, Ministry of Human Resource Development, Government of India, 29 July–8 August 2013.

'Karunanidhi's Gift—a Colour TV', September 15, 2006.

'Landslide Victory for AIADMK', *The Hindu*, 14 May 2001.

Madhavan, N. 'Class Act', *Business Today*, 9 August 2012.

'Maternity assistance for Sri Lankan refugees too', *The Hindu*, 24 April 2013.

'Milch cows a source of livelihood as well as nutrition in villages', *The Hindu*, 15 July 2013.

Murthi, P.V.V. 'Jayalalitha Avoids Local Issues', *The Hindu*, 7 May 2001.

Nambath, Suresh. 'Minorities in a Dilemma', *The Hindu*, 1 May 2001.

Nambath, Suresh, 'Jayalalitha Sworn in CM', *The Hindu*, 15 May 2001.

Nambath, Suresh, 'Karunanidhi to Be Chief Minister for Fifth Time', *The Hindu*, 12 May 2006.

Nambath, Suresh, 'People Want Me to Be CM: Jayalalitha', *The Hindu*, 9 May 2001.

Nambath, Suresh, 'Tamil Nationalism Is No Longer Useful', *The Hindu*, 7 May 2001.

http://shodhganga.inflibnet.ac.in/bitstream/10603/9999/8/08_chapter%203.pdf(accessed on 18 July 2017).

Narayanamoorthy, A. 'Functioning of PDS in Tamil Nadu Source', *The Hindu*, 24 November 2009.

'Opinion Poll Predicts "Edge" for DMK Front', *The Hindu*, 7 May 2001.

'Opposition Stages Protests', *The Hindu*, 5 April 2000.

'Orders on Jayalalithaa's Petition Today', *The Hindu*, 12 April 2000.

'PDS Malpractices: Govt. May Not Endorse Central Suggestion', *The Hindu*, 20 January 2000.

'Police Helped DMK Cast Bogus Votes: Jayalalitha', *The Hindu*, 18 February 2000.

Radhakrishnan, R.K. 'Karunanidhi, Ministers Sworn in', *The Hindu*, 14 May 2006.

Ramakrishnan, T. 'With universal PDS, TN lukewarm about Food Security Bill', *The Hindu*, 10 June 2013.

'Rs. 20-a-kg rice scheme gets overwhelming response', *The Hindu*, 28 April 2013.

'Send Back Sri Lankan Military Officials in Wellington: Jayalalithaa', *The Hindu*, 10 June 2013.

'Social Welfare and Nutritious Meal Programme: Performance Budget 2016–17', Social Welfare Department, Government of Tamil Nadu, 2016.

'Students Make a Quick Buck off Government Laptops', *The Hindu*, 6 June 2013.

'Success of "Uzhavar Santhais" has Silenced Critics: CM', *The Hindu*, 22 March 2000.

'Successor a Surprise Choice', *The Hindu*, 22 September 2001.

'T.N. CM reiterates commitment to minorities', *The Hindu*, 12 April 2001.

'TN Plan Outlay Fixed at Rs. 37,128', *The Hindu*, 11 June 2013.

'TN to Institute "Tamil Chair" at JNU', *The Hindu*, 5 April 2000.

Venkatesan, J. 'Another Judge Should Hear Jayalalithaa's Appeals Afresh', *The Hindu*, 8 September 2001.

Venkatesan, Radha. 'Egg Won't Be Served at Noon Meal Centres', *The Hindu*, 22 September 2001.

Venkatesan. 'SC Unseats Jayalalithaa as CM', *The Hindu*, 22 September 2001.

Venkatesh, M.R. 'CM Still Looking to the Left', *The Hindu*, 6 March 2000.

Venkatesh, M.R. 'Save State: Karunanidhi', *The Hindu*, 9 May 2001.

Venkatesh. 'False Propaganda Won: Karunanidhi', *The Hindu*, 14 May 2001.

Vydhianathan, S. 'Jayalalitha Has Not Changed: CM. *The Hindu*, 7 May 2001.

World Bank Independent evaluation group, Tamil Nadu and child nutrition an assessment.

ABOUT THE AUTHOR

S. Narayan was the Economic Adviser to the Prime Minister (Mr Atal Behari Vajpayee) during 2003–04. Prior to this assignment, he served the Government of India as Finance and Economic Affairs Secretary, Secretary in the Departments of Revenue, Petroleum, Coal and Industrial Development. His special interests include public finance, energy policy, governance issues, and international trade.

Dr Narayan belongs to the Tamil Nadu cadre of the Indian Administrative Service, and spent nearly two decades in the state, in several positions including District Collector, Secretary Planning and Development, and several years in Rural Development working closely with the political establishment.

Dr Narayan obtained his Ph.D. from the Indian Institute of Technology in New Delhi. He has an M.Phil. (Development Economics) from Cambridge University and Master of Business Management (Finance) from the University of Adelaide. He graduated with an M.Sc. (Physics) from the University of Madras (Madras Christian College).

Dr Narayan has authored one book, edited two books, and written numerous policy papers, reports, and book chapters. He also writes regularly in newspapers, both locally and internationally, on issues relating to public policy, governance, public finance, trade, and energy.

He has been the visiting Senior Research Fellow at the Institute of South Asian Studies, National University of Singapore since 2005.